Dug In, Along an Argonne Hillside.

The
Lost Battalion

By THOMAS M. JOHNSON
and
FLETCHER PRATT

INTRODUCTION TO THE BISON BOOKS EDITION BY
Edward M. Coffman

UNIVERSITY OF NEBRASKA PRESS
LINCOLN AND LONDON

Library of Congress Cataloging-in-Publication Data
Johnson, Thomas M. (Thomas Marvin), b. 1889.
The Lost Battalion / by Thomas M. Johnson and Fletcher Pratt;
introduction to the Bison Books edition by Edward M. Coffman.
p. cm.
Originally published: 1st ed. Indianapolis: Bobbs-Merrill Co., c1938.
ISBN 0-8032-7613-3 (pbk.: alk. paper)
1. Argonne, Battle of the, 1918. 2. United States Army. 308th
infantry—History. I. Pratt, Fletcher, 1897–1956. II. Title.
D570.33.308th.J64   2000
940.4'36—dc21
00-020518

This Bison Books edition follows the original in beginning the prologue
on arabic page 17; no material has been omitted.

INTRODUCTION

Edward M. Coffman

On 26 September 1918, the American First Army launched a massive assault along a front of some twenty miles, stretching from the depths of the Argonne Forest to the Meuse River. During the next six weeks, Gen. John J. Pershing pushed more men into the battle, and casualties mounted to more than 120,000. The number of men involved—more than a million—and the heavy losses made this battle even greater than the major American actions that would follow in World War II.

Later, Pershing recalled that the first days of October were the time of "the heaviest strain on the army and me." His hope that the heavy blow of the initial assault would break through the German fortifications had been dashed. Attack after attack simply could not breach the German line. Despite heavy casualties, Pershing continued to exhort his division commanders to keep up their attacks.

On 2 October, New York draftees and a smattering of midwestern and western replacements, in companies from two understrength battalions with some attached machine-gun units, took part in another attack. Under the command of a recently promoted major, Charles W. Whittlesey, they advanced and found a valley in the Argonne that took them beyond the German lines.

Whittlesey, a thirty-four-year-old Harvard Law School graduate who practiced his profession in New York City, and the other officers were all civilians temporarily in uniform. His military background consisted of a term at the Plattsburg training camp in the summer of 1916 and the experience gained training green troops and leading them through the battles of the summer of 1918.

He had protested the order to attack with his tired, understrength command, but when overruled he led his men to their objective. Meanwhile the Germans stopped the attacking French and American units on his flanks. Ordered to ignore his own flank security, Whittlesey pushed ahead and, once on his objective, placed his men into position along the slopes of the ravine and sent word back of his location.

Apparently the German commanders became aware of the significance of Whittlesey's advance sooner than their American counterparts. They realized that it was a breakthrough and presumed that the Americans would reinforce and exploit the advantage. That night only one company of the battalion sent to reinforce Whittlesey reached him. German troops quickly plugged the gap in the line, surrounded the small force, and squashed the efforts of the Seventy-seventh Division to relieve Whittlesey's command over the next four days.

They were in a desperate situation. All they had was the ammunition, rations, and water that the individuals carried with them. Rain helped quench thirst but there was no resupply of food and ammunition. Aviators who tried to drop supplies never hit their mark. To add to their problems, an American artillery barrage killed or wounded eighty of the increasingly desperate men. The Germans who kept pressure on them eventually mounted a flamethrower attack and called for the Americans to surrender, but they could not budge Whittlesey and his men.

While the five-day siege was in progress, war correspondents picked up on the story of what was then miscalled the "Lost Battalion." Everyone knew where they were. The issue was whether or not the division could fight its way to them. On the night of 7 October, troops finally broke through and rescued the fewer than 200 officers and men who survived from the 554 who had started out five days earlier. These men and their commander, who was promptly promoted to lieutenant colonel, were celebrated as heroes when they emerged from the Argonne Forest.

Correspondents gathered around the tall, lanky commander, who with his glasses and mild manner seemed more like a stereotypical schoolteacher than war hero. Whittlesey modestly diverted them to the other survivors. When the journalists talked with them, they heard universal praise for the commander who manifested outstanding courage and strength of character as well as concern for his men throughout those terrible days.

A few days after he got out of the pocket near Charlevaux Mill, Whittlesey put the best face possible on his harrowing experience in a letter to Max Berking, an old friend from his college days at Williams: "It's a great life. Finest thing in the world, and we'll never have the same small outlook on men when it's over. Some of these fellows are just finer than anyone can say."

Life would never be the same for Charles W. Whittlesey. The Army sent him home and awarded him and two of his officers Congressional Medals of Honor. He returned to his law practice in Manhattan but was beset with servicemen and their families who begged him for help. He supported them as much as he could and acceded to those who asked him to head the Red Cross Drive for New York City and to accept the colonelcy of his regiment, the 308th, which was then a reserve unit.

Family and friends thought that Whittlesey was haunted by the war. They also knew that he was racked by a cough that they assumed resulted from the gas that he had inhaled during the fighting. The burdens of his celebrity kept the war on his mind, although he rarely talked about it. On the third anniversary of the Armistice, 11 November 1921, he was one of the honored guests at the ceremony of the entombment of the Unknown Soldier at Arlington. When pressed by his family about the occasion, he said only that it made a deep impression on him. Nine days later, he was on the stage with Marshal Foch, supreme commander of the Allied forces on the Western Front, at a function in New York.

On 26 November, without telling anyone, he sailed on a passenger boat to Cuba. When the captain discovered he was on board, he invited him to dine with him that night. The conversation was about sports, and Whittlesey expressed particular interest in the day's Army-Navy football game. Afterward he joined a group for a drink and talked about the war for perhaps two hours before he excused himself.

The next day was rough and many stayed in their compartments, but on Monday, the twenty-eighth, a search revealed that Whittlesey was missing. His bed had not been slept in and letters to members of his family and a few friends were found in his room. He must have leaped overboard either late Saturday or early Sunday. All who knew him were shocked, as they had noticed that he had been more cheerful during the past week. When they had recovered from the initial blow, their reaction was that he had been overcome by his war experiences.

Whittlesey's comrades eulogized him at a memorial service at the Seventy-first Regiment Armory on 4 December, and the *New York Times*, which had covered the disappearance in detail, editorialized two days later: "As a soldier he never spared himself; as a citizen he wore himself out in service for others."

When his shipboard letters reached the States, the four friends who received them issued a joint statement: "The letters contain only personal farewells and in no instance attempt to explain the reason for his departure." They concluded their brief statement, which the *Times* carried on 9 December, with "His was a battle casualty."

In 1982, the brother-in-law of J. Bayard Pruyn, who was Whittlesey's best friend and former law partner and whom he designated executor of his small estate, gave the letter Pruyn received to the Williams College Library. Headed "S.S. Toloa" but undated, the letter opens: "Just a note to say good by. I'm a misfit by nature and by training, and there's an end of it." Then he explained his desires for the disposition of his estate and personal effects. He concluded: "I won't try to say anything personal Bayard, because you and I understand each other."

The story of the Lost Battalion and the mystery of Whittlesey's death intrigued Americans for years. Whittlesey, along with Alvin C. York and Samuel Woodfill, received special recognition from Pershing in his memoirs. In the 1930s small children learned about the Lost Battalion either from their fathers or from a story, printed in one of their grade-school readers, about the carrier pigeon Cher Ami that Whittlesey had dispatched to call off the barrage that was decimating his command. Despite losing an eye and a leg, the bird made it back with its important message.

In 1948, the Williams Club in New York City dedicated his portrait in a room named in his honor. George McMurtry, his second in command who also received the Medal of Honor, was among those in attendance.

The greatest tribute to Whittlesey and his men, however, is this book, *The Lost Battalion*. In the mid-thirties, two established freelance writers, Thomas M. Johnson and Fletcher Pratt, combined to work on what they considered "the supreme American hero-story of the World War."

Johnson brought more to the combination in that he had been a *New York Sun* war correspondent with the American Expeditionary Forces (AEF) throughout most of the war. Shortly after the rescue, he had visited the Seventy-seventh Division and talked with Whittlesey and others involved in the fight. In 1928, he had included a chapter on the Lost Battalion in his book on the Meuse-Argonne, *Without Censor: New Light on Our Greatest World War Battles*. In this earlier book as well as in *The Lost Battalion* he made good use of the wide range of acquaintances he made among AEF commanders and staff officers. He and Pratt also consulted with German participants and examined the records of both sides.

After completing what has remained one of the best battle studies of the American participation in World War I, the authors went their separate ways. Pratt's works in popular naval and military history made him one of the best known military historians in the nation before his death in 1956. Johnson went on to write books on military intelligence activities. When he died in 1970, he was the last surviving AEF war correspondent.

By the time the United States entered World War II, the fame of another World War I hero had surpassed that of Whittlesey and his men. In 1941, the movie *Sergeant York*, with Gary Cooper in the leading role, put the story of the conscientious objector who routed a German machine-gun battalion on big screens throughout the nation. The movie made in the early twenties about the Lost Battalion had gone into oblivion.

During World War II, the Tennessee hero often left his home to speak out in support of the war effort. Even after invalided by a stroke in the fifties, the affable York welcomed visitors and appeared often in the news. By the time York died in 1964, Whittlesey had been dead forty-three years, and not many of the Lost Battalion were left.

World War I was fading from the national memory when the Vietnam War came along in the sixties. During the fiftieth anniversary of the AEF's greatest battle, Americans were preoccupied with the frustrations of the war in Southeast Asia and paid no attention to those who fought in what they had presumed was the war to end all wars.

Recently there has been somewhat of a revival of interest in the Great War. A few Americans even visit the battlefields. An unforgettable experience for those who go into the still heavily forested hills and hollows of the Argonne is to drive down the 1918 road cut into the steep slope above the Charlevaux valley and find the small marker with an arrow pointing down to the position of the Lost Battalion.

It had been raining the day I was there, so the slope was slippery. I cautiously ventured a few yards down into the trees and saw the indentations of the foxholes, which were the Lost Battalion's front line. It did not take much imagination to envision the travail of Whittlesey and his men as I stood by those vestiges of the battle and looked down into the densely wooded valley that they occupied and then back and up across the road into the German position. As battlefield walkers know, there is an aura about places where such terrible things happened. On that overcast, misty day in the deep woods of the Argonne, it was as strong as I have ever experienced.

Anyone who is interested not just in World War I but in accounts of men who rise above themselves in extraordinarily difficult situations should welcome this reprint of *The Lost Battalion*.

I wish to express my appreciation to Sylvia Kennick Brown of the Williams College Library, who made available the Whittlesey letters that I quote. I am indebted to Heather Robertson Roberts for the biographical sketch that accompanies the description of the Whittlesey Collection. Finally, I am most grateful to Lillian E. Collins of the Hobart and William Smith Colleges Alumni Office for copying Thomas M. Johnson's file for me.

FOREWORD

THE SIEGE of the Lost Battalion endures after twenty years as the supreme American hero-story of the World War. Yet this unique, poignant episode has had no complete chronicle, and its luster has been dimmed by a tarnish of mystery and sensational rumor. To get and tell the full truth, we have joined forces: a sometime war correspondent who reported the episode at the time, albeit under censorship, and an historian who has specialized in military history.

As collated from many sources the complete story emerges far different from, and in many ways much more creditable to those participating than, the legend which has grown so profusely about it. The battalion was not a battalion but parts of four; it was never lost; it did not rush rashly ahead of the rest of the army and fall into a German trap set deliberately; if its commander, Major Whittlesey, had had his way it would not have attacked at all; he did not commit some fatal blunder that caused his suicide; he did not say "Go to hell!"

A few points remain shrouded in mystery, since human memory is fallible; for example, who was the captain that marked Lieutenant Putnam's map? (Page 119.) In a few other cases we have been obliged reluctantly to choose between conflicting eye-witness accounts, as in the case of the German flame-thrower attack, which survivors of the Lost Battalion have assured us with great earnestness occurred variously, on the 5th, 6th and 7th. The German accounts are all agreed in placing it on the 6th; and we have taken their word for it. We have found that the memory of the survivors for events and details is better than their memory for dates; they remember and usually agree astonishingly well on what happened and even on what was said. But they are apt to place these details, these accurately recalled conversations, many hours apart. To give authorities for certain statements, and elsewise to illuminate the main narrative without continually digressing from it, we have followed it with a series of notes drawn also from a variety of sources.

The men who came through those dreadful days and nights in the pocket are scattered the country over, but they have been extremely generous about submitting to cross-examination. Yet, as they themselves have wished, we have checked and pieced out with diaries, letters and whatever reliable data were available, including, of course, the official records in Washington and in the *Reichsarchiv* in Potsdam, for the German side of the story has been largely unknown in this country.

Wherever possible we have checked the American side of the story by German sources, unofficial as well as official. The tale of the captured Americans who successfully lied to the Germans with apparently important effect, was thus jigsawed together. And in general we have found our former adversaries most fair and willing to co-operate. Indeed, all the German sources, contemporary and present, speak of the Lost Battalion in terms of admiration so enthusiastic as to sound American. General Wellmann, the tough old soldier who tried to wipe them out, made them this tribute:

"Let all men pause before the picture of their high soldierly courage."

The Germans confirm what many Americans do not realize: that the Lost Battalion's courage not only left a glorious tradition, but broke the Germans' last line in the Argonne Forest, whence their retreat was then hastened by the American and French efforts to rescue the surrounded command. And the Argonne Forest was the strongest single natural obstacle in the path of the 1,200,-000 Americans then attacking to win their vastest battle, the Meuse-Argonne.

In the Lost Battalion's struggle in the forest, the principal actors were:

The Americans

ROBERT ALEXANDER, major general commanding the 77th Division; a regular, stocky, square-jawed, determined and aggressive.

EVAN M. JOHNSON, brigadier general commanding the 77th Division's 154th Infantry Brigade; slim, high-strung and somewhat mercurial, but a regular and willing to fight.

CROMWELL STACEY, colonel commanding the 154th Brigade's 308th Infantry Regiment; short, southern accent, twenty-four years a soldier since he started as a drummer-boy, but now nerve-racked and wellnigh exhausted.

CHARLES W. WHITTLESEY, major commanding the 308th Infantry's first battalion; tall, gawky, spectacled, serious; in peacetime a New Englander practicing law in New York City.

GEORGE G. MCMURTRY, captain commanding the 308th Infantry's second battalion; short, nimble, ruddy-faced, cheery; Harvard man, ex-Rough Rider, New Yorker.

JAMES F. LARNEY, private, signal-man for Whittlesey; young, slight, religious, apple knocker from upstate who kept a diary among the big city boys in the Pocket.

WALTER J. BALDWIN, corporal with Whittlesey's headquarters; one of the big city boys, short, faithful, with a flair for observation.

GEORGE NEWCOM, private in the 308th Infantry; a midwestern replacement; clearheaded, and realistic.

LOWELL R. HOLLINGSHEAD, private in the 308th Infantry; also a replacement; youthful, fresh-faced, imaginative.

EUGENE H. HOUGHTON, lieutenant colonel commanding the 307th Infantry; medium height, powerful, a seasoned fighting-man.

NELSON M. HOLDERMAN, captain commanding K Company, the 307th Infantry; light-complexioned, neat, optimistic and gallant.

JAMES B. CARROLL, acting first sergeant of K Company; tall, thin, aggressive.

The Germans

GENERALMAJOR WELLMANN, veteran commander of the I Reserve Korps on the Argonne Forest front; soldierly in appearance and action.

FREIHERR QUADT-WYCKRADT-HÜCHTENBRUCK, commanding the 76th Reserve-Division opposing the 77th American Division; of the best Prussian tradition; well-liked by his command.

HAUPTMANN VON SYBEL, Chief of Staff of the 76th Reserve Division; an efficient officer.

MAJOR HÜNICKEN, commanding the 254th Reserve Infantry Regiment; principal immediate adversary of the Lost Battalion.

LIEUT. FRITZ PRINZ, in early thirties, attached to the 76th Reserve Division as an Intelligence Officer to question American prisoners because he had lived in Seattle.

BECAUSE this narrative has been drawn from many sources, and because some of the key participants are now dead, we have adopted a special device for the indication of quotations. When a remark is quoted from official records, or has been supplied to us by the man who made it, or the exact words have been given to us from different sources, it is set apart by the ordinary quotation marks (" "). When we have been given only the substance of a remark, or when the source from which we received it is not sure of the wording, we have used the Continental European quotation mark, a long dash (—) before the quotation.

THE AUTHORS

CONTENTS

ILLUSTRATIONS

THE LOST BATTALION

The Argonne Forest, Near Le Mort Homme, September 28

IT WAS the third day of the drive in the Argonne by U. S. Division 77. Commands were getting mixed on the left wing. A new advance had just been undertaken after what Major Charles Whittlesey of the 1st Battalion, 308th Infantry, reported as a "breakfast of bacon, butter, bread and a one-pound cannon barrage from the Germans." They got through a defense system and crossed a German war cemetery toward twilight, pausing on the reverse slope of a hill bearing the ominous name of Dead Man's Mount, where latrine rumor said a Heinie lieutenant-general had been planted.

Nobody knew where the elements on the flanks were; maybe not there at all, all dead, but you could not tell in this forest, a jungle of second growth. It rained like hell. Toward midnight one of the runners came in to say he had been challenged in German. Major Whittlesey put out a night patrol which presently returned with news that the chain of runner-posts was indubitably broken and that there were "kraut" machine guns barking at them in the dark. "Pretty cold," commented the Major in his notes, but could only make the best of it till morning, as it was too dark to fly pigeons and the situation too confused to risk combat patrols which might fire on friends.

Daybreak had found the battalion P. C. on the edge of a little clearing, with the clouds pulling away, everybody trying to get soggy clothes dry and Corporal Baldwin cleaning the boss's pistol. Suddenly there was a rustle and a German officer stood gazing at them from the opposite side of the glade, a sergeant beside him.

"My gun, quick!" said Whittlesey; Baldwin passed up a handful of disassociated springs and bolts, just as all the rifles in the headquarters group went off together and down flopped the two Germans. There was still a little life in the Hun officer when they got to him.

—You will meet real opposition up ahead ... my company is only seventy men (he said and died).

"Our line of communication with the rear still cut at 12:30 P.M. by machine guns," said the pigeon message Whittlesey got off when the light was a little stronger. "We are going to clean out one of these guns now. From a wounded German officer-prisoner, we learned there is a German company of seventy men operating in our rear to close the gap we made yesterday. We can of course clean up this country to the rear by working our companies over the ground we charged. But we understand our mission is to advance and to maintain our strength here. It is very slow trying to clean up this rear area from here by small details. Can line of communications be kept open from the rear? We have been unable to

18

send back details for rations and ammunition, both of which we need very badly."

All day they had stayed in funk holes filled with mud, the four companies in square, beating off sporadic German attacks from all points of the compass. That was the day the negroes caved in leftward; the Germans, who knew all about the four companies isolated behind their lines, had kept filtering new men in to strengthen their intercepting detachments, and by afternoon had Whittlesey's little command in bad shape, with many casualties, no food, nothing to drink but the muddy dregs of the rain, almost no bullets, no response to the repeated pigeon-calls for help.

About noon Whittlesey had sent two patrols out; one, headed by Ben Gaedeke, brought back a German lieutenant, dead, but with a fine set of maps on him. The other, under Sergeant Anderson of A, worked two miles southwest and still encountered nothing American, only a forest full of machine guns, snipers and infantry who threw potato mashers. When Anderson came back, there was a conference; Whittlesey fixed on the device of sending out a powerful combat patrol under the best man he had, Lieutenant Arthur McKeogh, the battalion adjutant.

At the cemetery McKeogh had contacted the Germans; found them even stronger, both as to numbers and position than he had expected, sent a runner back to inform Whittlesey of these facts and then attacked. The runner, Quinn, never got through (they found his body four months later among three Boches he had killed), but McKeogh did, with Monson of A and Herschkowitz of C; he got a wound and a D.S.C., and started on their way the relieving force which reached Whittlesey that night.

"I went back to Rgtl. Advance Hqrs," wrote Whittlesey in his notes after that previous relief. "The blackest night I've ever seen and I had to be passed on from reserve post to post, holding the hand of each successive guide. Then back to the Bn. again, which I found with great difficulty in the darkness. Orders were to advance at daybreak."

OCTOBER 2

I

Western Edge of the Argonne Forest
(8:00 to 10:00 A. M.)

LOW CLOUDS went swinging across the sky under the press of the east wind. It had rained the day before; everything was still wet, shivering with the autumn chill of France, when the sergeants came down the line.

—Move in twenty minutes. Get ready, gang.
Eight-ten.

—I ain't seen a mess-wagon since the battle of Calais.

—What are you kicking about? You had your breakfast, didn't you?

—Yeah, hardtacks and corned willy.

The watch hand touched the half, whistles blew and Regiment 308, Division 77, stood up and went stumbling forward into the woods, depressed-looking woods, second growth and underbrush, with bullet scars all around and leaves showing drops of the last-night's rain.

—North straight ahead (the orders said, that Colonel Stacey had had from Brigade at night). North straight ahead, then bear westward up the ravine that climbs from the valley of Charlevaux Brook, 294.6—275.5. On

21

the crest above lies the Giselher Stellung, the main German line. Take it; push on through to the road and railroad on the opposite slope, above Charlevaux Valley. There the regiment will reorganize and await orders for farther advance.—

Major Whittlesey of the advance battalion had looked grave enough when he received those orders from the Colonel, and pointed out the difficulty of the country and the defense. The Colonel had protested, already, via 'phone to General Johnson of Brigade—his men had no blankets, raincoats or reserve rations, no rum, no hot coffee, no experience. Only ten per cent of them knew how to work a hand grenade, and as for the rifles, "I can't make the bullets go into this thing," said one of the men, who was found smoking behind a bush in a battle not long before, though he fought very bravely when the trick was explained. The French were cracking on the left, the woods too thick to permit good artillery support, the liaison was bad—why, two days before, the krauts got round the left of 308 in the tangle of woods and gave that wing hell.

Johnson of Brigade remembered it well, a tall skinny man, with sunken eyes; said that before receiving Stacey's protest he himself had protested to General Alexander of Division about making an attack in that direction and country with so few men. Alexander said nonsense; the French were attacking and their drive had sucked in all the Germans who could do any damage by

22

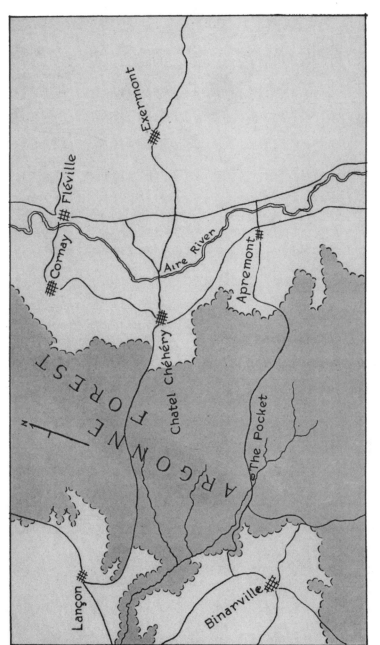

The October Offensive in The Argonne Forest Region.

flank attack. The orders from Army command were to drive on remorselessly. Go ahead; pay no attention to flanks or losses.

Therefore Johnson transmitted the go ahead to Stacey, very peremptorily, through a filter of bad nerves and sleepless bad temper; Stacey passed on the same order to Whittlesey in the language of an old regular—that is, harder rather than softer than he had received it. Battalion I, Regiment 308, Division 77, went stumbling into the wet woods with no bugles and only what breakfast they had been able to snatch from a fresh rations dump as they marched past.

On their left, out of sight through the woods, a division of French dismounted cuirassiers was moving forward in conformity, grumbling, taking no chances, waiting for the *soixante-quinze* to come up and blast out each knot of resistance. It was the French habit, a habit they could afford, being in open, if difficult country, where gun sights could be laid accurate to the millimeter

On the right Regiment 307 was sloshing forward through the same forest, and beyond that 306 and 305— but they would be fortunate to keep touch with one another, having a hill, a draw, and another hill to conquer before they could join 308 at the main line of the Giselher Stellung. Those four regiments made up the Division, the 77th, "New York's own"—draft boys from the melting pot of the lower East Side, who had come through the ooze and shellfire of the Vesle and there lost many

23

men. The inexperienced boys were replacements, fresh drafts from the West largely, strong and full of drive, good men to add pepper to the melting-pot stew.

They went forward then, brown uniforms flickering in and out among the brown trees, barely in visual contact with each other. Major Whittlesey and his headquarters company were up with the guides, a rather unusual arrangement, but someone had to find the way. Down a steep slope, some men bent double, a few more nearly erect, making their advance in quick jumps from one patch of cover to the next. There was not a German in sight, only the one—two—three—of shells dropping at random and the chatter and whistle of machine-gun bullets all around. Men were falling here and there. "First aid!" "First aid!" and the advance was slow. Major Whittlesey found a convenient patch of cover near the base of the marshy ravine, took stock, decided he was losing so many men he would have none left by the time he reached the German lines.

Halt. He considered while the battalion wriggled into cover around him, and the voice of Rainwater, the Indian miner from Butte, was raised in the plaintive wish for a chew of tobacco.

—North straight ahead (said the orders). But that would take the battalion straight up the ravine, and it was clear from occasional flash and ripping of leaves that the machine-gun fire was pounding into them from the high, wooded slopes on both sides. Straight ahead would bring that fire into both flanks, cost every life in the organization unless the French on the left, 307 on the right, kept level and took those machine guns from behind. Whittlesey's map showed this prospect unlikely; the French you could never depend on, while 307 had a steep hill to face, with wire and trenches, woods slashed with tunnels down which German machine guns blazed.

On his left, the hill beyond the ravine, La Palette the map called it, was open ground. A few trees and some houses dotted that hill, with a formidable trench system zigzagging among them. There were sure to be pillboxes, with staked machine-gun ranges. Oh, yes, the French would find it slow work against this sort of position. They were finding everything slow work in 1918 (no wonder!) and they were without the numerical superiority they needed, for the American negroes brigaded with them had been pulled out. That was after the attack a week ago, when the negroes broke, the Germans filtered in behind 308 and gave it hell.

The sound of German fire close behind Whittlesey's left flank told him there was no hope from the French even if the map did not. But the orders said bear westward; that meant that at a choice he should swing toward La Palette rather than toward the hill to the east of the ravine, Hill 198. Another glance at the map—yes, La Palette once gained, he would be astride the Giselher Stellung; the machine guns could not hit his command from either flank, he could then make his turn north toward the day's objective—that road and dinky rail-road, side by side, along the north slope of Charlevaux Valley, beyond the main German line.

There had not been too much loss and, thanks to the configuration of the ground, practically no scattering. The men were under good control. Whittlesey got them moving leftward among the caves and crannies at the foot of La Palette, with bullets chipping the limestone shelves all round them. But the minute they turned the last corner, the fire in their faces became a perfect hori-zontal hailstorm. There was no cover now for forward movement and fire from both sides. Without orders the battalion halted in what protection it could find, fired back in a rather desultory manner that advertised its presence without bringing any result. You can't hit 'em if you can't see 'em.

Whittlesey looked at his watch. Ten o'clock; still time for something to be done if it were done quickly, with help from the guns. He rushed a message back to Colonel Stacey, reporting that westward and north straight ahead progress was impossible without aid from both flanks. Stacey was at the telephone head—no wire up with the battalion—"You haven't got enough to reach where I'm going," Whittlesey had told telephone Sergeant Cahill—with a fairish view through the trees, and he had a liaison runner from 307 who reported that they also were making no progress. He called up Bri-gade—"Hello, is this Delaware One? Detroit One talk-ing"— and reported to Johnson; Johnson called up

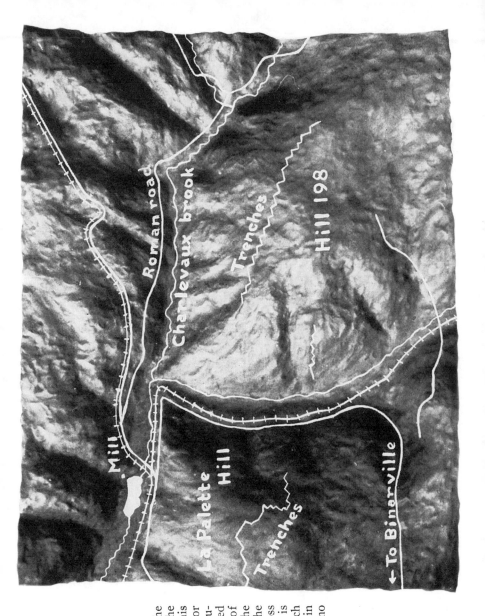

The terrain in which the action took place. The country is shown in this map as though bare for the sake of clarity. Actually, it was all wooded except for the summit of La Palette Hill. The railroad following the line of the road across the top of this map is shown on all French maps of the date; but in error. There was no railroad there.

October 2

Alexander to announce that the troops on the left wing of his line could accomplish nothing more.

II

Headquarters, I Reserve-Korps (German), Briquenay
(8:00 to 10:00 A. M.)

Regiment 308 was facing the extreme left flank of General Wellmann's I German Reserve Corps. The men in La Palette and on the height above Charlevaux Brook belonged to the 76th Reserve Division of that corps, mostly to Major Hünicken's 254th Reserve Regiment, Hessians. They were not the best troops in the German Army; second stringers, who were considered only fit for quiet sectors and had been placed here on the edge of the Argonne because the forest was one of the quietest sectors of all, a position where nature and engineering had united to build a fortress so powerful that only an insane enemy would think of attacking it.

East of the 254th, facing American 307 for the most part, was a detachment from the 122nd Regiment, 2nd Landwehr Division, old men, home guards, still worse troops than the 76th Reserve, who were rated fighters, if indifferent ones. "We brought in one crying bitterly," says one of the Americans who had struck these Landwehr in the September attacks. "He continued to cry and wipe his eyes with a dirty handkerchief. He thought we were going to kill him. He took out his cheap billfold

27

and offered Hanson all his money if he would not hurt him."

One must notice, though, that the Landwehr did not belong to Wellmann's command, but to that of his neighbor, von Kleist, head of the Army Group Argonnen. Wellmann, on the morning of October 2, was not even looking in this direction. At noon of the previous day the French artillery had come down hard on his right wing, and at twilight they charged him around the railroad station of Autry, with a gingery Breton division, the 71st, leading the attack. They got into his main defense line and began to spread; that night he had to throw in most of his corps reserve under the star shells to push the 71st out of Autry, and at dawn on the 2nd, this day, was still engaged in an artillery duel with that unit. About eight in the morning reports came through that the American artillery was tuning up; and not until then did he realize that the French attack had been a covering maneuver, designed to pull his reserves eastward so the Americans could hit a disgarnished line in the Argonne.

The position there was extremely strong, but Wellmann had been in contact with these transatlantic soldiers long enough to know by this time that their push would be far more serious than the French local attack. They always came on in overwhelming numbers, with a valorous ignorance that was both exasperating and difficult to meet. Outflank a French company and it surrendered or courteously retired, according to the rules; outflank an American company and it simply sat still and shot things out. About the only way to drive them was to catch them loose, at the crest of one of their attacks, when they tended to become disordered. The news from Major Hünicken caused a quick shift in the arrangements. Wellmann ordered the corps reserves with their artillery pulled out of line and switched toward the American front as fast as they could be disengaged. Meanwhile, he reached Freiherr Quadt-Wykradt-Hüchtenbruck, in command of the 76th Reserve Division, by 'phone; told him to shift any local reserves into the line and hold out till the corps reserve could arrive. He had no more than put down the 'phone when there was bad news from Autry; the persistent French had broken loose there again, and, as soon as some of the reserves had been removed from their front, smashed up a whole machine-gun company. Part of the already pitifully small corps reserve had to be put back.

III

Headquarters, 154th Infantry Brigade, U. S. A.
(11:00 to 12:20 A. M.)

It would be about eleven when Alexander received from Brigadier Johnson's command post by 'phone the latter's lugubrious report of the morning's operations. The General of Division was a bull of a man, mentally and physically; broad, red-faced, chesty, tough, a general out of a movie; had come up under his own power from an enlisted private in the ranks to be the youngest division commander in the American Army in France by sheer ability to lead and drive. Perhaps his nerves were slightly frayed; the first Argonne offensive had been a dismal business. A *failure,* if the word comes to mind, intended to pinch out the fortified wood by slashes on either side, which broke down when the French cracked on the left and the American V Corps on the right. There followed a series of red-hot remarks, signed "John J. Pershing, Commander-in-Chief," a few demotions *pour encourager les autres,* and instructions—no, not instructions but orders, extremely positive, that since the Argonne could not be pinched out the troops fronting it must drive right through, regardless of casualties.

Thus Alexander had left a 'phone message for Johnson at the latter's headquarters during the morning:

"You tell General Johnson that the 154th Brigade is holding back the French on the left and is holding back everything on the right, and that the 154th Brigade must push forward to their objective today. By must I mean must, and by today I mean today, and not next week. You report heavy machine-gun fire but the casualty lists do not substantiate this."

Yet the attack was stalled and Johnson had to say so; he did say so and listened to a magnificent piece of pyrotechnics in which he heard that the attack was to go on regardless of flanks and losses and, if he could not do it, Alexander would get someone who could.

30

October 2

At eleven-twenty Johnson 'phoned Colonel Stacey:
—The advance of the infantry will continue at twelve-thirty. The infantry action will be pushed forward until it reaches the line of the road and railroad, where the command will halt, reorganize, establish liaison to left and right and be ready for orders for a farther advance. The General says you are to advance behind the barrage regardless of losses.—

Stacey passed the message along to Whittlesey, but put in an addendum of his own, a sop to Whittlesey's reluctance to go on where he was, and this addendum turned out to be important. The bald height of La Palette was pretty hopeless; he gave the Major permission to try the other side of the ravine, Hill 198, which swung the direction a point or two east of true north. Whittlesey was still worried about his left flank.

—It will only be the same thing over again. We'll be cut off.

Stacey: "You're getting panicky."

Whittlesey: "All right. I'll attack, but whether you'll hear from me again I don't know."

IV

Hill 198, *Argonne Forest*
(*12:30 to 4:00* P. M.)

Unfortunately for the Germans there was a yawning gap in their line. The position above Charlevaux Brook ran for about five hundred yards along the hill crest, zigzag and strong till the trenches ended in a wild tangle of brush, piled limestone heaps, caves and a little precipice. This precipice marked the outer limit of Wellmann's sector; from that point on the line was von Kleist's care with his Army Group Argonnen. Now von Kleist had had plenty of trouble east of this point just a few days before when General Johnston's Pacific Coast huskies of the 91st Division had punched through his line. Most of his strength had been shifted facing them. For the protection of the westward tip, where his line joined Wellmann's, he was depending upon good position, good artillery, the fumbling of the Americans, and Wellmann's help.

The morning attack of the 307th fell upon the obtuse-angled elbow where the two corps joined and got a lodgment, not through the wire, to be sure, but enough to worry the defenders on the ridge. As the clock ticked toward noon while Whittlesey was away west of them at the foot of La Palette, most of the Germans in that line of trenches on Hill 198 came over to face the 307th, since there were no Americans on their immediate front; and most of the rest had been drawn away in the other direction by the French covering attack.

Whittlesey, meanwhile, surveying the eastern ridge above him, spied a chimney that led to the summit. Its walls would cover him against fire from La Palette; there did not seem to be much machine-gun fire coming down on him from the top of the ridge, and his strength had been augmented by the arrival of the 2nd Battalion of the regiment, the support battalion, under Captain Mc-Murtry.

The command was forward; the barrage arrived with the tick of the clock, not a good barrage, but at least something that made noise and a comforting dust of explosions among the German positions ahead. The two battalions together began working up the eastern height, crawling belly-floppers, sneaking from tree to tree, skirmishing by singles and twos as American soldiers have done since the days of Mad Anthony Wayne. There was some artillery fire from the Germans, but desultory, merely sprayed on the woods without aim, and therefore not serious; some machine-gun fire, but mostly from La Palette, across the valley on what was now their left-rear, therefore long-range, inaccurate; some sniper fire, and that was really pretty bad, taking fifty or sixty men as 308 sifted through the dense growth of the slope of Hill 198.

About two o'clock Whittlesey thought he had located the center of this sniper fire as well as a machine-gun nest somewhere on the right of his movement, and sent Lieutenant Rogers with B Company to clear the matter up. It was a machine-gun nest all right; Rogers dropped a few men behind trees to let off guns once in a while and keep the machine gunners amused, while he took the bulk of the company and worked round behind. The Germans kameraded without even offering to fight and, when Rogers closed in to disarm them, a whole batch more came up out of a dugout, till his bag amounted to a couple of officers and twenty-eight men.

They were disgusted with the war and glad to be captured, though not till they got back to the prison pens and questioning intelligence officers was it discovered why—some of Quadt-Wykradt-Hüchtenbruck's local reserves, supposed to be taking their rest, who had been shoved into the line just in time to be caught in the American barrage, and were feeling very sorry for themselves. There must have been half a dozen auto-rifles in the crowd; these the American officers rendered useless by breaking the spring of the breech mechanism.

No matter; the command is forward. They pressed on against isolated snipers who became ever fewer in number, isolated bursts of machine-gun fire from La Palette on the left, which were now all noise and hitting nobody. It must have been about four that the leading patrols stumbled on a trench protected by wire and scattered men back through the forest to search for the Major. He arrived presently; found the trench, a properly revetted, permanent line, dug a long time ago, now camouflaged by nature with weeds and creeping growths, but inside all in order—drainage sumps, firing platforms, machine-gun posts—the sort of place a military man could live in for years. This must be the Haupt-Widerstands-Linie, the main German defense line of the Giselher Stellung, the line which Whittlesey and every other officer of the A.E.F. knew the Germans had orders to hold to the last. The 308th was into it—with only that

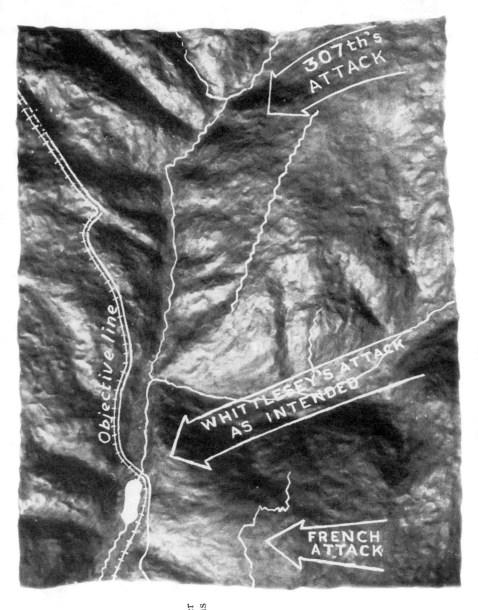

The attacks of October 2nd, in the morning as they started.

little sputter of B Company's against the thirty Germans to show for it.

But why? And how? Where were the Germans? Mystery.

V

Hill 198, *Argonne Forest* (*Half a Mile from the Last*)
(*10:00* A. M. *to 5:00* P. M.)

L had been the company of the 307th which effected the lodgment at the elbow on the crest above Charlevaux Brook. They lay panting in the underbrush from ten o'clock, the close of the morning battle, till half past noon, when the second began, nearly dead beat and much hurt.

They could not know it, of course, but the German troops opposite were in even worse shape. There were some men there from the 254th Hessians, some from the 122nd Landwehr; nobody knew who, precisely, was in command of the mixed detachment; there had been a good deal of loss from the American auto-rifle fire; their ammunition was running low. The barrage that came down at twelve-thirty finished them morally. Americans immediately began sifting through the wire in the most unexpected places and seemed to be shooting from every direction. They yielded; L Company went through the wire en masse, through the main defense line, and swung round like a line of skaters cracking a whip to flank the long arm of trench which Whittlesey found abandoned a little later and some distance west, though neither Whittlesey nor L Company of 307 was aware of the other's presence.

But this was L Company's last punch. Its captain, Kerr Rainsford, was a thin young man, artistic in tastes, not naturally a killer, upset by the losses his command had suffered. His runners could find no support at hand; instead they brought up Captain and Acting Major Crawford Blagden, a bluff, hearty officer, who had been sent forward by the Colonel to find out how things were going.

Blagden was a man with an active mind, perhaps too active. He heard Rainsford's story, which dwelt on loss and exhaustion, counted what few numbers L had left after the hard fight, and, knowing that the Germans always came back in a stiff counterstroke when a bit of their trench system was taken, decided on pulling out. "We can't fight the war alone;" and their orders said something about getting through the German line, then organizing for defense, which could be interpreted as Rainsford and Blagden chose to interpret them—that, having defeated the Germans on their front, they should return to the jumping-off point and "organize for defense" there.

This must have been about three o'clock, or just before Whittlesey stepped down into the trench of the Haupt-Widerstands-Linie. L Company pulled out, and it was not till ten years later in a New York hotel that its colonel learned that a portion of his command had really broken the German line that day. He nearly swallowed the glass from which he was drinking a Scotch-and-soda at the time.

VI

On the Bank of Charlevaux Brook, Argonne Forest (*About 4:00 p. m. to Sunset*)

Beyond the abandoned trench line Major Whittlesey took the lead with his headquarters company. The advance might be particularly dangerous here, and he was a man who felt strongly that anything his men were asked to do their officers should be willing to try. Besides, the whole situation was unclear, almost incomprehensible—why should that line of trench, undamaged by gunfire, be altogether tenantless? With the runners close at hand, Larney carrying the panels for signaling airplanes, Richards and Tollefson the pigeon cages, he wriggled across the ridge and out onto the opposite slope, glancing automatically at his watch as he did so and noting that it was just five-fifteen.

Out ahead the valley spread, Charlevaux Valley, not so wide as the Mississippi plain nor so deep as the Grand Canyon, but enough. Marsh green at the bottom; forest green and dirty brown to right and up the opposite slope, with the headland of La Palette blue in the west where the sun of the short October day was going down behind hurrying clouds that presaged a release from the rainy weather. Across the hill facing him ran a streak of livid grey—the road, the objective point; and not a soul was visible in all that expanse. No-yes! Two little figures in coal-scuttle helmets on the road.

A man at the Major's side raised his rifle and drew a bead. Whup!—and the two little figures scuttled into the underbrush of the hillside with a movement oddly bug-like.

—Missed (said the rifleman, and spat). I'd do better if I had some chow.

Several of the other officers came up and said a few words while the men streamed past, words important neither then nor later, reports of strength, comment on the country, a hail and farewell before they began sliding down the slope of the valley. Lieutenant Williamson was there with A, a shadow of a company, only eighteen men in line; Rogers of B, Captain Stromee, the new officer who had joined the night before the attack, with his lieutenants, Schenck and Trainor of C, the strongest company present; Wilhelm, Leak and Harrington of E in McMurtry's battalion, Buhler and Eager of G, Cullen and Griffin of H; and three machine-gun officers—Peabody, Revnes, Noon—with their apparatus and men from the 306th Machine-Gun Battalion.

Redheaded Cullen remembers a feeling of apprehension on that hill in the fading light. Perhaps he was psychic, perhaps his memory now accomplishes one of those transfers of time which memory often does.

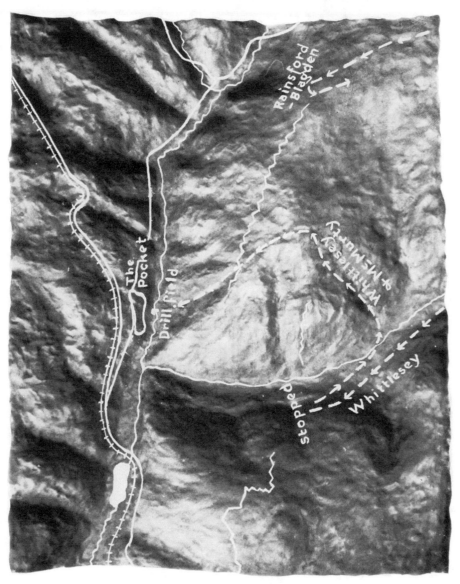

The American attacks of October 2nd, as they actually took place, showing the approximate route the Lost Battalion took in crossing Hill 198 and the pocket at which they arrived on the night of October 2.

October 2

—Take your men forward (said Whittlesey to each officer in turn).

Forward, down the slope, sliding and skidding among the trunks: At the bottom was an open space, where processions of ordered footprints showed a German drill field. They crossed it at a pace that suggested a herd of wild cattle to Newcom, the Kansas rancher in G Company. Beyond the drill field a rustic bridge crossed the stream that must be Charlevaux Brook through a scene that most of the men would have found charming had it not been for the long-range machine-gun bursts tearing the water at intervals from the direction of La Palette, where there was still a terrific racket going on. The command was halted briefly; the men crossed the bridge single file, with long intervals between, and even then a few were hit during the dash, but nearly all made it and as twilight closed in they were on the north slope of the stream, objective point, with the parapet of the road looming out of the forest above them.

Now all the officers became suddenly and intensely busy. The machine guns were set up first, mostly on the left of the position they surveyed, toward La Palette and the laggard French; the pieces carefully traversed to give avenues of fire by their own officers, then inspected by the Major. Positions were allotted to the twenty autorifles; guards told off. There was a business of rushing canteens to the brook for water; the men began to eat the corned willy and hardtacks they had brought, and a few to arrange swaps for a mouthful of beans or to coax favors from the fortunates who had tomatoes.

Whittlesey wrote a message and, calling Corporal Baldwin, told him to pass it back through the chain of runner-posts that had been dropped off every hundred yards during the climb up the hill, the journey through the German trenches and down the slope. The next question was liaison; a patrol was assigned to cross the road and railroad up the hill and see what, if anything, lay beyond; another patrol, a strong one, to push rightward. The French just possibly might have filtered some elements through on the left; McMurtry assigned Newcom and Hutt of G to push out in that direction and gain touch with them if so. "Keep under cover of the road," he warned them.

Shells were dropping, but mostly far, far away. The men of the original 77th had been in attacks before and found this one easy, especially since it was over. They groused about the food shortage, joked and kidded. A few apple knockers from upstate, over on the left of the position around an auto-rifle, began to talk about God in halting phrases and found to their mutual surprise that they agreed every man in the battalion was in His hands. The western replacements had not seen much of war, but were mostly from outdoor country and were ashamed to show themselves less virile than the city rats from the East Side. The wounded were relatively few; by general consent they had won an easy victory. Fritz must be on his way down the chutes.

VII

Headquarters, 76 Reserve-Division (German), Lançon (Afternoon to Evening)

THE Chief of Staff, who in the German Army is operations officer and practically brains, for the 76th Reserve Division (Hesse) was Hauptmann von Sybel. He had been under both Wellmann and Quadt-Wykradt-Hüchtenbruck earlier in the war; understood both, but that had not made this day of October 2 any more comfortable. In the early afternoon came the report of the French blow at Autry; Wellmann called for most of the divisional reserve to use with his corps reserve at this point, which left von Sybel as divisional reserve nothing but a single battalion of the 254th.

On the heels of this news came tidings from the front; the 253rd had yielded some ground west of La Palette, and what was worse still the Americans had broken through on a wide front near Charlevaux Mill and front-line communication with von Kleist's Army Group Argonnen was destroyed. The Herr Officer rendering the report begged to announce that the matter was urgent; the divisional bakery lay in the path of the American advance and what would our poor soldiers do for bread?

"Eine Schweinerei nie allein kommt," murmured von Sybel wearily. The reserve battalion of the 254th should be used west of La Palette to help out the 253rd. There was still a machine-gun company, supposed to be rest-

ing; let them go to the scene of the American attack, and he sent them off, to be gathered up by Rogers later in the afternoon. Obviously, there would have to be a counterattack in this quarter, but that was a matter for the corps to arrange, and von Sybel's present problem was that of saving the divisional bakery and getting enough men in position so that the counterattack would be a success.

What troops were available? He consulted maps and reports and found nothing but a pioneer battalion (376) and a couple of detached pioneer companies (76 and 77) who were working on roads near the bakery. Send them forward in the evening to form a new front across the line of the American break, ordered von Sybel, and issued orders that the pioneers were to be liberally supplied with machine guns and bombs.

Wellmann got the report of the break and the measures taken to stem it just about dark. He was much annoyed, but the night reports from the front line quieted his apprehensions, for the Americans who had breached his line did not seem to be coming any deeper than the Charlevaux Brook, nor even to be making efforts to widen their breach left and right. At the same time there was word that the French had once more been ejected from Autry. That set free the corps reserve, which was ordered out of the line and shifted eastward, and the same night report announced that the 252nd Regiment had beaten back the French west of La Palette, taken thirty prisoners and surrounded another batch of Frenchmen, who were still holding out at the time of the report, just before midnight.

At the same time Intelligence officers announced that they had pieced together some air photos taken on September 30 and October 1; bad pictures (given the rain) but they confirmed the indications in front-line dispatches that the Americans had brought up much artillery opposite the extreme left flank of the corps in the Argonne, and were now evidently mounting a full-dress offensive in the forest, peculiar as the idea might seem to a German soldier.

That made the break near Charlevaux Mill even more serious, for it meant that, if the Americans were allowed to hold the position they had gained there, they would widen and deepen the hole, possibly flanking out La Palette and breaking the whole line in that sector. Therefore the Haupt-Widerstands-Linie must be recovered. Wellmann got through to von Kleist, who had served with him in the old brigade during the advance to the Marne four years ago, and asked him for co-operation in closing the breach made by the Americans. Von Kleist was himself heavily engaged, but everything seemed to be holding on in his front; he would spare some detachments to join hands with his old friend. The rest was detail; the artillery were assigned to the task of holding the French around Autry; a counterattack by the 252nd was ordered between Autry and La Palette; the reserves of the 76th R.D. were ordered in to close the break, and the 254th released from other tasks to head this movement.

The German staff officers were awake half the night working out timetables and road movements, so that every man should be in the right place when the guns started to shoot. Through the dark the weary regiments stumbled eastward, and all night long the 252nd continued to heave potato-masher bombs and *Minen* into the little group of French cuirassiers who had broken the line.

OCTOBER 2—NIGHT

I

Above Charlevaux Brook
(About 6:00 P. M.)

"VERY hard digging," reports the diary of Private Jim
Larney, one of the two men who were keeping diaries
(the other was a Colorado Dane named Christensen), in
faint pencil-traces that had to be read later by the impression they made through the paper. Faint and laconic
were his words, since the man was tired, doubtless feeling
the nervous reaction of having come through a battle and
crossed safely the bridge of death at the valley bottom,
and finding the physical difficulty of clawing at the
limestone ledges with a bayonet nothing to cheer about.
There did not seem to be any shooting at present, but
both battalion commanders were familiar with the German habit of fierce counterattack and were concerned
over the problem of arranging their men and getting
them dug in before it became too dark to work.

It was dusk; leftward through the dying light Newcom and Hutt were shoving through the underbrush toward the French, five yards or more apart, both with
rifles ready. Above them, and almost touching their

hips on the right, towered a line of masonry, heavy blocks cunningly joined without mortar—the terrace of an ancient Roman road, solid as on the day it was built, topped now with the facing of the modern route.

They must have been four or five hundred yards on their way when both at once heard voices on their right, uphill above the road. Newcom had just pushed into a thicket of particular denseness; the voices came from a trifle behind him.

"What outfit is that up there?" he heard Hutt say, and turning cautiously, could see his partner standing at gaze, framed in an opening where the trees fell away on either side. His own vision was cut off by a screen of shrub; he ducked to look through the lattice of stems below, and missed a heartbeat when he saw a German corporal with one, two, three, four—nine other men, and a machine gun, pointing straight at Hutt.

"Go nod pack, but come up here," the corporal was ordering in labored English, and Newcom noticed he had a Lüger in his hand. The Kansan moved his rifle forward and drew a bead on the man, calculating swiftly that he could not miss this open-sight shot, he would be protected against the return blaze of the machine gun by the lip of masonry, could drop the gunner all right with the second shot . . . but no, the machine gun was pointing at Hutt; the moment the corporal was shot they would turn loose on him. Newcom made himself smaller in his bush and saw his companion go uphill to the Germans, who immediately began to feel through his pockets for souvenirs.

Photograph U. S. Army Official.

The Pocket: A close-up view from the valley bottom. Right: The commander of the 77th Division; Major General Robert Alexander.

October 2—Night

He was not to return to the regiment till after the Armistice, and then pale and staggering, clothes in rags, his body covered with white louse sores, his stomach starved for a taste of anything sweet, which a bumptious Y.M.C.A. secretary refused him because he had no money. The night that happened there was something which the Y reported as a riot, and a profitable supply of chocolate mysteriously disappeared.

II

Headquarters, 154th Infantry Brigade, U. S. A.; and Hill 198, Argonne Forest (Night)

At about eight o'clock in the evening, when the forest was already pitch-dark, General Johnson of the 154th Brigade heaved a sigh of relief. Early reports from Colonel Houghton of 307 admitted no progress on his front and, as there had been nothing more encouraging since, it was probable that no progress represented the sum of that regiment's efforts for the day. But now Johnson had a messenger from Whittlesey with the cheering news that 308 had burst the German lines and was sitting down on its objective for the night. For once Alexander would have no fault to find with him.

The Commanding General had been at him all afternoon, following the eruption in the morning, though the arrival of the German machine-gun prisoners seemed to mollify him somewhat.

The Lost Battalion

—How is the advance? (he asked about four).

When Johnson said the last reports showed it still going forward, the General began to worry about flanks. The French did not appear to be making material progress, and Whittlesey's left ought to be covered. What troops had the brigade?

The Brigadier mentioned Battalion 3 of 308, his brigade reserve, and Companies D and F of the same regiment, which Colonel Stacey had withheld from the twelve-thirty attack and which were now doing flank guard.

—I'm sending you another battalion from the division reserve (said Alexander); you had better push that 3rd Battalion of the 308th forward to plug the gap.

Johnson ordered the 3rd Battalion up under Captain Scott. However, it was a weak battalion, the weakest in the regiment since the September fighting, in which it had suffered severely. An effort to maintain direct physical contact with Whittlesey's left would result in its being swept away in detail by the inevitable German counterattack, there being too few men for the amount of ground there was to cover; and moreover it was by this time so dark that any such delicate maneuver as pushing the formation through a kilometer and more of forest would succeed only through the most fantastic good luck. He had the battalion halt at the road running east from Binarville into the forest, dig in, facing north and connecting solidly with the French who were in Binarville. This, he considered, would put it in an ideal position to flank any German counterstroke against the two battalions that had gone forward. General Evan Johnson was a man who would give considerable weight to that sort of consideration, above all, a tactician, who could not come into a room without thinking of some ingenious way of doing it better than it had been done before.

The news that came at eight o'clock helped matters still further. A battalion of the 307th, as he ascertained by field 'phone, was up in close support. It could be shoved in between the 3rd Battalion of 308 and the two up with Whittlesey, giving a line almost or altogether continuous. In the morning this battalion of 307 would join with Whittlesey, facing half right, and covering his right flank. The Major, by holding hard with his left, could pry rightward, ripping up the German line with the crowbar of this battalion; 307 would take up the move, then 306, and so eastward along the whole line. A pretty combination!

Johnson ordered Houghton of the 307th to send up his third battalion in support of Whittlesey at once, the map having shown a path by which it could move. It was murk night, but the moving troops could guide by the slope of the hill. When they reached the ravine they would swing north back up the crest, across the abandoned trench line and so down into Charlevaux Valley, following Whittlesey's runner-posts for this part of the journey. The orders were that 307 should resume its frontal attack on the German lines in the morning, while Whittlesey was taking the same adversaries in flank and rear.

Houghton's battalion was composed of four companies, K, I, M, F, all pretty strong and in good condition. They had lain in support, taking a little shelling, but nothing serious; had had a hot meal and dropped off to sleep when at nine Lieutenant Currier appeared with the guides and orders to move up. Many of the men had to be shaken awake by the noncoms.

The lead of the movement fell to Captain Nelson Holderman of Company K, a hearty young man from California, who liked soldiering so much he even liked its discomforts, the whole business a perpetual party to him, and the best war he was ever in. Lieutenant Tom Pool, a cotton classer from Texas, who had been in temporary command of the company when Holderman joined, led the Indian-file advance through the scrub and forest down the trail, Holderman in the rear, and the men so close they could almost touch each other. The night was cloudy, dark as the inside of a dog's belly, and the only illumination an occasional German star shell, far away toward La Palette. M Company trailed K; behind came I and F. Progress was slow and slower as deceptive chimneys and cuts ruffled the slope by which they were steering, the men frequently stumbled and fell, there were halts to keep from breaking the chain. The clock ticked on; touched midnight, then the half. The four companies made a long halt, there was some confusion and men dropped off to sleep where they were.

October 2—Night

At about two-thirty Currier came stumbling along, passed from hand to hand down the line. He reached Pool, told him that everything was all right, a guide had been found, they were to go on. Pool passed the word back, mouth to mouth; the men were got to their feet again and shambled onward. Pool, at the head of the file with the guide, thought he heard German voices (which was not impossible) and passed back word, "No talking, boys, keep quiet and follow the lead man."

As before, there were bunchings and frequent halts; during one of them Lieutenant Shelata at the head of Company M, never a strong man and now utterly exhausted, sat down to get a little rest. When he fully recovered himself, the man whose belt he had been holding was gone and his own little troop was lost in the forest. Guide by the slope, his instructions had been; he made a tentative effort here, another there, and then, too weary to care what happened next, set outposts and lay over till daylight.

F and I broke loose when M did and, though they kept moving, got onto a track that led them into a valley with water in it and a bold escarpment of rock looming out above against the midnight sky. They climbed a little way and got into some old German dugouts, now covered with moss, where they bedded down for the night, planning to cross the crest of the hill and link up with Whittlesey in the morning. Without lights or guides they had no way of knowing that the path they had taken led them in the wrong direction and that they were just under the headland 308 had tried to circle in the morning attack, the headland that was the last turning before La Palette. Nor would they discover these things till morning.

III

Hill 198, *Argonne Forest* (2:00 A. M. *to About* 4:00 A. M.)

Holderman's K alone held the true line. They could have covered but a small distance after the two-thirty halt when, mouth to mouth, word passed up from the rear that they were to about face and march back. Both form and content of the order struck Pool as strange; Colonel Houghton's messenger had told him personally to see that the advance was executed and the four companies used to prolong Whittlesey's right. No—retreat could not be a genuine order, unless written. "In place, halt!" he ordered, and slipped back down the line, telling each man to take orders from the head only, disregard everything that came from behind. Too late— the last two squads had dropped off and with them Company M had disappeared into the darkness behind.

It must have been twenty minutes later when Pool got back to the head of his column and got the men moving again; an hour later when they happened into a little clearing on a shelf of rock. Under two scalped birches at the far side, they stumbled on three soldiers—men of the runner-posts Baldwin had dropped behind.

—Where's the 308th? (asked Pool).

—Beyond the hill and the valley on the other side (replied the runners). There's a double trench line on the crest and another runner-post just beyond it. You can't miss it.

Pool picked up one of the runners as a guide to the next station, and the little company, seventy-nine men now besides their officers, pushed on into the dark, negotiated the abandoned German trench line without difficulty and, as the first runner had said, found a post just beyond it.

—You can't miss it (repeated the men). There's a field and a bridge at the foot of this hill and the Major is dug in just beyond.

But Pool found the next runner-post vacant; could see nothing of field, bridge, or next hill, nothing at all indeed and, with the slope dropping away from him in all directions, felt that it would be fatally easy to take the wrong road in the dark woods. Moreover his mission was support, and his position now ideal for such a purpose. Holderman set outposts and let the men get a little shut-eye for the few remaining hours of the night.

IV

The Pocket Above Charlevaux Brook
(6:00 P. M. to 10:00 P. M.)

Major Whittlesey had assigned his men to their positions and had his top kick, Ben Gaedeke, out making a checkup on losses during the advance. The message announcing his arrival had gone back at seven.

He sat down in the funk hole grubbed out as a headquarters for a brief chat with McMurtry, while the men of the headquarters company around them shared puffs from the carton of Lord Salisburys brought up by Jim Larney, the signal-panel man.

Battalion headquarters was at the center of the banana-shaped position, center and north, just under the edge of the road. Below it Company A was strung out, down near the bed of the stream, the position least likely to encounter trouble, for A was the weakest company and the one most frequently called on for runner details. E and G, under local orders of Lieutenant Wilhelm of E, held the right flank with the two machine guns from Company C of the 306th Machine-Gun Battalion, with their officer, Lieutenant Noon, who also had one of Company D's seven guns. On this flank just beyond the road and a good few yards from the position, a twenty-foot precipice jutted out from the hillside above.

The left flank, three hundred and fifty yards away toward the French and the valley mouth, was the dangerous one. The other six machine guns were there with Companies B, C and H, the latter the heaviest company present, and the whole in charge of McMurtry, with Lieutenant Cullen of H as his second. Stromee of C was a captain; therefore outranked the latter, but Stromee was new; he looked like a good man and might turn out a heavyweight, but knew none of the men or the little regimental customs which have the force of law in such

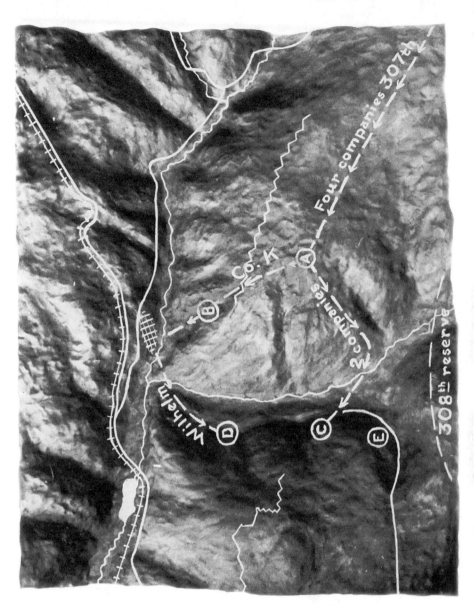

Movement on the night of October 2 and the morning of October 3. (A) is the point where the chain of men from the 307th broke, sometime during the night. (B) is the spot where Holderman spent the night with Company K, 307th. (C) is where the companies following him in spent the night. (D) is where Wilhelm's command encountered Germans on the morning of October 3. (E) is the night location of Lieutenant Paul Knight with Companies D and F, 308th. All these locations are approximate, as is the placing of the 308th's reserve.

an organization and was unknown to the men, while both the Major and his second were sure of Cullen—a redheaded man with square features and a high sense of his own value, yet by that very token not likely to let down in a pinch. When he barked, men jumped.

Orders had said "along the line of the road and railroad generally." Whittlesey felt and McMurtry confirmed that the final adverb qualified the phrase permissively enough to allow them to leave the railroad out of their lines. They could see the slope, how it fell away beyond the road offering less good cover, would be subject to artillery fire from La Palette and even beyond, and to raking long-range machine-gun fire from a number of points; would be farther from water, and in general a weaker position than the steep hillside where they were now dug in.

Better where we are, since top kick Gaedeke is back from his checkup and reports less than five hundred and seventy-five men present for duty, not enough to grip both hill crest and stream.

The Major and McMurtry agreed that the most serious lack was that of creature comforts for the men, no rations but iron rations and not enough of those, no coffee, almost no tobacco, no blankets—not that either officer was a sentimentalist, but both liked things done *en règle* and had thought this whole Meuse-Argonne offensive smacked of the costly and ignorant optimism of 1914. The plans of the high command are not usually explained in all their details to junior majors, but the main outlines of what was taking place were fairly clear to an analytical mind, and there were two of them considering the matter in the funk hole above Charlevaux Brook. Obviously there had been an effort to pinch out the difficult country of the Argonne by sweeping round both sides of it; that was the offensive of late September and it had faltered when neither flank attack made enough gain. It was equally obvious that the mission of their own division during that ill-starred drive had been that of a containing force, expected to advance rapidly and to sleep in billets; the lack of blankets, overcoats, trench mortars, tents, tanks, bespoke the idea that the high command did not intend them to do any slugging. Such shortages could be borne, it is true, especially if the intent had been translated into fact—if they had mainly the forces of nature to overcome. The rub was that they were now being asked to assault the strongest German positions of the whole front without any of the usual equipment and preparation for such assault except some not very effective artillery protection. Unfair.

An indistinguishable homunculus rose at them out of the darkness, and by the slow-motion lightning flash of a German star shell, flickering through the pattern of leaves, they could make out that the man was saluting. The voice was that of the battalion sergeant major.

—Beg pardon, sir, but Private Powers thinks he heard someone speaking German back where we just came from.

—Private Powers is having nightmares. Tell him to go back to sleep.

OCTOBER 3

I

Headquarters, I Reserve-Korps (German), Briquenay
(Dawn to About 9:00 P. M.)

GERMANS preferably attacked at dawn, having by observation and logic arrived at the conclusion that at
that hour more of the variables—weather, visibility, our
artillery fire and the enemy's, our morale (strengthened
by early breakfast and schnapps) and theirs (weakened
by lack of the same if you come early enough)—more of
the variables are favorable than at any other hour. Before
the day that morning, everything was ready for the
counterstrokes the corps had ordered; when the sun
jumped up, red and cloudless for the first time in more
than a week, both Wellmann's and von Kleist's counterattacks moved forward, cheerfully and with confidence.

There had been a little confusion during the night. Of
all days this American break had to fall on the one when
Wellmann's Chief of Staff, Major Becker, departed to
take up new duties with von Hutier at the high army
command, and the new staff man, Major von Ditfurth,
knew neither the corps nor its sector. In addition
Becker had begun his plan in the full confidence that

57

von Kleist and the Army Group Argonnen would be able to make a strong effort toward closing the gap made by the Americans and during the night von Kleist had 'phoned that his wing regiment, the 122nd Landwehr, was not very good for offensive operations.

Becker ordered the covering attack during the night by the 252nd Regiment at the spot where the French had made their incursion between Autry and Binarville. Information from an American prisoner that two battalions had come through near Charlevaux Mill, however, did not make his other plan for a simple recovering attack by a battalion of the 254th look hopeful. Two battalions of Americans, even allowing for losses, could not number much less than fifteen hundred men, which was about the strength of a whole German regiment in that part of the line. Therefore von Ditfurth had to mount a much more elaborate operation than his predecessor had counted on, especially since von Kleist could not give much help.

He planned a slide left and eastward by most of the troops in the corps area; the 9th Landwehr Division would take over around Autry, where the French advance was now thoroughly stalled; the 76th Reserve similarly moving eastward, with its strength concentrated toward the left wing.

The details of the 76th Reserve Division's portion of the slide naturally fell to Hauptmann von Sybel, Chief of Staff of that division. He arranged for the 252nd Regiment to take over the ground around La Palette and a little westward; the 253rd should hold La Palette and the ravine to Hill 198. This would release the whole of the 254th for the counterstroke along that hill, and he would still have the reserve battalion of this last regiment, together with what extra troops could be swept up, to surround and wipe out the two battalions who had made the break. Count up: one battalion of the 254th; one of foot-Uhlans; the pioneer Battalion 376 and the two detached pioneer companies, beside what von Kleist could send; that ought to do the business.

The men were sent up to Charlevaux Mill through the night in trucks; behind the troop trucks followed others with extra supplies of machine guns and potato-masher bombs, especially for the pioneers who, not being normally fighting troops, would need particularly heavy supplies of these mechanical weapons.

Naturally, all these arrangements took time, with the necessary requisitions on the ammunition dumps, traffic to be got moving, men to be found in the dark. It was therefore later than the optimum hour when Major Hünicken's 254th moved down the valley behind La Palette and began to climb the spur toward the end of the lost portion of the Haupt-Widerstands-Linie. Yet the news that came to Wellmann in the early day, as he sat in bed sipping his coffee, was good—the night attack on the besieged French group had been so brilliantly delivered as to bring the congratulations of von Einem, the Army Group commander, and had resulted in the capture of two officers and fifty men. An hour or two later the remaining French officer surrendered with the thirty who were all that remained of this little command and the breach was closed.

II

Hill 198
(*Early Morning—Hour Uncertain*)

Hünicken's men moved forward slowly. They understood the general situation better than the Americans, but were not aware of all its details and may have suspected a trap when they were permitted to climb the spur opposite La Palette without drawing fire. The spur was steep but wooded, with good cover. One would normally expect American auto-rifle nests all over the place, and Hünicken had brought along a *Minenwerfer* section to stamp out such cores of resistance, but there were none. There was no resistance of any sort as the 254th worked on into the red rising sun.

Northward, a man with good eyes or an officer with glasses could doubtless have made out that there were Americans in considerable number along the Roman road, just as Whittlesey, from almost the same spot, had looked across the valley and seen the two Germans on the previous evening. Whether there were eyes or glasses good enough to pierce the distance in those first faint streaks of day we do not know; we only know that the 254th was filtering eastward in small parties, each grouped around its light machine gun, the advance parties spread across a wide front as required by the Ludendorff system, all following the general direction of the Haupt-Widerstands-Linie.

Along the trench they organized machine-gun positions, alternately facing them north and south. Now it was after six, not yet full day in the gloomy forest. There was some artillery firing off toward La Palette and pennons of smoke occasionally drifted past. Two of the flank patrols chanced on American runner-posts and expeditiously dispatched the men in them, but without finding either messages or food—worse luck!—on the bodies; and another flank patrol came in to report that a body of Americans from the hornet's nest on the north was moving toward the rear of the newly recovered trench line in attack formation.

III

The Pocket Above Charlevaux Brook
(About 6:00 A. M.)

Just before dawn two men in the leftmost outpost, down toward the mill heard something grunting and squashing in the underbrush ahead of them. They flattened and, when the grunts, which had an unmistakably Teutonic accent, were near enough for them to do business, rose simultaneously with their rifles at the ready.

"Kamerad," said the subject docilely enough, and

threw his own rifle down—a young man, who had once been fat, but whose pouched cheeks now hung limp to give him a peculiar chuckleheaded appearance. No food in his pockets—worse luck!—but there was a good Lüger which one of the sentries appropriated, while the other marched the prisoner off toward the funk hole where Whittlesey and McMurtry had slept side by side.

The Major understood a little German, but not much; he called over Interpreter Manson who, to put the man at his ease before questioning, offered him the half-sack of Bull which was all the tobacco that remained to him. The German instantly produced from his pocket a porcelain pipe of approximately the content of the Mammoth Caves of Kentucky, dumped the entire sack of tobacco into it and politely returned the empty sack to Manson, while smiles flickered briefly across the faces of the officers.

—What is your regiment?

—The 254th Reserve Regiment, from Hesse.

—We know your regiment; they are good troops. Are there many of you near here?

—Very many. You will be wiped out.

—The whole regiment is here?

—And more yet.

The questioning went on, Whittlesey and McMurtry standing thoughtfully by and trying to wring a connected picture from the mass of confused and often contradictory details which are a private soldier's recollections of a night movement in war. Whittlesey, a lawyer with a little experience in cross-examination, handled the prisoner like an unfriendly witness, courteously, with interspersed irrelevant questions to keep the man from building up a connected tissue of lies. But everything had to be filtered through the mind of the interpreter, so it was slow going.

—The food was not famous. They had made a night march in trucks; had been in reserve beyond La Palette on the previous day. American tobacco was not like German—it was too sweet, not enough *Brennstoff* in it, went out in your pipe. The Herr Major had made them a speech; they were to make a counterattack against the Americans, but it would not be difficult, for they would be surprised and taken in flank. He was not married, not yet.

And the questioning was interrupted by the patrol which had gone to the hill crest, who reported that they had both seen and heard Germans in numbers beyond the road, got a fleeting shot at one—"I think I hit him, sir"—and had received the fire of a light machine gun in return.

Whittlesey stared at the ground in silence for a moment, then consulted his watch and his map.

"Ask Lieutenant Wilhelm to report to me," he said.

IV

The Pocket; Whittlesey Thinks
(6:00 to 7:00 A. M.)

The same thought, the thought of the cutoff on the 28th-29th, had occurred to both Whittlesey and Lieutenant Paul Knight who had been assigned to the command of the flank-guard, companies D and F. If the French failed in keeping their end up in this attack as the French and negroes had failed before, there would be trouble on that left flank from German infiltration; the Major and the Lieutenant were agreed that the safety of the wing depended upon that possibility being well watched.

As the attack was planned, keeping touch with that flank would not be too difficult a matter, but to provide for emergencies Whittlesey had made an agreement with Knight, that when he, the Major, reached his objective, he would send a company back to link up with D and F, which in turn would link through the 2nd Battalion with the regiment. The situation had changed radically since that agreement was made, for the agreement had contemplated neither the right-oblique movement across the brook and Hill 198 nor the ploying of the 1st and 2nd Battalions into a single force for the successful afternoon attack.

The battalions had, indeed, been intended to attack in depth, a somewhat idealistic arrangement inherited from a period when the division was operating in open country, and an arrangement which assumed that both battalions would be somewhere near their full strength of nine hundred men apiece. Actually the two together were little more than half this figure; and when Mc-Murtry came up to confer with Whittlesey during the lull in the fighting just before noon of the previous day, the two officers agreed that to attack in depth would so disperse the few men at their disposal that they would be subject to defeat and destruction by squads; and the two were made into one, for the final thrust.

Thus the oblique had stretched the communications with Knight's two companies; and the ploying together of the battalions had brought into the fighting line units that might otherwise have been covering that left wing. It was therefore important to contact Knight's two companies and keep the private agreement; yet when the command reached its objective the night before it was already too dark and too late to make this contact. There were too many chances that a company sent back would lose its way feeling out toward the left; Newcom's report showed there were Germans very near on that side, the linking company might easily stumble into them and be lost to a man.

Besides, there was little danger of infiltration at night; the Germans never attacked after dark without a parade of star shells, artillery, and assorted whatnots as easy to remark as the second coming of Christ, and they never pulled night attacks over such ground as this. His runner-posts had been doubled to be sure that regiment, brigade and division headquarters knew accurately what he was doing and where he was; he had sent reports back every half hour; and with the experience of the 28th in mind, it would be odd indeed, if these higher units failed to clean up the rear areas for him or to keep communications open and his left flank closed.

The Lost Battalion

The news brought back by the outpost which had captured the prisoner, the fact that there was a prisoner found on that left flank, was Whittlesey's first certainty that the rear elements had not closed up to him, or that the French had not made any advance. One expected this of the French who, after four years of war, had not exactly the zip of raw recruits. But the question before Major Charles W. Whittlesey, commanding 1st Battalion, 308th U. S. Infantry, as he sat on the edge of a funk hole with dawn beginning to streak the sky over the Argonne was not the moral one of apportioning blame for something he could not have prevented, but the practical one of protecting that left rear, through which some German elements had evidently filtered already; and, considering this practical question, he remembered his agreement with Knight.

He remembered also that the German infiltration tactic consisted of small parties, which became strong only by accumulation; the time to stop them was before the accumulation became serious. So he summoned Wilhelm, and while waiting for him wrote a message telling what he was about to do:

At: 294.7—276.3
Date: 3 *Oct*. 18 *Hour*: 6:50 AM
To: *Detroit* 1

Have sent order to D and F Co's. to advance rapidly
   to rejoin us.

October 3

Am sending E and H down west side of ravine to
assist this movement.
Will await orders here.
McMurtry is with me and we are working together.

Whittlesey.

V

The Tip of Hill 198, near the Pocket
(7:00 A. M.)

Captain Holderman, who had exchanged messages
with Whittlesey in the hours before dawn, came over
the brook early and the two officers compared their
orders. Holderman's bade him prolong the 308th's flank
along the line of the road.

—And there are two or three more companies right
behind me (he added) which should be along here any
minute.

—Oh, then we're all right (remarked McMurtry, who
was taking part in the conference, with relief in his
voice).

The Major nodded agreement.

—Have your company report here, then (he said to
Holderman).

He turned back to McMurtry, who thought that
sending H Company with E would hardly be necessary;
H was the strongest company present; if there were
Germans out on that left flank a dangerous dispersion
would result.

67

—Let E alone go then (said Whittlesey, and so it was). Wilhelm, Karl, 1st Lieutenant, A. E. F., was from the heavily Germanic city of Buffalo, the best German-speaking officer in the command and an intelligent, quick-witted leader. His company, E, was on the right flank where the menace was least; could be replaced by those men of the 307th whose helmets were now occasionally visible in the thin early light, bobbing through the undergrowth of the Charlevaux bottom; and it had two other lieutenants (Leak and Harrington) which assured the little command of good tactical control for its mission. There was a brief conference for orders; Wilhelm and his company trotted off toward the stream, across it, and, while the day began to open up, began climbing the hill above Charlevaux where they were to meet the advance of Hünicken and the 254th Reserve Regiment.

VI

The Ravine Under La Palette Hill
(Morning—Hour Uncertain)

Companies I and M of 307 woke in their mossy dugouts to find themselves under slow shellfire from somewhere to the north and the same accurate crisscross of machine guns that had stopped Whittlesey and his men the previous morning. Obviously they were in the wrong place. As soon as the officers could get a bearing on landmarks they backtracked and formed on the rest of the regiment.

VII

The Pocket
(7:00 to 9:00 A. M.)

Half an hour after Wilhelm and his company left, Holderman and Pool with Company K, 307, began to filter across the bridge and into the position, filing away rightward to cover the flank E had vacated. It was now full daylight; most of the men, with little else to do, were digging in industriously at their funk holes or working on the latrines which the Major had ordered dug at the first peep of day. A few lucky enough to strike soft spots made good progress—"Regular caves they had," Powers the signal-man described it enviously, he having hit a limestone shelf that nothing short of blasting powder could remove. There was no remaining doubt about the German voices up on the hill now; and shells were beginning to drop all round the position. Most fell far below at the edge of the brook, sending up elegant geysers of muddy water; a few beyond the road, none among the men. Steep hillside, nice position—it would take a good gun to find us.

It would be just after Wilhelm left and Holderman arrived that a message came in down the chain of runner-posts:

To: C. O. *Red*

Plenty of rations at your P. C. of last night. Send
  for them if you want them.
Believe railroad will prevent details from getting
  lost.
Am making every effort to get up blankets, overcoats and slickers.
Be prepared to move forward at 7 A. M. but do not
  advance until you receive the order from me.
At daylight try and establish liaison with troops on
  right and left.
Why not try one-pounders on observation tower?
Will try and have overcoats at ration dump by midnight.
Two companies reserve 3rd Battalion are now at
  your P. C. of last night.

DETROIT 1

Whittlesey regarded this message with considerable
internal disquietude. "Detroit 1" was the code signature
for Colonel Stacey and he knew the handwriting besides; there could be no doubt of its genuineness. But
there were several things about it not altogether pleasant.
He had no one-pounders; he did not feel he had men to
spare for a ration detail; it was now after seven in the
morning and no orders for the advance indicated in the
message had reached him; and most singular of all, the
message was timed at seven P.M., that is, the previous
evening, which meant that his runner-chain was working so very badly it had taken all night to get a message
through. He immediately wrote out one of his own:

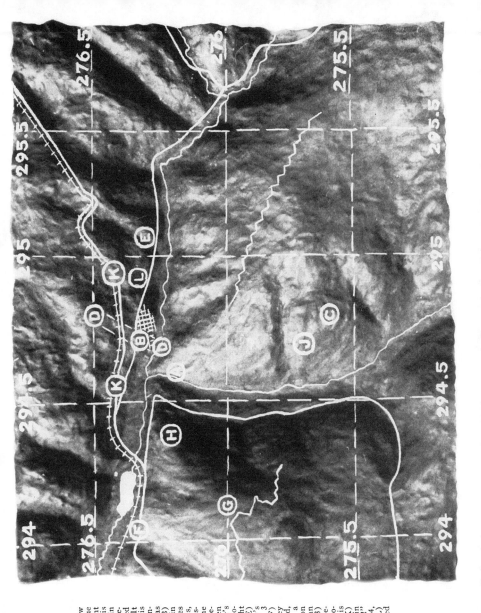

Co-ordinates. The lines show the exact location of the true co-ordinates. (A) is the point where Whittlesey placed his command in the one message in which he erred, the message beginning "I have just received your message about rations." It will be noted that even in this one he is not far off and the runner who bore the message was killed before it was delivered. (B) represented the location given in all the other Whittlesey messages and in McMurtry's messages, right at the edge of the cross-hatching that represents the pocket. (C) is the spot represented by the co-ordinates given in Lieutenant Teichmoeller's message. (D)—(D) are the co-ordinates given in the night message of October 2. (E) is the spot where Whittlesey's morning message of October 3 reports meeting Germans. (F) is the spot at which Whittlesey reports a German mortar located, and (G) is where he reports a German machine-gun firing on him. (H) is where the German prisoner (morning of October 3) said he left his truck. Whittlesey's message, morning of October 3, by pigeon, reported his runner-post broken at (J). (K)—(K) is the line mentioned in the "For God's sake, stop it!" pigeon message of October 4, during the friendly barrage. (L) is where the aviators sighted Prinz' fake panel.

October 3

At: 294.6-276.2
Date: 3 Oct. 18 Hour: 7:40 A. M.
To: Detroit 1

Have just received your message of last night about
rations. Don't dare send back for them if we are
to advance. Can't you send them to us? Also
overcoats and blankets if possible.
Have sent only E Co. back to join D and F as I feared
too much dispersion if we must advance again.
Casualties yesterday (estimated in B E G H and I
Cos., the ones now here) 8 killed 80 wounded.

Not long later it occurred to him that neither regimental nor brigade headquarters would have a very accurate nose-count on his men, and that the Q. M. boys
were strong on paper work; he sent off another message
giving a formal requisition for the number of rations
required.

After it had gone, McMurtry, who had been arranging
patrols, came up, a precise, careful man. There was a
brief conversation. Whittlesey thought Holderman's
company coming through demonstrated that the line of
runner-posts was all right; the fact that Pool had found
one post vacant and Stacey's message had taken twelve
hours coming up probably meant nothing more than
man-failure or the advance of a few wandering and ad-
venturous German parties. It was the beginning of an
infiltration to cut them off, not the completion of it.
McMurtry was inclined to agree, but as they discussed

the matter decided it was a good idea to test the runner-chain by sending another message through.

At: 294.6-276.3
Date: 3 Oct 18 Hour 8:20 A. M.
To: Detroit 1

Capt. Holderman with K Co attached to 2nd Bn. 307th is here with his Co. They were sent to get in touch with 308th and last night came up our runner line from our advance telephone station. Mr. Holderman says that at 9 P. M. last night the two advance companies of 307th (G and H) were at 295.4-276.45.

A few moments later it occurred to McMurtry that in asking for rations to be sent up Whittlesey had not mentioned the headquarters companies and machine gunners. He therefore got off another note, a note which was to turn out more important than its face value:

At: 294.7-276.3
Date: *Oct 3 Hour: 8:42* A.M.
To: Lieut. Taylor Co K 308 Advance Tel. Station

Do not forget to send following rations for the Bn. Hqts. and Mgs.
1st Bn. Hqts—32
2nd Bn. Hqts—43
Mg Detachs—50

G. G. McMurtry

At the same time it was important to do something

about that German artillery; sooner or later they were apt to straighten out their co-ordinates or get a gun over behind La.Palette, and then there would be grief for the command on the hillside. Whittlesey asked for Omer Richards, the York State French-Canadian who was the number one pigeon man, and sent off a message by one of his birds, which would get through quicker than any runner:

At: 294.6-276.3
Date: 3 Oct. Time: 8:50 A.M.
To Delaware 1

We are being shelled by German artillery.
Can we not have artillery support?
Fire is coming from northwest.

Preparing these messages, the discussion of their precise terms and the general situation had swung the clock to nine; there was now a good deal of machine-gun fire in the direction Wilhelm had taken, so he must be having trouble connecting with Knight, and now another machine gun in the rear somewhere was sending up a shower of minor splashes among the big geysers from the shells in the brook.

The artillery liaison officer, Lieutenant Teichmoeller, of the 305th Field Artillery, was of course present when the subject of these messages, particularly the last, came up, and at the same time offered to get in touch with his own organization through division headquarters and see what he could do about getting some help from the guns. It was apparently just after Whittlesey and Mc-Murtry had gone to start the patrols and sent their messages that he got a pigeon and sent off his message:

To: C. O. 305th F. A.

We are being shelled at this point.
Cadence 1 per minute.
Caliber Minen 77HE
Fire—northwest.
  Give us artillery; work quickly
  Place: 294.8-275.6
      J. P. TEICHMOELLER, Liaison Off 305 FA

This pigeon was found in the loft at division HQ at ten-fifty-five and the message at once telephoned through from division to the command of the artillery brigade.

VIII

Consideration on Co-ordinates

In all of these messages the most important thing, and in most of them the only important thing is the co-ordinates, those mysterious little sets of numbers following the word "At." The French had covered the whole northern portion of their country with an imaginary grid of parallels like those of latitude and longitude. The bars of this grid were exactly one thousand meters, one kilometer, apart; and each bar was represented by a number. In employing this system a man identified any spot he was on by recognizing some landmark on the French Army map he carried. These were very detailed maps which showed every house and in some cases even the larger and more impressive trees.

For example, he found himself in the shadow of a house by the bend of a stream; by looking at the map he discovers that stream approaches house exactly at the point where longitudinal bar 46 crosses latitudinal bar 192, and being himself one hundred meters north of this point, sends through his message, stating that he stood at 46.0-192.1. At headquarters officers glancing at their exactly similar maps now know exactly where he was when he sent the message.

In the American Army strict general orders had gone out to state the co-ordinates of every position from which a message was sent; and the officers with that attacking force of the 308th Infantry were all men pretty careful about doing this sort of thing. On the previous afternoon Whittlesey had sent messages through his runner chain every half hour. These messages have survived and are still in the archives, countersigned with the hour of their receipt. They trace his progress in a perfectly good line across Hill 198, never deviating from that line.

Thus at three-fifteen Whittlesey reports himself on lateral 275.9; at three-thirty on lateral 276.15; at four-forty-five on lateral 276.2. Lateral 276 cuts the crest of Hill 198; evidently Whittlesey was almost absolutely accurate with these reports. Another message, apparently his final one of the night says that C Company is now at 276.25, which is two hundred and fifty meters north of lateral 276, and vertical 294.7; B Company is at 294.8-276.5. "Sending scouts to railroad," the message adds. "308th has reached objective."

These co-ordinates are almost perfect in their accuracy; they err only in placing B Company a little too far forward; that is, about a hundred yards beyond the line of the railroad. However, it was sent the moment Whittlesey arrived, and it is just possible that B was up that far before the two battalions settled down.

Of the morning messages Whittlesey's reporting the arrival of Holderman, McMurtry's asking for rations for the headquarters companies, and Whittlesey's pigeon message about the German artillery also give the position with great accuracy. Whittlesey's message with the requisition for rations was apparently captured by the Germans; it never turned up. Whittlesey's "Have just received your message of last night about rations" gives co-ordinates wrong by a hundred yards in one direction and a hundred and fifty in the other, though why he should have sent wrong co-ordinates in between two messages giving right ones is a mystery. This message was found by a soldier of the 302nd Ammunition Train on a dead runner; so it was never delivered.

Teichmoeller's message to the artillery, however, instead of putting the command on lateral 276.3, planted it at 275.6—that is, seven hundred meters, or just about half a mile behind where it actually was. What is more, a glance at the map shows that 275.6, the position given by Teichmoeller, was an eminently reasonable place for the battalion to be. Like its actual position beyond Charlevaux Brook, this was on a reverse slope, behind a front of headland that protected it from German artillery. It was just short of a powerful defensive system with a line of trench and much wire, the Haupt-Widerstands-Linie, which was marked on the map then in use both with Whittlesey's command and at 77th Division headquarters; and it was so far forward as to occasion no surprise at the idea that the place was being shelled and subjected to German attacks.

Apparently someone (we shall never know who) at Division headquarters looked at the Teichmoeller message, looked at the map, found everything in order, and passed it along to the 305th Field Artillery. Apparently this someone was a person familiar with the general order of battle, who had not seen the messages from Whittlesey on the previous evening, nor from Whittlesey and McMurtry on that morning. (For that matter, all but the "artillery" message from Whittlesey came by runner and some of them arrived after Teichmoeller's.) We say apparently because this is the only possible method of accounting for what happened, of which the first step was the transmission of Teichmoeller's request to the 305th for artillery support.

Now the gunners had their directions.

IX

The Pocket
(*About 9:30* A. M.)

Hardly had the patrols been started out and Teich-moeller gotten his pigeon into the air, when things began to happen, none of them pleasant. The first was that Leak and Harrington of E came staggering in from the outposts on the left. Leak had a bloody bandage round his head; Harrington was helping along Chiswell and Habeck, two privates, also badly wounded. Of the fifty men who had gone out with Wilhelm a few hours before, there were only eighteen left, most of these wounded, all sober and grim after a savage ordeal.

They had crossed the Charlevaux and started to climb the slope of Hill 198, cutting across its foot in preference to going around the nose, which might bring the La Palette machine guns down on them. When they were about twenty yards from the crest a voice called suddenly from the woods:

"Americans?"

The accent was right; it could hardly be a trap. But why ask? A moment's hesitation, then a little Greek answered, "Yes."

"What company?"

"E," replied the same man who had spoken before.

The questioning voice snapped something in German.

"He's giving them our range!" shouted Max Probst, who had a brother in the German Army.

There was a terrific crash of grenades, and at the same

moment machine guns began to chatter. They took cover and tried to work around one of the guns. Another caught them in flank, then another and another, dozens of guns, the worst they had ever seen. Snipers opened up from their flanks; men dropped all over the place, Leak was hit and Harrington. Private Henry Miller snuggled through the underbrush like a snake, flanked one of these snipers as the sniper had flanked the company and drilled him with a rifle bullet. "I got him," Miller said, turning his head, but just at that moment a machine gun got Miller in turn, and his D. S. C. was posthumous.

With his company half gone and both the other officers hit, Wilhelm had finally ordered the others back. He himself, with thirty-three men tried to push on through, and he ultimately made it, though with a wound and only four men left when he got to regimental headquarters.

Leak had not even finished telling the story when there was a rumble, then a terrific crash; everyone in the headquarters funk hole was deluged with dirt and twigs. That could come from only one thing; *Minenwerfer*. Berroum!—Crash! Again. Whittlesey was on his feet now, spotting the angle of fire from the thing. Crash! and someone called for first aid.

A voice floated up: "The wop got whacked that time. Do you suppose he's got anything to eat on him? I saw him with something this morning"—and that was the epitaph for Hero Tomasso Cavello.

Over at another part of the position Farncomb, the

Californian, who had been hit through the ankle crossing the bridge on the previous evening, lain out all night
and been picked up by the morning patrol, had his whole
funk hole turned over on him like a blanket. Otto Volz
pulled him out, eyes and mouth full of dirt, and got him
into another one, something Farncomb was never to
forget.

Whittlesey rapped out orders for Lieutenant Schenck
of C to take a strong combat patrol and eliminate that
Minenwerfer, pointed the direction for him and waved
him away. Another man was clawing for the Major's
attention with a half-salute and the news that the Germans were up beyond the line of the road; several men
of Company G had heard them.

—What did they say?

—I don't know, sir. We couldn't understand.

—Then why come to me about it? I know there are
Germans there. Go back to your position.

Shano Collins was at the Major's other side; one of
Baldwin's runner-post men. He had been driven out of
his post by heavy machine-gun fire; the other two runners in the post were dead, killed in a sudden blaze of
fire which he had escaped by the miracle of being lower
down, bending over to pick up something when the
gun let go. One of the men from the next post he had
heard crying out was probably wounded and a prisoner.

—Which one?

—Don't know his name, sir. He wasn't from my
company.

October 3

"What do you think of our chances, Major?" said someone from a funk hole.

The Major was too busy to think of chances, his own or others. There was a machine gun up beyond the road now, and another across the stream, on one of the spurs of Hill 198, their bullets crisscrossing overhead and "chirping like a flock of canaries" as Private Wade expressed it. The patrol was back from the eastward flank; had seen six Boches in the woods in that direction, from them receiving machine-gun fire and a rain of potato-masher bombs. Worse still, the patrol that had been sent out westward was not back at all, five men become suddenly nil; up above, Schenck and his combat patrol had stirred more machine guns into life. They were chattering vigorously and the *Minenwerfer* continued to dump its ash cans of dynamite into the position with maddening persistence.

Whittlesey asked for Holderman. A runner brought the Captain, with his lieutenant. The Major wanted the 307th company to go back the direction they had come, get that machine gun across the stream and open up the runner-chain once more. It was important to get rations and ammunition up to the command. Holderman perked up at once at the prospect of vigorous action, but Pool seemed doubtful.

—We haven't men enough for such an operation.

"You have your orders. Proceed."

The men of the 307th trailed away behind their officers into the scrub, bending low, helmets over one eye at an angle, which somehow seemed to make them feel that the steel bowl offered more protection.

—Have Private Tollefson report to me with a pigeon (said Whittlesey, seating himself at the edge of his funk to compose another message).

—Sir, Tollefson was wounded by that last trench-mortar shell.

—Richards, then.

It was ten-forty-five:

At: 294.6-276.3
Date: 3 Oct 18
To: Detroit 1

Our runner-posts are broken. One runner captured. Germans in small numbers are working to our left rear about 294.6-276.2. Have sent K Co 307th to occupy this hill and reopen the line.

Patrol to east ran into Germans at 295.1-276.3 (6 Boches)

Have located German Mortar 294.05-276.3 and have sent platoon to get it. Have taken a prisoner who states his company of 70 men were brought in here last night 294.4-276.2 from rear by motor truck. He saw only a few infantrymen here when he came in.

German Machine Gun constantly firing on valley in our rear from hill 294.1-276.0.

E Co. (sent to meet D and F) met heavy resistance at least 20 casualties. 2 squads under Lieut. Leak have just fallen back here.

October 3

X

Further Consideration on Co-ordinates

It is important to note the co-ordinates given in this hasty message. That for the Germans "working to our left rear" is quite possibly accurate, though it is the same co-ordinate as given in that earlier message in reply to Stacey's about rations, the only one in which Whittlesey failed to give the co-ordinates of his position with almost absolute accuracy. That for the position of the German *Minenwerfer,* or trench mortar was admittedly guesswork on Whittlesey's part, and apparently not a very good guess, for it placed the mortar way over behind La Palette, where it would have nearly a kilometer to shoot. If the mortar had really been that far away he would not have thought of sending a patrol after it.

The error, however is of minor importance and the message itself contains the material for its correction. It would be precisely at 295.1-276.3 that the patrol found the six Boches; the position is on a spur and just where the pioneers of the German encircling force would be, moving along the Roman road. The German prisoner must have left his truck during the night at a spot not more than fifty yards from 294.4-276.2; the German machine gun firing from the flank would certainly be somewhere around 294.1-276.0. And if all these spots be marked on a map they form a rough and irregular outline, enclosing the exact position of the command.

XI

Headquarters, 77th Division, U. S. A.
(Morning)

Both General Johnson of the 154th Brigade and General Alexander of the 77th Division woke to the new morning with something like cheerfulness. Their attack had gone well, the German line was punctured and the general of Division had congratulated the general of Brigade via telephone. The only worry for both men was the question of that left flank, where Lieutenant Knight's two companies had reported the Germans still in considerable force and fighting with enthusiasm, and where the French cuirassiers had sent in no report of the gains they should have made around La Palette. Regiments 306 and 305, which were the 153rd Brigade, had not accomplished anything on the right of the divisional sector either, their night regimental reports speaking of interlocking belts of machine-gun fire from well-manned trenches. 306 indeed, had come through the day so much hurt that it had to be pulled back to a support mission.

Under the circumstances Alexander prepared a directive for the day calling for an attack on his right flank by 305—since the German reserves would be attracted to the break made by Whittlesey and his two battalions, 305 ought to find it fairly easy going—and renewed pressure on the left flank by the rear elements of 308 to close up on the battalions that had reached objective.

The orders were prepared, and the attack was directed to start in the early morning.

Now the 3rd Battalion of 308 was, as we have seen, along the Binarville Road; it had been the brigade reserve; was therefore under Johnson's direction and not Stacey's. The only troops directly under the Colonel's control in the early morning were Paul Knight's two companies, about one hundred men, and they alone made the first attack, trying to link up with Whittlesey's left wing, as per the Whittlesey-Knight agreement. They had not gotten far before they ran into concentrated machine-gun fire from La Palette and Hill 198, as well as a frightful tangle of barbed wire, much of which appeared to be newly strung.

The brigade reserve did nothing at all; simply sat still, waiting for roast larks to drop in its mouth while the Germans were toilsomely closing up the gap Whittlesey had opened in their line. The 307th did not attack either; it investigated, sent officers on reconnaissance, pushed out patrols. It was noon and after noon, late in the day, almost twenty-four hours beyond the time when the Major went through, before any effort was made to occupy the Haupt-Widerstands-Linie and hold it in force.

XII

Headquarters, 76 Reserve-Division (German)
(Morning to Noon)

By ten o'clock in the morning von Sybel at the headquarters of the 76th Reserve Division had worked out a fairly clear picture of the situation. Something like two battalions of Americans had come through his line on the previous afternoon and had established themselves on the reverse slope along Charlevaux Brook near the mill, but they apparently had no supports close at hand, and his men were succeeding in the effort to close behind them the gap in the Haupt-Widerstands-Linie. By half-past noon, indeed, he had a report in hand from Major Hünicken, announcing that the 254th had joined hands again with the 122nd Landwehr of von Kleist's command, and that the pioneers on one side, the 254th on the other had succeeded in delineating the position of the *"Amerikanernest"* with a good deal of accuracy.

The problem presented by the Americans was then, one not new to the war or to the 76th Reserve Division. It was essentially the same as that which had been solved on the day before west of La Palette, and the day before that at Autry—that of gobbling up the morsel they had bitten off. The only inconvenience was the uncomfortable size of the tit-bit; if the beleaguered Americans were to discover how great was their own strength in comparison with that of the forces opposed to them, they might break out again.

A front-line report from the early morning hours showed that this had come near to happening already; a group of the beleaguered Americans, estimated as a strong company, had made a powerful effort to break back to their own lines under the shoulder of La Palette. It could be considered the merest of good fortune that a patrol had spotted their advance in time for an ambush to be set against them.

The size of the detachment of Americans thus introduced a variable into the equation normally used in such cases. Von Sybel felt it could be canceled out by first making sure of the Haupt-Widerstands-Linie against any attack, either from the Americans in its rear or from the forces that would undoubtedly try to relieve it from in front. Extra supplies of wire were accordingly sent in, and some of the pioneers brought down to string it. Extra machine guns were sent forward at the same time, with orders to station them at intervals not exceeding ten meters apart, as the men in the Haupt-Widerstands-Linie would have to fight facing in two directions.

At the same time the artillery were to fire a shoot along the line of Charlevaux Brook, just enough to keep the Americans in their nest. As soon as Major Hünicken was sure of his main line, he was to render the Americans as uncomfortable as possible; *verpflaster* them with his *Minenwerfer* section, make regular bombing attacks, use snipers and light machine guns freely. The appearance of enormous strength on the part of the besiegers was to be set up and maintained by every device of bush-warfare—heavy fire from the machine guns, even though it hit nothing—shouts and movements in the woods, every kind of activity. The Americans would either surrender or spend their strength in attacks against the automatic weapons.

By eleven Hünicken said he had everything going

nicely. The line was secure and had already beaten off one rather weak and tentative effort from the south. The *Minenwerfer* section was *verpflastering* away with energy and its accompanying machine guns had turned back a vigorous but inexpert effort to put the *Minenwerfer* out of action.

About that hour the Americans, true to type, made an energetic drive to clear their skirts toward the rear in the direction of the Haupt-Widerstands-Linie. Hünicken succeeded in shunting it into a belt of wire and stopped it, working snipers around the wings of the movement while he held fast in front. By noon the attack was driven back across Charlevaux Brook.

The program of pressure by snipers, with shouting through the woods to impress the Americans did not come off quite so well. To every rustling leaf they replied by bursts of rifle or machine-gun fire, often painfully accurate, and producing casualties which the 254th could ill afford. Nevertheless orders were categorical; and as the sun crossed zenith Hünicken was busy preparing a serious effort to break down the left flank of the American position.

XIII

The Pocket; Whittlesey and McMurtry Consider *(Noon)*

When Holderman's company came back across the brook, swearing and dirty, with many wounded, there was something like a council of war at the headquarters funk hole. Schenck was back from the attack on the trench mortar as well, to report having lost a couple of men and made no progress; the confounded thing was protected on every side by continuous streams of machine-gun fire, so that not even a mouse could have crawled through to it.

Holderman reported briefly; he had had to send his men forward in a single-file crawling position under intense machine-gun fire. The hill, Hill 198, was alive with Germans, who had strung some new wire since he crossed that slope in the night. When they reached the first belt of this obstruction Pool, who was in the lead, formed his men in a wedge with the four sergeants at the point and himself in the center. They got through; but at the second belt of wire hell broke loose around them; there were machine guns not only in front but on both flanks as well, and a number of snipers, who seemed determined to work round the rear of the little command and cut the men off from the brook. Two of the sergeants were hit; Pool himself had gallantly dragged one in under fire.

Pool interrupted to remark on the bravery of one of the other sergeants, Carroll, whom he had seen helping Art Fein back—Fein with three bullets in him, and Carroll walking slowly, half-supporting the man through all that hail of fire, saying, "You gotta keep going. You can't let go. I'll help you."

Good, but never mind that now. The sum of it

was that Holderman could not gain an inch, and judged it best to beat his way back before he should be cut off from the battalion as well as the rear. The Major had ordered him to avoid that at all costs.

The question was what to do next? It was now noon, the methodical Germans had apparently knocked off for lunch, and they had time to consider the matter.

Whittlesey nodded slowly with some remark that the only thing to do next was wait until relieved. The question, as it presented itself to him, was partly a moral one. It was possible that the strictly sensible course of action was that of taking the whole command and smashing into the German line that had just turned back Holderman, effecting a lodgment in their trench system and again establishing communications with the division, or, failing the latter, to retreat through that line to wherever the rest of the regiment now were.

Yet there were equally sensible objections to such a course. What Holderman had said about the progress of the 307th on the day before indicated that it might reasonably be expected to break through and fall in on the right of Whittlesey before very much later in the day. Evacuating the considerable number of wounded would severely hamper the command in any effort to work rearward and might bring on serious disorganization. Above all, the position offered better opportunities for defense against the developing German counterattack than any the Major had seen since yesterday's attack started.

This would also be retreat; and it had been unceasingly drummed into Charles W. Whittlesey, as into every other officer of the A. E. F. since the beginning of the Foch offensive, that any retreat, even local, would include a loss of the ascendancy in morale which the Allied Armies, and especially the American, had gained during the summer at the price of so much blood. Whittlesey was a New Englander, who had emigrated from his native state to become a New York lawyer of the higher type; he had the combined moral prejudices of both backgrounds and there would be a strong question in his mind, whether under any circumstances, he had the moral right to deprive his men of their morale, to inflict upon them the consequences of such a loss. The 35th Division had executed some local retreats in the last offensive; things got mixed, and the division was in such bad shape as to be considered no longer a front-line unit. So had the 79th.

Yet it was not a moral question on these grounds alone. For one thing, he had been ordered to advance to the objective regardless of flanks. He had done so. It now became the duty of Stacey, of Johnson, of Alexander, to provide for the safety of those flanks. He had no moral or military right to assume that his superiors would fail in so important a duty. In fact, it was altogether likely that they would succeed; that although his present position looked grim, before the afternoon was out, some thundering barrage, followed by a parade of infantry, would come crashing down on the German

lines, or some whirlwind French attack sweep them out
of La Palette. If he, retreating, were to meet such an
advance, of whose success the presence of the little knot
of fighting men in the pocket above Charlevaux Brook
was an essential element, he would hamper an entire operation, destroy for the battalion the credit it had right-
fully earned and he would stand convicted of constructive disobedience.

And not of constructive disobedience alone. Less
than sixty days before, as the 28th Division was slashing
forward among the ruined buildings of Fismettes on the
Vesle, at the top of that swing which had so surprised
and hurt the Germans—at the top of this swing, when
the division had crossed the stream and was mopping up
without meeting any opposition but that sniping which
is the last effort of an exhausted defense, something queer
had happened. A number of men appeared suddenly
among the front-rank troops. "Go back!" they shouted.
"Retreat, they've got us surrounded. Captain Friedenberg says to go back."

Captain Friedenberg was a perfectly good captain of
the 28th and a good many of the men recognized his
name. They went back; the advance stopped a mile or
so short of where it should and the Germans were granted
time to organize a new position. Division HQ fumed; a
checkup followed which revealed that nobody recognized the men who had done the shouting, and that
at the time it had taken place Captain Friedenberg was
a prisoner in the hands of the Germans. That settled it;

it was a German trick of a type played before on the other Allies and by us on the Germans. Word of the device was passed along the line, with the warning that it might be repeated.

Major-General Robert Alexander, commanding 77th Division, was one of the officers who received this warning. It touched some secret spring of fury in his nature, for he was about to embark on a drive into difficult country, and it was easy for him to conceive of the troops of his green division being gulled in a similar manner. When the drive started, he issued a general order with instructions to have it read through the division, all the way down to captains:

"Ground once captured must under no circumstances be given up in absence of direct, positive and formal orders to do so emanating from these Headquarters. Troops occupying ground must be supported against counterattack, and all gains held. It is a favorite trick of the Boche to spread confusion among our troops by calling out 'Retire!' or 'Fall back!' If, in any action, any such command is heard, officers and men may be certain that it is given by an enemy. Whoever gives such a command is a traitor, and it is the duty of any officer or man loyal to his country, who hears such an order, to shoot the offender upon the spot. WE ARE NOT GOING BACK, BUT FORWARD!"

Some officers remarked later that they "did not pay too much attention to the order—there was always something like this coming down from headquarters."

But this particular order was stricter than most of its kind; it was fresh when the offensive opened on the morning of October 2, and Major Whittlesey, with his New England background and lawyer's training, was just the man to take this or anything like it literally, and he seems to have done so.

It is unlikely that he thought any man in his battalion would seize the opportunity offered by the order to put a bullet through his head in case he violated it by taking the command back across Charlevaux Brook. It is still more unlikely that the possibility of someone taking a shot at him would have deterred him from making such a retreat if he thought it the right thing to do. The point, as far as he was concerned, was that this order constituted a definite and positive command. It fitted exactly the case in which he and his battalion stood at the present moment. He had no "direct, positive and formal orders" to retreat from Division Headquarters; on the other hand, the general order, itself from Division HQ, constituted a direct, positive and formal order to stay where he was, and it was reinforced by his attack order of the day before—"The command will halt . . . and be ready for orders for a farther advance." And only that morning he had received Stacey's night-order again emphasizing that he was to be ready to advance during the day.

Both the general order and the specific attack orders constituted for Whittlesey not only a military obligation which he must fulfill or risk a court-martial but also a moral obligation. It must be emphasized that he understood them with a New Englander's organs of perception; that is, according to the most strict and literal sense of the words. It would never occur to him that there might be a general doctrine superior to his orders, just as it would seldom occur to a lawyer that there would be a general principle of justice superior to law.

For he was a wartime officer, an emergency man. He would not think, as not a few West Pointers have thought since, that Alexander's general order violated both the letter and spirit of the Army Regulations or that in his present position he was beyond Alexander's control, and therefore in a military sense, a free agent, himself the high command, head of his own little hierarchy.

Nor was there anyone in his command to suggest such ideas to him. McMurtry, his senior and most valued associate, lay under many of the same moral compulsions as Whittlesey himself. Fifteen years after the war, when asked why the battalion stayed where it was on that morning of October 3, he was to glance up in surprise—"Why, what else was there to do? Those were our orders." Stromee, the only other captain of the 308th, was an utter stranger; Holderman was enjoying every minute of the fight—would not have been out of there for anything in the world; Cullen was frankly ambitious of heroism; Wilhelm was gone, Leak wounded, Buhler and Eager new men, transfers from the negro regiment, Schenck and Peabody too new to their rank to question any decision from above or even to offer advice, and the other lieutenants were without that special force of character which imposes ideas on others.

... McMurtry pulled from his pocket a pad of field-message blanks, wrote briefly and handed the result to the Major. The latter read and nodded. "That ought to cover it," he said, and began copying the text in triplicate, looking up to speak to Baldwin, "Have three runners report to me at once."

To all officers:

Our mission is to hold this position at all costs. No falling back. Have this understood by every man in your command.

XIV

The Pocket
(Noon)

—Shall we eat one cracker apiece now, or half a cracker and then smoke a cigarette?

Gaedeke, Larney and Baldwin, perched on the edge of their funk hole in the warming sun of the afternoon, debated the question with the gravity of senators. They were feeling neither comfortable nor heroically uncomfortable. They were merely, in the phrase with which hospitals fend off anxious relatives, doing as well as could be expected. The German trench mortar was out to lunch; snipers, who only worked sporadically at any time, were quiet except for a shot or two off toward the flanks, the machine guns silent, only the ceaseless beat of the faraway artillery furnishing the background of battle; that and the fact that wounded men in the funk hole not far away moaned occasionally.

It was half a cracker and a cigarette; with the latter Larney unexpectedly produced from inside the signal-panel roll a copy of *Adventure* magazine he had carried up through the advance, and began to read a story about pirates on the coast of New Guinea.

The Major had a party out improving the latrines; everywhere the tenseness of the morning had been succeeded by an atmosphere of relaxation. On the left flank where the machine guns were, Bugler Leonard lay back behind a bush, stretched flat, and remarked to Private Tolley that it was a dismal landscape and it didn't look like they would ever get out of there.

—No, you can make your will now, all right. Got anything to smoke?

—Butts on Jim Lonergan's cigarette. He's got a package. Hell, it makes a guy kind of sore. We'll never live through this. I wish we had something to eat.

Actually that bugler was not thinking about eating at all, nor about smokes, nor whether they would leave the dismal hillside, though the prospects were bad, the cigarettes low and the food all gone that morning and all three things forced themselves upon his attention. He was talking from the lips outward and thinking about his mother—"I wonder whether I have done all I could for her?" but it was only the last remark that Lieutenant Peabody caught as he slithered along from post to machine-gun post of the left flank.

—I have a can of jam (he said suddenly to the two, his voice making them jump, for they did not know he was there) and I want you two to share it with me. Anybody got any crackers?

They had no crackers and felt they ought to refuse the jam, eyeing it greedily, torn between hunger and what the Field Service Regulations had drummed into them about eating with officers.

—Oh, for heaven's sake let's not pay any attention to that stuff here (said the Lieutenant.) We're all in this together.

He jerked at the lid of the can with his knife and they ate it off the blade with contortions of their tongues to avoid the cutting edge. Momentarily all three were happy.

XV

The Pocket; Another Part
(Afternoon)

Out beyond the last nipple of hill within the lines of the position on the right, at the spot where Holderman was in charge, a limestone cliff jagged from the hillside. Here the brush and trees were thick, and from here, just as the light began to turn, the afternoon lull was shattered by a sudden and violent crash of potato-masher bombs, and at the same moment all along the line the German machine guns began to chatter and the bass cough of the *Minenwerfer* took up the melody. Hünicken was clamping down.

Holderman's company fired at will toward the bluff, but hit little behind its protecting brow; on the left, where the potato mashers had also come down, stoopshouldered Cullen was moving along the line, his eyes snapping.

—Cease fire! Cut it out, there! Stop it! Sit tight till you see them.

He wanted no wild shooting, and knew that habit of the men behind the guns that made one of them say later, "When they're coming at you, you don't care so much about where your bullets are going as you do about having something coming out of the end of that thing you got in your hand."

In the momentary silence that followed the first volley of grenades voices came clear from the screen of woods:

"Rudolph!"

"*Hier.*"

"Eitel!"

"*Ich bin hier.*"

"Fritz!"

Calling the roll, a long roll. Did any voices answer twice with the intent to deceive the listeners? It is possible, though no one noticed. The roll ran to its end, then, "*Sind deiner Menschen da?*" and when the answering "*Ja, ja,*" came, high and loud, "*Nun, alle zusammen!*" There was a patter of feet among the trees, a crash of bodies through the underbrush, a whine of bullets from the thuttering machine guns and then bang, bang, bang, another shower of potato mashers, right into the lines.

Little Griffin, the one-hundred-and-ten-pound lieutenant from the West who had sat in the dark last night talking to McMurtry about his wife, was hit through the shoulder by a bullet; went down and had to be led back. His face was puckered with pain, curiously resembling that of a little boy about to burst into tears over being punished for a fault he had not committed, but he didn't say a word. Stromee got a bomb hit, a great tearing wound down back and shoulder.

McMurtry was up there on the left where the main pressure was coming. Both he and Cullen had seen German bomb attacks before; both knew that the explosive auto-cylinders required close range or enclosed space to be really effective—trench-warfare weapons, more dangerous to morale than to bodies among those woods and from a distance. Both knew also that the Germans had a curiously unlimited confidence in the power of their potato mashers to lay down a barrage under which nothing could live. Presently they would come rushing in behind the curtain of their bombing.

"*Alle zusammen!*"

Closer through the trees. Germans do not throw like Americans, from the shoulder and with a snap of the

100

wrist, but in a ponderous sweep that brings into play the muscles of back and thigh, requiring an erect position. They were volleying beautifully with their bombs, the whole line together, with a flicker of *feldgrau* cloth visible now through the trees as they let go the third barrage, then scuttled forward in the shelter of its bursts. At the word of command for the fourth, they were close, close enough to be dangerous, the whole line visible to Companies C and H, all swinging back and up together. Neither Cullen nor McMurtry had to shout "Fire!" and if either man did his voice was drowned in the universal rippling blaze of fire that ran along the line, every shot aimed. There was a choir of shrieks; half a dozen bombs burst at the feet of the men who had meant to throw them as they collapsed under that surprise shooting. Somebody on our side began to yell.

"Shut up!"

The attack was stopped.

XVI

The Pocket
(*Afternoon to Dark*)

It must have been late in the afternoon when Major Hünicken compared his orders from above to the fact that he had not made the slightest impression on the besieged Americans, and that he had suffered losses—always losses!—he could ill afford. The movement that followed in the falling light of the evening was less a formal attack than an informal explosion of senseless fury, the intent of which was to wipe the annoying little knot of Americans from the face of the earth under a whirlwind of burning metal.

The *Minenwerfer* section opened up as fast as it could fire; a battery of artillery ranged on the position of the besieged, all the machine guns that had been cautiously sifted into position earlier in the day let go together and snipers cracked at everything that moved.

For the time being the men in the pocket had nothing to do but endure, heads and bodies low, while their own machine guns and auto-rifles replied as best they could. The left flank got it worst; one of the machine guns got a direct hit from the *Minenwerfer,* the whole crew with Sergeant Graham was killed and the gun smashed. Lonergan, who shared his cigarettes, was wounded; Lieutenant Peabody got the whole burst of a machine gun in one leg just below the knee. Somebody put a tourniquet on the leg while somebody else called to Revnes that he was in command now.

The fire of the machine guns was beginning to fade; they had lost too many men. Revnes got a runner across the open ground to Whittlesey for reinforcements, and he sent back a detachment from H and the already depleted A, but not more than half of them ever reached the flank. Those not hurt were driven flat to the ground, simply unable to move in the torrents of German fire; and before any of them arrived Revnes himself was hit, a bullet through the ankle, and Sergeant Hauch had to be left in charge of the guns.

The storm must have lasted for over an hour; as it died down a trifle Major Whittlesey got off another pigeon with an urgent message:

At: 294.6-276.3
Date: 3 Oct
To: Delaware 1

Germans on cliff north of us in small numbers and have tried to envelope both flanks. Situation on our left flank very serious.

Broke through two of our runner-posts today near 294.7-275.7. We have not been able to re-establish posts today.

Need 8000 rounds rifle am 7500 chauchat, 25 boxes MG, 250 offensive Grenades.

Casualties yesterday in companies here (A, B, C, E, G, H), 8 killed, 80 wounded. In same companies today, 1 killed 60 wounded.

Present effective strength of companies here 245.

Situation serious.

As the bird winged away into the now rapidly fading light there was another burst of fire from down near the edge of the brook, and a few minutes later word came along the line that Private Judd had been killed at the water hole trying to take some of the canteens down to get a drink for the wounded.

As dark came down the German machine guns one by

one tailed off to silence and the trench mortar's fire also died out. Their artillery kept on with a few shells, usually in sets of three, a star shell with two H. E.s following quickly after it. By the fitful glare the men of the 308th could be seen moving about the pocket, burying dead and caring for wounded under Major Whittlesey's orders. He had most of the latter moved to funk holes near the headquarters position, which had been moved a little down the slope, so that he and the other officers could give the injured men whatever comfort was possible by personal attention. Something along this line was needed, for the three medical detachment men had used up their supply of bandage by six o'clock and now there was only what could be scraped up from first-aid packages and similar "invisible" sources. Lieutenant Peabody was a tower of strength to the seriously wounded. Kept awake by the pain of his own utterly smashed leg, he laughed and joked as easily as though he were in a parlor, keeping the spirits of the rest up. Night pickets were set and a few patrols sent out, especially to the right, where there seemed a possibility that the 307th might have accomplished something.

XVII

Headquarters, 77th Division, U. S. A.
(*Afternoon*)

The reports that reached division headquarters during the day were confused and contradictory. At two o'clock in the morning a telephoned message had come through from Johnson's brigade headquarters, confirming a previous message that said Whittlesey was on his objective. Someone at Brigade added that it was extremely probable the line of runner-posts had been cut. "It must be confessed," said Alexander later, "that this did not make a very great impression at that time." Runner-chains had been cut frequently in the push into that forest and, humans being what they are, it was not altogether unheard of for the runners themselves to straggle back to the nearest chow-wagon, alleging clouds of German attackers when they were picked up later.

There was, moreover, a question of personalities involved. Colonel Stacey of the 308th was a good officer, a regular with two gallantry citations, but his nerves were in bad shape. On the other hand Alexander knew Colonel Houghton of the 307th for one of the best officers in the division or in the American Armies, a true man of iron, who had come through seventeen particular hells with the Canadians earlier in the war. If Stacey could push his regiment through the Giselher Stellung, surely Houghton could be trusted to bring his up in tune, exploit the gap and keep step with 308. Renewed attack orders had, therefore, gone out at daylight; and during the early morning hours some runner messages came through from Whittelsey, of no great importance in themselves, but sufficient to show that the line of communication was open.

At about the same time a 'phone message came down

from corps headquarters summoning all division commanders to a conference with General Liggett for the afternoon. Alexander prepared by calling for reports from his brigade commanders as to the disposition and prospects of their forces. His right brigade was perfectly clear on both; the 305th regiment had been driven to ground by crisscross belts of machine-gun fire and was accomplishing nothing, while the damaged 306th was supporting it.

The report from Johnson, however, was a shock; he did not appear to know where half his troops were or what they were doing. Two battalions were with Whittlesey, up on the objective. The 3rd Battalion of 308, the brigade reserve, had not been put in where Alexander expected, on Whittlesey's flank, but in position for the elaborate tactical plan conceived by Johnson, which was now clearly not going to work. The 307th had been paralyzed in the morning by the wandering of its companies during the night, and the situation of Holderman's Company K was uncertain. M, I, and F had just returned from their nocturnal meanderings, and Lieutenant Shelata was under arrest.

On the heels of this there came a message from the pigeon loft, where a bird had just flown in with a request for rations from Whittlesey, which indicated that they had not reached him yet as they certainly should have.

It was, accordingly, with a disturbed mind that General Alexander went to the Corps conference. Before he could bring the matter of the doubtful situation of Whittlesey's battalions before that body, General Liggett announced that a full-dress attack by the whole American First Army would be staged at daybreak on the following morning. The weight of the effort would be rightward of the 77th, on the east edge of the Argonne and up the Aire Valley. The French on the left, where the cuirassiers had failed the day before, had been reinforced and had promised to knock a hole in the German line on their side, outflanking La Palette and forming the second horn of a double advance which would join behind the west end of the forest and pinch out all German elements on the 77th Division's front by cutting their lateral communications.

The plan, if carried out, would remove most of Alexander's difficulties and the mention of it was enough to resolve his doubts. He immediately determined to throw the weight of his division toward the left flank, next the French, putting in both the brigade and divisional reserves to smash through to Whittlesey's position along the same track that officer had taken going in, allotting to the 305th and 306th the duty of merely keeping enough pressure up to hold the Germans in position and prevent them reinforcing the weak spots in their line.

When he returned to division headquarters Johnson was directed to make this attack as part of the morning's general movement. He had the 3rd Battalion, 308th, the

3rd Battalion, 307th, all of the 306th Machine-Gun Battalion but the two detachments with Whittlesey, and some headquarters troops. There was plenty of artillery support. Zero hour was set for 5:30 A. M. while everything was still dark in the woods; this would help an attack that had to work through wire.

OCTOBER 4

I

The Pocket
(*Dawn to 5:30 A. M.*)

THE night patrols had encountered nothing but German
sentries, but Whittlesey had hardly expected more from
them, their mission having been defensive and their orders not to move far. Morning made some action essential. The seriousness of the command's position was now
manifest, they were evidently surrounded by Germans,
were battered by that trench mortar to which there was
no good reply, and ammunition and food were running
very low. Both the Major and McMurtry had heard
men talking under cover of the dark.

—How the hell can we get out of here?

—Well, if you crawled along that line of bushes . . .

—Too late tonight, but if we get by tomorrow . . .

The sprouts of the black nightshade of disorganization; and Lieutenant Schenck reported the same thing
taking place in his company.

Oh, the men were sound enough stuff, you could not
ask better. But they needed leadership. Privates cannot
be expected to realize that when an organization dis-
solves into individuals, each seeking the personal safety

of A, by that act the personal safety of all is jeopardized. Even quite good officers often forget the necessity of discipline when under trench-mortar fire.

Whittlesey was sure of his own ability to hold in line as many men as he could keep within sight or sound, and of McMurtry's ability to do the same. Holderman, Cullen, Schenck, could similarly be counted on in all cases, and probably some of the others. But already he had lost Wilhelm; Peabody, Griffin, Stromee and Revnes were so badly hurt as to be of little use as officers, and Leak and Harrington had lesser wounds. It would be useless to blink the possibility of some chance bullet or T-M shell removing him from the scene, or McMurtry, and the movement of panic that such an event might set off would be extremely difficult for the juniors to stop.

To this consideration was added the strong possibility that neither regimental nor brigade headquarters knew how serious the situation of the organization was. He had sent numerous messages, but how many, if any, of them had got through, he was uncertain. There was no reply, nor had there been any roar of battle along the line of Hill 198 to indicate that a serious effort at relief was being made. It was altogether likely that only the pigeon messages had been received; and Whittlesey knew enough of messages at the front to be sure that the written word always stands at fifty per cent discount, never fully represents the situation as it can be brought out by questioning a fairly intelligent man who can describe what is going on.

It had thus become, as far as Whittlesey was concerned, a matter of considerable urgency to get a personal messenger through the lines; and since no single messenger was likely to get through, he sent a strong patrol under Corporal Holgar Peterson of G. They were to work across the creek, which, with its banks, had been churned into a marsh by the previous afternoon's shelling, keep low, sliding up Hill 198 in the unearthly dawn light to the shelter of the trees and then shift through the trench line as best possible.

On the previous day the Germans had pressed the left hard but had made little effort against the right except to toss a few bombs from the cliff over Holderman's command. Two more patrols went out up the valley in this direction, in the hope that the pressure had been so much relaxed there that contact with the 307th or 306th could be established.

Just as the patrols left the clock touched five-thirty and guns began to go off all over the place, American guns, French guns, south, east and west in a crash that could only be the opening fire of a big push. Beyond Hill 198 the besieged command caught the sudden grunting of the Chauchats—an attack!

II

H. Q. I Reserve-Korps (German) Briquenay
(5:30 to 8:30 A. M.)

From Wellmann's headquarters at daybreak everything seemed in good order. It was true that the late report from Hünicken of the 254th Reserve Regiment said that he had been unable to break up the two American battalions that had penetrated his line, but he could be pardoned for that in view of the weakness of his formations. It was enough for the time being to have held the Americans and to have hurt them; and that they had been hurt there could be no doubt, for the *Feldwebel* who brought Hünicken's report to divisional headquarters said that during the night the besiegers had heard shrieks and groans from the Americans, though he was forced to admit that his regiment had taken from them neither prisoners nor ground.

During breakfast, artillery suddenly began to growl in the distance and field-telephones to clamor at Corps headquarters. The French were setting up a preparation fire along the whole front, and a little later there was a message from the Army Group Argonnen, saying von Kleist had been heavily attacked along the valley of the Aire. That made everything clear; the Allies were trying Mackensen's classic "two-horns" advance, which would presently be followed by pressure from the American 77th Division at the spot where the imprisoned battalions had broken through two days before. To throw the plan out of gear, it was only necessary to hold the French within bounds, then hit the Americans hard as they came up what should have been the alley between the two entering horns of the attack.

Wellmann ordered in whatever reserves were available

to hold La Palette and the ground between that point and Autry, the more willingly since the high command assured him that an infantry regiment and two artillery formations of the 45th Reserve Division were on the march to reinforce him. His (or Major von Ditfurth's) calculations proved eminently correct. By eight in the morning the French were knocked out, their attack had sunk to peevish artillery bombardment without any particular meaning. Seventeen prisoners were taken together with four machine guns and a dozen Chauchats.

III

The Ravine Under La Palette Hill
(5:30 to About 9 A. M.)

Just what caused the confusion at the left wing of the 154th American Brigade that night we shall never know, but confusion there was. Knight's efforts to get through to Whittlesey on the previous day had brought his two companies from one hundred down to fifty-four men and this fragment, these two companies that now aggregated less than half of one, were the only troops directly under Colonel Stacey's control. The 3rd Battalion of his regiment, the one which had been in brigade reserve, was now also under his tactical orders, but even with this addition his position practically was that of a major with Captain Scott as his second in command.

The Lost Battalion

Over the battalion of 307, which had been division reserve and was now brought up in preparation for Alexander's attack by the left, Stacey had no authority at all; and as those two reserve battalions formed the left wing of the 77th Division Johnson was in command of them. This made the brigadier's position practically that of a colonel commanding a curiously mixed regiment. All orders still had to come down from division headquarters to Johnson at brigade headquarters and then to be transmitted, in the case of 308, to Stacey and through him to Scott; in the case of 307 to the commander of the reserve battalion. The route was too long and the process too slow for the size of the units engaged; nor does Johnson seem to have been quite certain of the exact position of his front-line troops.

Alexander had impressed on Johnson the importance of personally supervising the attack. He called Stacey to the field 'phone and had Stacey call Paul Knight who would take the lead.

—Are you equipped with grenades? (he asked).

—We are.

—You don't sound very enthusiastic. It is vitally necessary that your men get through and reach Whittlesey.

—We'll do the best we can.

The 'phone emitted some inarticulate gurglings that sounded like profanity and then went dead.

In addition Colonel Houghton of 307 was pessimistic about the project. He had studied the map with some care, had made personal reconnaissance along the line and talked with his juniors. When he heard that his battalion was to be used in the attack he got in touch with Alexander and told him it was perfectly hopeless to send good men up against the side of that rocky and wooded ravine, right at the spot where the Germans were certainly expecting an effort to break through to Whittlesey.

Alexander insisted that the attack should be made as ordered. His obstinacy snapped the string of Houghton's patience, a good and experienced officer who thought first of the men under his command. He called his captains and lieutenants together.

—This attack that you're going into (he told them) is a forlorn hope and I don't intend that your men shall be cut to pieces. As soon as you make contact with the enemy, stop; unless you find a gap in his line report that you are held up by rifle and machine-gun fire. I don't want any lives wasted in the German wire.

The total result was that Johnson's left-wing mixed regiment attacked late, after eight o'clock, and without as much help as the brigadier expected from the artillery, which totally failed either to cut the wire or to knock out the German machine-gun nests. They stormed up against the hills, La Palette and 198. Three strong efforts we count at this point; D and F were hard hit, Lieutenant Knight twice wounded and driven to ground, though he made his effort so boldly as to win a D. S. C.

He came back with his clothes almost torn from his

body and long wire-scratches across his hairy legs and arms, a strapping big man, pale with loss of blood. There was a 'phone message waiting for him from Division through Brigade; Sergeant Cahill, who had the 'phone farthest forward passed it on—He must have his men inside the German wire at a certain hour or face a court-martial. "Nuts!" said Paul Knight and made his way to the dressing station, which was the end of the attack.

About this time it would be when an excited Chief of Staff telephoned Alexander that the French were in Lançon, three kilometers behind La Palette and directly in line with it. The French were our gallant allies, but Alexander would no more believe that (after what they had done or failed to do before) than the one about the Germans building a gigantic tunnel whose outlet was to be in Paris. Still, one had to be sure. Liaison Officer Captain Klotz and his aide, Lieutenant de Coppet, were summoned and forthwith sent off to the headquarters of the nearest French division in a staff car with a request that the French mark on a map the exact line occupied by their troops.

IV

Along Charlevaux Brook
(6:00 A. M.)

Corporal Peterson and his patrol pushed into the marshy bottom with water soaking into their bellies, and guns held carefully to keep the mechanism out of the ooze, an inch a century. He was a garage mechanic from New York City, skinny and blond, with a deceptive slowness of movement, which had kept his superiors from giving him stripes sooner, but since the start of this fighting had been proving himself true officer material.

It was still dark in the valley, a massive spur beyond Hill 198 cutting off the low eastern sky where alone some streak of dawn might have been found, only the electric-blue lightnings of the distant artillery marking a horizon. In spite of the undertones provided by the racket of guns the rattle of every dry stalk, the squish of every knee in the mudhole seemed to fill the silence in which the patrol moved.

The stream. They edged cautiously along it, looking for a crossing place, hand almost touching hand, taking a step or two, then throwing themselves flat and waiting for the noise of the step to bring a burst of machine-gun fire. But there was no burst of machine gun, no sound, all dark. Peterson, crouched double, trying to make out objects in the dark, felt someone jerk his ankle. He turned; the man was pointing silently ahead, where the stream curved just above them. Faintly silhouetted against the indigo line of water, Peterson could just make out a shape that moved like a serpent's swaying head, the shape of a man half erect. It was crowned with a coal-scuttle helmet, German helmet, and as he watched there came to his ears the faintest of rustlings to one side. A German patrol.

The corporal flattened out, his rifle pushed forward, aimed on the formless shape, and waited. The rustlings persisted, moved forward, coming straight toward them. To go back, to turn aside were alike dangerous, equally noisy. Peterson pulled the trigger and the whole valley seemed to echo with the crash of the shot, as he flattened again and rolled over and over to dodge the return fire which came in a doubled flash from either angle in front.

Peterson came up, shooting at the flash on the right; there was a cry that told of a hit, a Very light from somewhere in the German lines hung like a star above the scene and in its ghastly glare a third German stood for a moment revealed, half-erect, arms pendulous and mouth open like an ape. Peterson fired his third shot before the light died, and down went the German; the next moment there was an appalling rattle of machine guns from high up on the hill, firing into the backs of the patrol, and another Very light arched across the sky.

"Back!" shouted Peterson; they scuttled up the hill through the brush to the battalion lines and the leader heard a wugh! from Oscar Wallen as a bullet got him.

V

The Binarville Road
(*About* 10:00 A. M.)

—Establish an observation post up there with the 308th Infantry. They have a couple of battalions up forward somewhere beyond the German lines (they told Lieutenant Putnam). Get them to locate where they are and we will fire to protect them.

He was new to the job of observation officer for the 305th Field Artillery, having replaced Chester Burden the night before. The 308th was not hard to find, a group of officers all looking very grim and sour as they ate their picnic lunch. They had just made an attack and been repulsed; part of their regiment was cut off and the high command was giving them hell for not breaking through.

—Where are they? (asked Putnam).

A captain (he does not remember who now, nor could ever identify the man afterward) produced a map and pointed out a spur just back of Charlevaux Mill.

—Right here (he said, indicating).

Putnam felt in his pocket for the piece of toilet paper he was carrying against sudden emergencies, and laid it over the map, making a rough tracing.

—Let me get the co-ordinates on that (he said). There we are; 294.2-276.4. Runner! Take this back to Major Wanvig. Tell him this shows where Whittlesey's battalion is.

The captain's error was only half a mile.

VI

The Pocket
(*7:00 to 7:30* A. M.)

The Major's watch said after seven when the patrols

119

were all in. Their report was encouraging; if Peterson had been unable to get through across the stream on the route to the rear the two smaller patrols sent out to the right from Holderman's position had encountered nothing, which meant that the Germans had probably pulled out on that side during the night and the way to the 307th was open. Still, there was not even any discussion of the advisability of taking the command out of the pocket through this gap. They had suffered, it was true, but men do suffer in war and both Whittlesey and McMurtry knew enough of tactics to realize that merely by staying where they were, driven into the German front, they exercised a paralyzing and irritating effect on the whole German line for some distance, like the fester of a porcupine's quill. The attack on them last evening proved that.

Moreover, their orders of Wednesday, not having been canceled or altered, still held good—"Organize along this line, establish liaison to left and right and await orders for a farther advance." The problem facing them was not that of closing on the remainder of the division, but of staying where they were and permitting the rest of the division to close on them, especially since the efforts to establish liaison to left and right had not proved fruitful.

Omer Richards had only four pigeons left. Whittlesey used one of them in order to send his morning report:

120

October 4

At: 294.6-276.3
Date: 4 Oct   Time: 7:25 A. M.
To: Delaware 1

All quiet during the night.
Our patrols indicate Germans withdrew during
   night. Sending further patrols now to verify this.
At 12:30 and 1:10 A. M. six shells from our own
   light artillery fell on us.
Many wounded here whom we can't evacuate.
Need rations badly.
No word from D or F Companies

VII

Headquarters 76th Reserve-Division (German)
(Early Morning)

In his early morning report, made by the mouth of
one of his *Feldwebels,* Major Hünicken applied for reinforcements. The imprisoned Americans could be
swept up if he had a few more men but, as matters stood,
he considered himself actually outnumbered along his
front. Part of his troops were those pioneers, doubtless
good men at their specialty, but not storm troops. Division headquarters replied, shortly after daybreak, that
no reinforcements could be sent; the line was being attacked westward by the French and every man was
needed there. Division submitted as the best program
that of keeping the *Amerikanernest* quiet by the free

121

use of mechanical weapons, snipers and the *Minenwerfer* section, wearing down the enemy's morale and numbers till an attack would be more fruitful. The enemy must be short of food. They would certainly surrender if held in the pocket long enough. They should be encouraged to do so.

VIII

The Pocket
(7:30-11:00 A. M.)

The burial parties were having a hard time, exhausted as they were and hungry, the ground full of rocks and proper tools lacking. Dawn came late, but frightfully clear, with a bright sun, to find them still at work, and almost instantly the trench-mortar section tuned up and gave them an hour's bombardment, searching the length and breadth of the position. Most of the shells pitched right over to the foot of the hillside and into the stream, but the noise shattered nerves, keeping every man on edge, and the diggers had to bend double, lie flat as they labored, taking out earth by the handful.

The machine guns began soon afterward, laying down a crisscross barrage, cutting away cover and dropping twigs into the faces of the men where they lay. Every shout, every cry from the wounded, brought a burst of fire and sniper bullets. McMurtry got up, and in spite of a wounded knee, began to limp among the injured men, trying to comfort them and keep them quiet.

"It pains like hell, Captain," said one, shot through the stomach, as the officer paused beside him, "but I'll keep as quiet as I can." He tried to smile, but the effort dissolved in a grimace.

Peabody laughed softly, smoking a cigarette. He was keeping them all alive; one would never know he was hurt but for the weakness of his voice. Water was the worst need; two men had been killed already trying to get it, but Zip Cepeglia, the little Italian runner, took a string of canteens and hunched, rolled, slid, toward the nearest shell hole where muddy liquid had collected. His foot struck a gravel pile, sending a miniature avalanche down inside the blouse of the soldier who lay behind it.

"You son-of-a-bitch!" said the man softly but with feeling. It was too much for the overwrought runner's nerves; in spite of the singing bullets he leaped to his feet, snatching at the buttons of his tunic.

"You wanna make something of it? All right, I fight you right now!"

Someone grabbed him by an ankle. "Pipe down and lay down, you crazy wop!" Another voice—"If you want to fight, fight the Germans."

Nine o'clock, ten. The trench mortar had stopped, but the scouts sent eastward were unreturned, so after all the Germans must still be in position along the right flank. More potato mashers began to come from that confounded cliff over Holderman's position, and then a tentative shower from the ridge beyond the road, one landing right at the feet of Shepard, the Californian, who thought he was a goner sure, but jumped on the thing with both feet, squeezing it down into the mud, and emitting a sigh from every cell of his lungs when it failed to go off.

The nearness of the delivery was serious, portending attack. Whittlesey moved up to the ranks of C Company, calling for volunteers to meet the German rush, and Schenck with ten men went hitching across the steep ground, taking an auto-rifle up to support the position.

Another shower of the potato mashers, nearer. Then the phunk of the Chauchat, a crash of isolated Springfield reports, and Schenck was back, successful for this time. His face was set, with deeply incised lines, and he seemed to be under some frightful inner strain beyond the strain of the war itself and their position. A strange officer, always low-voiced, always courteous, every command a request—"Will you please fire a burst or two in that direction?"

There were only three pigeons left, but the emergency seemed so great that it was worth using one, with murmurs going up among the men about getting the hell out of here, now audible even in daylight. Whittlesey called for a bird:

October 4

At: 294.6-276.3
Date 4 Oct. Time: 10:35 A. M.
To: Delaware 1

Germans are still around us, though in smaller numbers. We have been heavily shelled by mortar this morning.

Present effective strength (A, B, C, E, G, H, Cos) 175, K Co 307th, 45; MG Detachment 17; total here about 235.

Officers wounded: Lt. Harrington A, Capt Stromee C, Lts. Peabody and Revnes M. G., Lt. Wilhelm Co. E missing.

Cover bad if we advance up the hill and very difficult to move the wounded if we change position.

Situation is cutting into our strength rapidly.

Men are suffering from hunger and exposure; and the wounded are in very bad condition.

Cannot support be sent at once?

IX

Headquarters, 77th Division, U. S. A.
(About Noon)

By noon it was evident to General Alexander that his division's part in the general offensive was a frost. The 305th had found no weakening of the German resistance; the 306th made only a few yards before it got into crossing belts of machine-gun fire. Westerly, the mixed

125

regiment on the extreme left flank had suffered a more complicated but equally unpleasant fate. The 307th reserve battalion had been caught in German shellfire going up and lost some men; they now reported themselves stopped by heavy rifle and machine-gun fire. Colonel Stacey reported the same, but Alexander formed the opinion that he had not pressed the attack with any too much energy.

He talked to both Johnson and Stacey, ordering the attack driven home, and left word at the telephone station that there would be wigs on the green unless it were done. But about half-past eleven Johnson reported that the attack had resulted only in shattering what fragments of 308 remained; the men lacked equipment and he lacked men for pressing matters further. There was no possibility but that of heavier loss.

At the same time an airplane that had gone over in the morning reported Germans in the Charlevaux Valley. Klotz and de Coppet had not yet returned from their mission to the French headquarters, but the General was more than ever dubious about the glowing report he had received in the morning. If our allies were in Lançon the Germans would certainly be pulling out of Charlevaux Valley in a hurry, whereas the resistance in that direction appeared, if anything, to have stiffened.

However, the general offensive was one in which his part was co-operative; it did not now worry him so much as the situation of Whittlesey's two battalions. The loss of that many men and the practical destruction of the regiment it would entail, would be a black mark against him personally and would set back the whole offensive movement. There had been two pigeon messages from the Major during the morning, of which the second was couched in terms of distinct pessimism, speaking of many wounded, no food and an urgent need for support.

The divisional artillery, after having fired several shoots during the early morning hours, was now cooling its guns. They were ordered to fire in support of the beleaguered battalions, punching hard against the German trench line, then lifting and hitting the Germans surrounding Whittlesey's command. Meanwhile the 50th Aero Squadron was to send some planes to identify the exact position of the battalion, and when the planes had found them to drop food, ammunition, and medical supplies. The first machine was to go immediately, that is, just after noon. For one of the later planes Alexander prepared an order to Whittlesey, to be dropped on his position:

"Defend yourselves in your present position. Help is coming to you."

That message turned up later in the official papers, with the annotation of the man who picked it up— "Dropped at Supply Co. 307 Rond Champ"—and a marginal annotation on this annotation, in the handwriting of the General—"Seems to have been dropped too far south!!!" To say the least this was understatement, Rond Champ being at least seven miles behind the lines, even behind the divisional headquarters from which Alexander had sent the order.

X

The Pocket

"The trouble with this outfit," remarked one of the privates sententiously, when the 308th had first gone into action along the Vesle a month and a half before, "is that all the officers come from below Fulton Street and all the men from above it."

In addition to the usual polarity between the man who gives orders and the man who has to obey them, accentuated in the case of National Army organizations by the fact that neither officers nor men had been in the service long enough to learn the point at which legitimate orders leave off and despotism begins—in addition to this—there was thus in the 308th the special polarity between comparative wealth and comparative poverty, between "berled ersters" and a Harvard accent. The privates, the "berled erster" delegates, were not shirking the war itself or the necessity of winning it; it was their job which they had to do, and most of them accepted the necessity without question. But covertly, and without being conscious of it themselves, they were waiting for their officers to crack.

To begin with these officers were rich bastards, and most of the men (again without being fully conscious of such a feeling) suspected that beneath the glacé accents these ninety-day wonders were men like themselves, who would break down into honest Boweryese under pressure. That is, they felt that the whole busi-

128

ness, educations, Wall Street offices and shoulder bars, were only the signs of an assumed superiority which covered a genuine inferiority. It was part of the system.

The officers of the 308th thus had a special problem of their own in the business of making their command a military unit. It was connected with, but not the same as, the usual problems of leadership; and satisfactorily to solve this problem they must show themselves not only as good as their men, but better. Captain McMurtry had solved this problem as long ago as the training camp by means of a certain easy courtesy that took little account of shoulder bars, an ability to understand the problems of the men under him. Even his manner of speaking was confidential rather than hortatory; when giving orders he seemed to be taking the men into a secret rather than commanding them. His company had long ago decided that McMurtry was all right, and when he succeeded to command of the 2nd Battalion the word was passed along to the rest.

Cullen achieved the same result through sheer physical impressiveness—his rolling gait, red hair and square jowl. Without difficulty his men could picture him stepping six fast rounds with Mike Gibbons. Holderman was the best shot and best scout in his company, full of sheer energy; Peabody had acquired the accolade through unflagging spirit and careful attention to the wants and needs of his men; Schenck by his willingness to undertake the hard tasks himself and the almost apologetic manner in which he asked others to follow him, a peculiarly winning character. Toward most of the other juniors the men were neutral; many of them were new and none had made any special impression. Ten or fifteen years after the event the privates found it hard to recall their names; they were merely lieutenants, who might as well have been ventriloquists' wooden dummies with phonographs inside to give orders.

Major Charles W. Whittlesey had belonged to neither class when the regiment went sliding and pushing through the forest on the afternoon of Wednesday. First of all he was a major; and in the American Army, whose organization is really based on regiment and company with the battalion largely a theoretical unit, the major is a kind of fifth wheel, seen by the private only as a vehicle for transmitting orders in their most unpleasant form. Second, he was a New Englander, alien in spirit to the more volatile New Yorkers of the organization, stricter than they, a man who thought in terms of the abstract concept, Duty. "Don't stand there looking at me!" he would cry to Baldwin, as the corporal paused for a moment to assimilate the snapped-out order, "Goddamit, get me a messenger!" To those who overheard it this was merely an evidence of bad temper; they failed to understand that he was one of the kindliest of men or what an effort it cost him to say anything like that.

"Galloping Charlie" the men of the 1st Battalion had nicknamed their major during the Camp Upton days, not altogether in affection, as they watched him go past on his stilt-like legs, and it probably occurred to very few of them at that time that he was anything more than

130

a local tyrant, a kind of drill-sergeant with brass on his shoulders.

The change in their feelings may be said to have turned most sharply on the afternoon of the 2nd, and fortuitously, when the two battalions reached their objective with so little loss or difficulty. That they had done so was not, as we have seen, entirely Whittlesey's accomplishment but, as the man in charge must often bear the stripes for things that are none of his fault, he may also receive credit for pleasant situations he has not brought about. Such of the men who thought on the subject were also impressed by his night arrangements on arriving; probably a great many more were impressed by the minor fact that the Major had ordered the latrines dug and used, to the exclusion of other places, first thing in the morning. This was strictness, yes, but a reasonable strictness, the value of which they could appreciate.

Whittlesey was never too busy to stop for a word with the wounded, which was another fact noted with approval. But what made the deepest impression was the Major's conduct during the fighting of the 3rd, when the trench mortar opened up, the machine-gun barrage came down and the bombing attack started. The privates were ducking into fox holes with bullets peening overhead, elevating a cautious eye from time to time— and every time the eye was lifted it caught the crane-like figure of the Major striding about the position, not indeed as though on parade, but like the worried president of a corporation, perfectly oblivious of the noise and death all around him. "Remember, there are two million Americans pushing up to relieve us," he would say, and pass on to the next funk hole, where he would criticize the sight-setting of an auto-rifle team.

By noon on the second day in the pocket, the pendulum of opinion had swung to something like admiration. About that time an airplane caracoled overhead, its tricolor cockade flashing in the sun. The pilot fired a rocket and the men felt that they had been seen. Relief could not be far away.

XI

Headquarters, 308th Infantry Regiment, U. S. A. (About 3:45 p. m.)

Captain Bradley Delehanty, operations officer of 308, was at regimental headquarters shortly after noon. Stacey was there; the Captain noticed he was looking bad, his eyes sunken and a bullet hole in his coat which he had acquired that morning during the fight at the German wire. Lieutenant Hattemer of the divisional artillery dropped in for a moment on his way back from a liaison mission. The officers discussed the big news of the day, all about Whittlesey being cut off behind the German lines and the efforts to relieve him, and Hattemer remarked that as no infantry attack was scheduled for the afternoon the guns were to fire on the Germans surrounding him, "harassing and neutralizing fire," which would knock out some of the Boche machine guns and give the besieged companies long-range support.

"Where's your line of fire?" asked Delehanty.

Hattemer had a map. "Right along this line here, where the Boche must be."

The operations man and Stacey both jumped as though they had been struck. "Those are the co-ordinates of Whittlesey's position!" cried the Colonel, and Delehanty echoed, "Good God, man, support them—you're firing to destroy them! That's exactly the line Whittlesey is occupying!"

The Lieutenant stared.

—Are you sure?

—So sure that I'm going to call Brigade about it. Where's that telephone?

XII

The Pocket
(Noon to 3:30 P. M.)

There was the usual noon lull in the German fire and the sound of French and American shooting on the flanks had also died down. Nothing to do but wait; the men left their funk holes briefly and sat on the edges, talking mostly about something to eat. The wounded were moaning, and the three medical detachment men, Sirota, Bragg and Gehris, were doing their best with strips of torn shirts. There were several cases of gangrene and this worried them.

A violent explosion, then two more, then three on the heels of the two, drew every eye in the pocket. They saw tall columns of brush and muddy water rise in the air from the valley, and before they had subsided a whole new series of bursts, shellbursts, all along the line of the water's edge, parallel with the position occupied by the command. Shells give warning by a preliminary screech, and these screeches were from the south, from the lines whence the battalion had come; they were American guns.

For a few minutes every heart lifted; and then the line of fire moved forward as precisely as a line of advancing troops, came to a halt square on the position where the battalion lay and stayed there, shells bursting right in among the funk holes, killing and maiming the men of the hard-beset command. It was futile and horrible; Cavanaugh was hit, Bill Johnson hit and killed and so was Sergeant Mike Greally. The trees crashed down, the brush flew into the air, the men of the 308th had the cover stripped from them and lay bare to the German machine-gun bullets which were not long in coming. The pigeons were cooing and squeaking with fright in their narrow pens.

All over the position men were shouting, screaming, trying frantically to burrow deeper into the ground. McMurtry was wriggling to the left, trying to keep the men there steady under this cruel and undeserved blow from their friends. Twenty years later four men out of every five who lived through it were still to recall that

The Pocket: The Northern Slope of Charlevaux Valley, stripped of cover by shellfire of the "friendly barrage", revealing the foxholes dug by the Lost Battalion. Right: The Lost Battalion's commander, Major Charles W. Whittlesey.

horrible period as the worst of the siege, the worst moments they had ever been through anywhere, under any conditions.

Cullen was shouting in his deep voice to hold the men of the left steady, Holderman moving from post to post on the right under cover of the bushes, Schenck pleading with Company C, but in the midst of that terrible barrage, redoubled by the efforts of German snipers and machine guns, Galloping Charlie was on his feet, stalking gauntly about the whole hillside, carrying everything on his shoulders.

—Take it easy, there, take it easy. We're all right. This won't last long.

He was back at the hole where the headquarters men lay, coming along stooped double now, followed by Omer Richards and his pigeon crate, trying to find a quiet spot from which to get off an emergency message. As he sat down to write it Larney noticed a trickle of blood on his face. "Are you hurt, sir?" he asked. Whittlesey lifted a hand and dabbed briefly to reveal a diagonal shrapnel cut across his nose, shook his head irritably and went on writing.

Richards fumbled at the pigeon crate—two birds left—and in the excitement and shock, let loose the handles too soon so that one of the birds whirled out through his hands and away upward without any message. Whittlesey swore; Richards steadying himself with an effort, and clenching his teeth, reached into the cage and pulled out Cher Ami, the last pigeon, the last mes-

135

sage, the last chance this side of hell, for they were all dead men if that barrage endured.

At: 294.6-276.3
Date: 4 Oct.
To: Delaware 1

We are along the road parallel 276.4.
Our own artillery is dropping a barrage directly
    on us.
For heaven's sake, stop it.

The message was clipped on, Richards tossed Cher Ami into the air. He rose in a spiral while they all watched, open-mouthed, circled two or three times, and then, apparently shell-shocked, or not liking the atmosphere that day, or for some other bird-like reason, spiralled down to roost on the limb of a torn tree and began preening his feathers.

"Hey!" shouted Richards, "Boo!" yelled Whittlesey. Cher Ami was oblivious. They began to throw sticks and pebbles at the obstinate fowl, ducking as each shell burst near them. Cher Ami leap-flew to another branch and settled down again, perfectly comfortable. Richards looked around.

—What the hell (he muttered).

Then he began to shin up the tree, grunting, till he reached the branch and shook it. Cher Ami took off and began circling over their heads. The Germans had spotted him now, they knew that whatever message the bird carried it was important, and were shooting at him from the hillside above. Richards shouted at the bird again; a few circles of indecision and it took off, sailing away, definitely out of sight for this time.

The shelling went on. Galloping Charlie had left the headquarters hole before the pigeon made its final effort, was down at the base of the position, supervising the removal of the wounded to a spot farther right, where the shelling was less intense and a few fallen logs gave a little protection. Above the noise of the constant explosions the whir of an airplane was audible, and as it did a barrel roll the men below saw it was an Allied machine.

—Can you get the panels out? (Whittlesey asked Larney).

The signal man spread the white sheets across ground and bushes, unashamedly ducking at every new whine and shock, while the Major moved off, not a nerve unco-ordinated. The funk hole where the headquarters men were sheltered seemed to be the center of the trouble; a shell tore away its parapet. McMurtry encountered the Major just below and there was a discussion in clipped phrases as to whether the position of the battalion should be changed to get out of the shelling.

"No," said Whittlesey, "that would be out of the frying pan into the fire. At least the German artillery can't get at us here, nor their trench mortars very much, and our own guns can't keep this up forever."

A new command post, nearer the base of the slope, where the wounded had been taken away, might be better, though. Pass the word along. Larney saw Bob

Manson, the interpreter, crouching at the crest, under the road parapet and turned to join him, up there where the shelling was not so thick. Just beyond, on the other side of the road itself, they marked a man, face down in the ditch, and out there were no shells at all. Larney leaped across the road, flopped like a football player who has missed his tackle, and a moment later felt Manson fall across his feet.

But just as Manson hit, a German machine gunner somewhere up the line let go with his piece, the bullets whizzing right past their faces, filling Larney's mouth with bark and dirt. "We've got to get out of here!" shouted Manson, "Let's go!"

He went first, bent double; when Larney saw him next, which was after dark that night, he had a finger missing. Just as the signal man got back across the road and floundered into the ditch one of the bullets hit him, too, right through the leg above the knee. He felt nothing at the time, nothing but the blow of the bullet, and angrily pushed his rifle over the parapet, trying to get a shot at the man who had pinked him, but not a chance. The third man, a big fellow, came last, and drew a bullet that went through his body. He fell, sprawling and rolling among the trees down the steep, lying there for half an hour before he could gather strength to go down and have some kind of crude dressing put on his hurt.

There was an auto-rifle team near where Larney had come to rest, the men less interested in shelling from the rear than in their weapon, with which they were questing about toward the Germans up the slope. The signal man heard voices, and turning, saw Ben Gaedeke, with Baldwin and a wounded man.

"Hello, Jim," said Baldwin, "This is Sam Feuerlicht of C Company. He's wounded."

Ben Gaedeke said they ought to get down to the new command post, Whittlesey might want them; and they started off in a straggling group, into the middle of which there was suddenly a flash and a tremendous roar. Ben Gaedeke had been right on the spot; he disappeared as completely as though he had been a name wiped from a blackboard. Feuerlicht sagged from Baldwin's hands, his chest torn out; Larney went down with a chunk of iron in his right elbow, and Baldwin was beside him, tearing a shirt to pieces to stop the blood. Together they rolled down the hill and began to scratch at the hard earth, Larney with his one good hand and a bayonet, Baldwin with a trench shovel he had picked up from the side of Paul Andrews, the Boston Jew-boy, who had valiantly volunteered to get water earlier in the day and valiantly done it, but now lay dead with a piece of American shell in him.

—See if you can find Tollefson and get me another pigeon (said Whittlesey, appearing from nowhere, to Richards).

The pigeon man crawled sidewise to where he had last seen the Minnesotan. The smashed pigeon-cage was there, empty, and beside it the body of a man with half his head shot away; Tollefson, who would never raise pigeons again on his little farm. Richards did not bother to report it and so Tollefson went into the records as missing.

"Anyway," remarked Richards to himself, "I got something to eat," and crouching in the shelter of a tree root, pulled from his pocket the two packages of pigeon-food he carried—cracked corn, split peas and birdseed. The shelling went on.

XIII

The Pigeon-Loft, 77th Division, U. S. A.
(*4:00* P. M.)

Cher Ami got to the loft just before four o'clock. He must have been caught in the shellfire, for he was nearly done when he came in, with one eye gone, his breast-bone broken and a leg cut away. They gave him a medal and a pension, which he did not understand in the least, and he died in 1919.

Corporal George Gault was the pigeon-loft man on duty that day. He had been very excited ever since it became known that Whittlesey was cut off. When he read the message Cher Ami carried, he was so upset he could hardly hold the 'phone on which he called Major Milliken at division headquarters.

"Major, listen to this one"—and he read the message, in code.

"You don't *mean* that. Give it to me again in clear, no matter who may be listening in."

Gault repeated, and it was just as bad as it was the first time. "My God, isn't that awful? Get that to me quick, the original."

There was a motorcycle outside, with a driver. Gault jumped in; as the machine bounced over the road, he noted that the clamor of guns was already dying down. Still it could not have been more than four-ten when Division telephoned artillery brigade and told them to stop that barrage. Artillery replied they were not firing a barrage and had already stopped what firing they were doing.

The French liaison officers, Klotz and de Coppet, had come back to Division by that time with their map, which showed that the French on the left had made no advance at all. De Coppet remarked that an officer over there said he had been in Whittlesey's position during the afternoon and talked to the Major. Alexander only growled some remark about the accuracy of the Gauls.

XIV

The Valley of the Aire, East of the Pocket
(All Day)

Easterly the Argonne ends in strong bluffs and jutting mountains, forest crowned, looking down on the valley of the river Aire, where it flows north toward the Grand

Pré gap. The hills in the sector run east and west; among the trees on their summits and reverse slopes were the German artillery positions. The valleys and lower sides are mostly bare but for limestone caves and patches of grove; here the Germans had their machine-gun nests, every post a fortress. Square in the center of this tangle looms a huge mountain called the Montrefagne, and on this day, without preliminary bombardment, without warning, there burst from cover against the Montrefagne men in khaki with a shield-emblem on their shoulders enclosing a big red 1.

A German counter barrage flew in their faces, machine guns rattled from front and flank. They kept straight on, United States Regulars, one of the best divisions in the army and the world, with a liaison service that never cracked and French 155's to help their own guns, which unfailingly dropped shells just ahead of their advance. The Germans here were hard stuff, too—Bavarians. They held to the last and all morning long there was on the slopes of the Montrefagne that rarest of events in the World War, hand-to-hand fighting with pistol, knife and bayonet. By noon the 1st was in Exermont, a mile within the German lines; their artillery had already rushed forward to a position beyond the original jumping-off point and was blazing into machine-gun nests at point blank range. All up the slopes of the Montrefagne the fighting was going on and von Kleist of the Army Group Argonnen was shouting frantically to the whole front for help and reserves.

October 4

Late in the afternoon von Gallwitz, himself hard pressed, but realizing the seriousness of the situation if the American Regulars were not stopped, sent the First Prussian Guards, the best troops in the Kaiser's Army. A message to Wellmann said that the elements of the 45th Reserve which had been intended to reinforce his front must be diverted to the help of von Kleist and the Army Group Argonnen. All traffic was cleared from the roads except that bringing up more shells to the support of the menaced Montrefagne, and during the afternoon grave-faced officers planned and planned, making ready for a counter attack the next morning. Orders were to drench the American troops with non-persistent gas during the night.

XV

The Pocket
(*4:15* P. M. *to Twilight*)

At four-fifteen the shelling stopped. Baldwin, examining himself, found the sleeve of his jacket ripped from shoulder to elbow by a shell fragment which had miraculously spared the skin, and he began to pray audibly. Before he had finished the Germans laid down a machinegun barrage all over the position. They were masters of grazing fire and it kept every head down, every head but one or two, the blond unfortunate head of young Corporal Peterson who had led the patrol, one of those.

He got a bullet through it, and so his D.S.C. went to his family.

Then the machine guns also crackled down into silence. "Kamerad, vil you?" an exasperated Teutonic voice cried from across the road somewhere above the position.

"Try and make us, you Dutch bastards!"

The reply was a shower of bombs and the reply to that the fire of Chauchats. For a few minutes—ten?—twenty?—half an hour?—nobody seems to remember how long, there was a determined effort at this point, an effort to rush the position from the north and center and break it in two. Schenck and his company bore the brunt of it; twice parties of Germans got across the road and into the outpost lines. Each time they were shot down or driven back, and when the burial parties went looking for corpses that night they found there German corpses, one with twelve bullet-holes, another with nine, but neither had any packages of food on him.

It was quieter now, except for the bursts of shooting with which every sign of movement was greeted. Clouds had been piling up and it was already growing dusk, with a hint of rain.

—Go around (said the Major to Baldwin) and make a check on how many killed and wounded in the battalions. See each of the officers in command of the companies.

Baldwin worked his way along cautiously, returned with the news that eighty men had been killed or

144

wounded in that fatal artillery fire, including two of the captains—Stromee, for a second time wounded, and Holderman, who had four slashes, none serious, but all bleeding badly.

The unit was down to a mere eight men now, and both the wounded officers, Leak and Harrington, were missing, together with many of their men. McMurtry says that after the Armistice Leak came back from Germany and told him that he had spread his men to escape the fall of shells, and then looking up from his fox hole saw a German standing over him with a pistol pointed at his head. He went away to Texas after the war and lost touch with most of the veterans.

There was another brief conference between the two battalion commanders after Baldwin returned with the results of his check. Subject—shall we change positions? Not back toward the brook or across it, certainly, for any post there would be open to German artillery. A change north and east in the direction of that cliff from which the German bombers did their throwing was a possibility. Such a move would certainly get rid of some of the sniper fire, and possibly of some of the machine guns. But the discussions always came around to the same point—exact co-ordinates of the position had been sent back, there was likely to be more American artillery fire and it was certain as anything that it would fall right on the spot where the proposed move would take them. There was now no means of notifying Division of any change—all the pigeons gone.

No, there was nothing they could do but stay where they were, hoping that whatever triple-distilled idiot had arranged the barrage that nearly finished them that afternoon would have fallen downstairs before morning. The discussion closed on this melancholy note. Both officers went round to set night outposts and start patrols. It was growing dark.

XVI

The Pocket
(*About* 6:00 P. M.)

On the right flank and front under the cliff, the machine-gun fighting had come to a close in a queer battle of words, punctuated by sniping.

"Gaz masks!" shouted a voice as the chatter closed. Words good, but accent foreign. "Gas masks hell!" replied an American voice and there was a shot that brought a howl from the forest, undeniably German, for while Americans groan or grunt when hit, the Heinies wailed like banshees in torment.

The exchange seemed to start a series. "First, Second and Third Companies, this way!" shouted an authoritative voice, very American in accent this time, which might have been deceptive but for the oddity of the words, there being no first, second or third companies in the U. S. Army. "Bring ten machine guns over here on the left!"—and then a long cackle of hoots and objurgations. "Order your coffins, Americans!"

146

October 4

There was only one possible end to it, given that there were more German-speakers in the 308th than English-speakers in a whole German division, and that end came when Corporal Georgie Speich covered himself with glory by bellowing, *"Ach du wint Betebren!"* which, being translated, is "Oh, you bunch of stink experts!" It brought down the house, also a shower of bullets, machine-gun and sniper, their sparks flashing redly through the gathering dusk.

"Goddamn it!" ejaculated one of the machine gunners, bending over the pierced jacket of his weapon. Captain Holderman slid cautiously through the leaves—cautiously because the hurt of his wounds made him grimace when he moved.

"Anybody think they can stop some of that sniping?" he asked in low tones. There was a moment's silence.

—I'll try, sir. It was Bob Yoder's voice, a Minnesotan from the Lake of Woods, who had shot hawks on the wing.

—Go ahead. You can take cover along the edge of the road there.

—Gimme some more bullets (said Yoder). What do you say, George? Coming along?

It promised at least a change from the strain of endurance without positive action which wears one so. George Newcom touched hands with Yoder in silence and the two slithered forward. They had perhaps covered twenty feet, when Newcom felt a touch, and looked around, startled, to discover Frank Martinez, the Indian, who had been following in the silence of his race. Yoder made the arrangements, a kind of rude *abri* where a triplicate tree stem sprang from a single root, arranging a branch screen so the leaves would mask the flash of firing, but leave sufficient interstice for aim.

On the slope below them something moved and they could hear moans from where the wounded lay. Bang! went a German sniper's gun, not ten yards above and to the left. Before the flash had died from their eyes Yoder's rifle cracked in sympathy and they heard a Teutonic shriek.

Three times more Yoder fired at the flash during the evening, and twice Newcom. The Minnesotan never missed, every shot brought its dividend of a yell. It was now quite late, though, the Germans were sending up Very flares every now and then. Down below some of the officers were trying to keep the wounded quiet. You could hear them moving and the voices. "Oh, lieutenant, for God's sake, turn me over."

The Germans still had that machine gun bracketed on the water hole, and fired it every time one of the men let a canteen clink against trunk or stone. Farther up the creek on the lower right of the position, some of the boys from Company K were also slipping down for water to the hole dug by trench-mortar shells. To their ears the tiny rustlings sounded like thunder, but no German shots came, so they got their drinks all right. Sergeant Hatch and Kaemper, a Montanan replacement, were in one of these parties; half way down, there was a sudden rush through the bushes, and they thought they were gone sure till the dark shape went right on past them like the old hoss making for home.

—Jeez!

—What was that?

—A wild hog. If I only hadn't left my gun back there. Think of the pork chops on that baby.

Some time before dawn Yoder's head slipped forward and he went to sleep with his cheek against the action of the Springfield. It rained on him during the night.

XVII

Headquarters, 76 Reserve-Division (German) Lançon (About 7:00 P. M.)

Just as the officers were sitting down to dinner in what had been the Salle de Réunion of some provincial society, one of the orderlies brought in a message from Major Hünicken to say that he had taken several prisoners from the *Amerikanernest*, including two officers. Officer-prisoners from that group were just what von Sybel had been wanting, for most officers belong to one of two large classes—the kind who can be persuaded with careful handling to tell everything they know, and the kind who remain silent about military matters, but whose very reticences permit information to be deduced. To be sure privates fall into the same categories, but even in their most expansive moments of confidence are not

149

so useful, because they are not so well-informed and they will repeat rumor as fact.

The Herr Hauptmann leaped to his feet so quickly that he almost upset the second gramophone, the one on the little table beneath the Kaiser's portrait. Then it occurred to him that there was very little sense in rushing such a matter. It was too late to make any use of information from questioning that night. A rain was falling that would hinder movement in the dark woods; besides the time to ask questions is after dinner, not before. He sniffed the perfume-laden air emanating from the kitchen.

—With the private you should take the usual steps (he said). Give the officers some potato-soup. Herr Hauptmann Bickel and myself will speak to them after dinner.

When the meal was over he strolled round with Bickel, who did the questioning, having a fair English accent. The first prisoner seemed a surly fellow; he gave his name, which was Harrington, and very little else, refusing the offer of a cigarette. A glance passed between the two staff officers and they dismissed him to try the other one.

This chap, like Harrington, was wounded, but seemed a better case. Reluctant at first, he softened under the atmosphere of *gemütlichkeit* which they managed to infuse into the proceedings, informing his questioners that he belonged to the 308th Infantry of the American 77th Division, which they already knew, and that with

150

German Official Photograph.

German snipers on the southern slope of Charlevaux Valley fired into the backs of the Americans along the northern slope.

other members of his regiment he had been in the position north of Charlevaux Brook since the night of the 2nd.

—We walked right through your lines.

All this was interesting, but not very helpful. Another glance passed between the two Germans as Bickel put the important question:

—How many of you are there?

—Oh, two battalions (said the American, easily). We were not up to strength, of course, when it began, but there must have been fourteen or fifteen hundred men.

Bickel shook his head, trying to hide his surprise; von Sybel had to use an effort to keep from starting.

—So many of you Americans. But then, your people have not the war experience of we others. We have found that even our best regiments do not stand well under such an experience.

—That is not like our regiment (said the American with evident relish). They are from New York, the gangster type. Very brave people.

—It is hard to keep courage up without enough to eat.

—Oh, for that matter, we have plenty; a big issue of rations just before we moved up. We're all fat as shoats.

The last word puzzled both Bickel and von Sybel, but its intent was obvious. They talked with him a couple of minutes more, then sent him away; and the idea coming over them slightly to doubt what he had said, sent for the other officer again, the Harrington.

The Harrington, faced with the admissions his companion had made, allowed the information to be dragged from him that everything Leak said was perfectly true, adding that the Americans in the nest were particularly well supplied with machine-gun ammunition; and when Bickel got around to questioning the captured privates he found them adding other confirmatory details. (How could either of the Germans know that the American prisoners had been left together on the road coming up for just long enough to rig up their story in advance?)

After it was over, both questioners went over to report to General Quadt-Wykradt-Hüchtenbruck that the earliest impression about the besieged Americans had been correct. There was really an immense number of them in the nest, and Major Hünicken would doubtless need very strong reinforcements properly to deal with them.

Division got through to Corps during the night and asked Wellmann for these reinforcements. He had none to give, but passed the request along to Army, with the annotation that special storm troops would probably be necessary before the Americans could be heavily and properly attacked. Army answered that all reserves for the present were being sucked into the whirlpool of the Aire Valley, where there had been a bad break in the line around Fléville and Exermont during the day. Army suggested that the information about the unusual strength and good condition of the detachment that had broken through the line might be false or misunderstood.

October 4

The men should be questioned again by an expert examiner. If the examiner reported the same results as those obtained previously, it would be a good idea to confine the operations against the *Amerikanernest* to attacks of sufficient intensity to keep them in position until more troops could be spared.

OCTOBER 5

I

Headquarters, 154th Infantry Brigade, U. S. A., and
Binarville Road
(Dawn to 8:30 A. M.)

DURING the night messages had been flying to and fro
between division, corps and army headquarters and toward morning Corps and Army, aroused by divisional reports and Alexander's repeated calls for aviation, which
was under the jurisdiction of Corps, realized that the
situation on the left flank of the 77th Division was very
tense. Army intimated that this was a situation in which
the standing orders to give up no gained ground might
be disregarded. Alexander's plan for the day was another attack by his left, the French to help. Airplanes
were to carry provisions and munitions to Whittlesey,
artillery to shell the Germans surrounding him. To this
was now added that a plane should drop him a message
directing him to attack rearward at the same time Johnson's brigade made its drive, thus taking the Germans on
Hill 198 between two fires.

Headquarters passed the word along to Johnson and

154

Johnson to Stacey. Stacey had been on nerve-point for days, and now he snapped.

"Am making every effort," his last message of the night had said, "but believe it is impossible to push through with these tired, disorganized men. Fresh troops will have to do the job. Request I be relieved."

When the new attack order came in the morning it was worse still:

—Scouting and patrolling are almost impossible (he told Johnson over the 'phone). We have no officers who know how to perform these duties. I have seen National Guard regiments who have never been in Federal service a day more generally efficient than this regiment. I don't mean to say that these are not good men. The material is excellent. They are brave and loyal and willing to do anything they can. But they don't know how to do anything; they have no instruction and no equipment, and they are now tired and thoroughly disorganized. I don't believe the General understands the shape my regiment is in. I must refuse to assume responsibility for any further attacks until we have some equipment and reinforcements.

Johnson, carried away by this torrent, got in touch with Alexander again.

—Colonel Stacey refuses to assume responsibility for an attack this morning.

"Relieve him! You should have done that without reporting to me. The responsibility for this attack is not on Stacey but on me. I'm ordering it. Refuses to assume responsibility!" The General's snort was sulphurically audible down a mile and a half of telephone wire.

"But relieving the Colonel will leave the regiment under the command of an emergency captain. The Major is up there in the pocket, and after all Stacey is a regular officer with twenty years' service."

"I don't care if it leaves the regiment in command of an emergency corporal, as long as he'll fight. Relieve that man at once and send him back to headquarters and relieve any other officer who talks in that way. You will take personal command of the attack."

Johnson, caught between the upper and nether millstones in this fashion, went forward to carry out the detail of the relieving attack. Stacey was sour and nervous (the matter left a black mark on his record, which it took four years and a court of inquiry to erase); not disposed to talk much about the operation. He went straight to a hospital.

The replacement was Captain Lucien Breckinridge—bright, active, full of ideas, which he instantly began to develop. Frontal attack against the German lines at that point (he said) had conspicuously failed. Moreover it was exactly what the Germans were expecting. Was it not therefore indicated that some other course should be taken? And heedless of the warning in the grim smile now playing around the Brigadier's lips, he explained his own plan, which he had worked out with the help of Colonel Douglas Campbell, the division machine-gun officer. It called for all the divisional trench mortars, the divisional 37 mm. guns, and special weapons generally to be put in against the front of Hill 198.

He had his map out now, and was going on, with a finger on it. The German line ran nearly east across La Palette, then jogged south to the crest of Hill 198, then east again, roughly. The position made a triangular salient, with the point lopped off square; those special weapons would direct attention to the angle and the square face, the French should make a demonstration against La Palette, while the 308th made an attack that swung like a boxer's left hook against the flank of the salient. It would burst in right up to Charlevaux Valley and make a—

Johnson burst into frank laughter.

—I'm afraid you don't understand all that is involved, Captain. You should be aware that the trench mortar and 37's have been left back and the men in those special platoons have been trained to use captured German artillery. Now, which is your strongest company?

II

The Pocket
(Dawn to 9 A. M.*)*

Dawn broke wretched and misty behind veils of rain. The downpour stopped about sunup, but the ground was still covered with fog, the fine fog of sunny France that chills to the bone and the marrow of the bone. Nearly all the men were weak with hunger. Baldwin was off behind a bush, his tongue greedily following the convolutions of an old condiment can in which there were still a few grains of coffee. Richards was in another hideout with his banquet of birdseed. Nobody had shaved; eyes were popping out and cheeks were falling in. The burial parties, which commenced work with the first light, were for once free from sniper fire, save when metal touched stone and the krauts tried a random shot or two into the fog. Yet progress was slower than on the previous day, the men so feeble and the soil desperately hard. Whittlesey watched them at work, spoke a few words to McMurtry, and then had the men cover the dead with logs, boughs, or whatever débris could be easily reached, the results of digging not being worth the wearing effect on men's strength. Ammunition was low too; they were beginning to turn out the pockets of dead men to find cartridges.

—Major, do you think we'll ever get out of here?

—We'll get relief all right. Didn't you hear those auto-rifles last night? There are two million American soldiers coming for us.

Whittlesey was not debonnair, he did not strike attitudes. He was merely matter-of-fact, which in the long run turned out better.

—That's right (they would agree, as the tall form ambled past on the morning tour of inspection). That's right, there was a lot of them sho-shos going last night.

The Water-Hole, where men of the surrounded force crawled
for a muddy drink—or a sniper's bullet.

If he had said Woodrow Wilson was coming in a hand-cart to get them out, they would have believed him since yesterday and the barrage, when he pulled them all through.

Down where the wounded lay was the worst, with calls for water. Cigarettes were passed from lip to lip after a few puffs taken. The whole place stank frightfully of dead men and gangrene. Holderman's wounds were gangrened too, and he was in great pain, had had another glancing hit from a sniper bullet.

In the shelter of a tree root the Major came on a man squatted down. He raised his voice:

—What do you think I had those latrines built for? If you want to do that, go down there and use them. The next man I catch at that trick goes on report.

The mist was getting thinner under the influence of the morning sun and now occasional sniper shots were falling, together with bursts from that damned trench mortar, which blew a hole as big as a house every time it hit—fortunately not often a hole in the middle of the position. The German machine guns rattled sporadically and a man trying for water got hit. Whittlesey drew a couple of riflemen from Company C and posted them as guards over the route to the water hole, with orders to shoot any man who tried to reach it without authorization.

He did not expect there would be any shooting; but his present business was to save lives, and the mere posting of the guard would do that, at the same time putting the water-details in the hands of such men as he himself would select. Zip Cepeglia, little, active as a monkey, with his nutcracker jaw and his funny Italian-Bowery accent, had shown a remarkable talent for getting the precious liquid in a manner both silent and swift. A brave little man—the Major made a mental note that when they got out of that hole, if they ever did, he would recommend the little runner for a decoration.

III

The Valley of the Aire, East of the Pocket
(All Day)

During the night von Kleist pushed his Prussian Guards forward into the lines of the Montrefagne, where the position had been stabilized at dark with the Americans holding the western lip of the mountain along a line that stretched forward toward Fléville. East of the Montrefagne was another big hill which had been turned into a perfect fortress. An oblique ravine protected it in front and slanted down to the foot of the Montrefagne itself, and the Guard had placed both artillery and machine guns in quantity at the head of this ravine, on a spot called the Ariétal Farm. Unlikely that any attack would come toward this wing of the front, Ariétal being so strong. The German planned, therefore, to hold hard there and use his Prussians for a vigorous counterstroke down the Montrefagne slopes, which would take the American salient in flank, break through, and with fortune our aid, capture a regiment or two before they could work rearward across the Exermont ravine.

There was a thick mist in the morning, favorable for this attack. The artillery preparations began under the fog of night, and at about six-thirty Prinz Eitel Friedrich's Prussians took off in their counterattack.

It bucked head on into that renewed charge of the 1st Division which, so far from being satisfied with its gains of the day before, had planned during the night to storm the rest of the Montrefagne, Ariétal Farm and another hill, Hill 272, all at once. Barrage crossed barrage; both American 1st Division and Prussian Guard had their machine guns right in the front line, batteries as close in as they could be brought and good telephonic communication; both were on razor-edge for battle.

The result was a wild tangled struggle of offense against offense—fire-fight, artillery-fight, bomb-fight and hand-to-hand, all at once in different parts of the same field. At least fifty Americans were shot down in front of one machine-gun nest; not two hundred yards away another was blown to pieces by a single grenade; farther on still a whole German platoon was down, every man with just one bullet-wound and that one fatal. Both 1st and Guard were, for all practical purposes, picked men, but the Germans had four years of war under their belts which, though it gave them more experience, left them with less zip, and zip weighed more than experience on the slopes of the Montrefagne with everything shrouded in morning mist, artificial smokes whirling through the groves and shell-bursts so thick a man could hardly see. By noon the Montrefagne crest was definitely American; the 18th and 16th Infantry were pushing down its northern cheek. They were winning not so much by driving the Guard back as by killing them—privates, noncoms, officers all the way up to majors lay among the dead, whole battalions wiped out to the last man.

Hill 272 and Ariétal were still holding out as the day passed zenith. The advance American elements, badly cut up, had to pause, reorganize, ask for more artillery preparation. The whole divisional gun-power concentrated on the fortified slopes of 272 and Ariétal; Regiments 26 and 28 tried them a second time, just after two o'clock. Fire was coming at the Americans from front and both flanks as they worked up a narrow ravine, but the Prussians were catching it pretty bad themselves now, long-range machine-gun fire from the captured Montrefagne on one flank, and such an artillery concentration as was rarely seen—ten shots a minute, the 7th United States Artillery fired till its barrels grew too hot to fire more.

It was in this two o'clock attack that an intelligent sergeant of the 26th found a chink in the defense system behind Ariétal and led a platoon through it; they got into a little wood behind the German main line, and were squarely across the runner-post chain for the whole defensive system. Runner after runner they captured or killed, and cut the 'phone wires. The German liaison collapsed, their supporting artillery began to miss, Regiments 26 and 28 never stopped driving, and by five o'clock the Dutch were confessing defeat by firing mustard gas onto the slopes. Westward the 16th Regiment was in the outskirts of Fléville and the line was broken.

IV

The Pocket, Left Wing
(*Morning—About 9:30* A. M.)

A little after nine the mist cleared away and the Germans began to lay a paste of trench-mortar shells all over everything again. Usually this was an indication that an attack was about to start, especially since the mortar was reinforced by the machine guns, which fired at everything that moved. The snipers tuned up; and the shooting was heaviest on the left flank, up toward the road where Cullen was. To his funk hole, as one of the largest (he had found a soft spot when the command moved in), the German prisoner taken on the morning of the 3rd had been assigned, and the Lieutenant had been trying to draw him into conversation.

—*Leben Sie dies?* (Cullen would ask, trying to make up for faults of grammar and pronunciation with the

163

energy of expression, when the trench mortar began to heave over its surprise packages.)

"*Keine ahnung,*" replied the prisoner and ducked.

Half-past nine, and the machine guns were adding their contribution to that of the mortar. Cullen, as he afterward remarked, "wanted to duck myself, but didn't think it would look good while that Heinie was there." Besides, the repetition of "*Keine ahnung*" which seemed the man's only phrase and which Cullen did not understand in the least, was becoming a bore. The Lieutenant turned and pointed downward toward the funk hole which held the P.C. and what was left of the headquarters company.

"*Du, heraus!*" he said with enthusiasm, pointing in that direction. The German looked puzzled, then pained, then scared, then shook his head vigorously.

"*Keine ahnung,*" he remarked.

—Oh, goddam it, *Heraus! Raus aus! Dort unten!*

Cullen produced his pistol, assumed as ferocious an expression as possible, and again pointed toward the P.C. The lad began to crawl away, his face wearing the expression of a cat which is being put out for the night. He got through to the P.C. all right, in spite of the machine-gun fire from his countrymen. There he found Lionel Bendheim, the Yorkville man, who had had a leg smashed during the artillery concentration of the day before, and it was a relief to both of them to talk German together. They entertained each other with tales of how tough life was in the army.

In the Air, Above the Pocket
(9:00 to 10:00 A. M.)

Morse, of the 50th Aero Squadron, shot over two observation planes as soon as the mist had cleared a little, in an effort to locate Whittlesey's men by visual observation, and to carry up to them a few baskets of chocolate, medical supplies and ammunition, these last being attached to the little parachutes taken from flares. The position of the besieged companies, as reported to him from Corps, who had received their co-ordinates from Brigade and Division, was "at the bottom of the ravine."

One of the planes got caught in archie bursts, lost a couple of bracing wires and came back; the other whirled on, circled low over the treetops without seeing any sign of Americans or their signal panels, let go two or three packages at the bottom of the ravine, and in circling out got over the hill of Charlevaux.

There was a clearing here, beyond the road, with the new earth of a fresh dugout at the edge of it. From this dugout presently emerged two or three soldiers, who were assuredly German by the shape of their helmets and the fact that they instantly began to shoot. The aviator whipped out his rocket pistol, pointed it up and released into the heavens a flare whose message said, "Fire on me."

It fell out that the observation officer of the 305th Field Artillery just at that moment had his glasses glued to his face in the tree-camouflaged observation post of

165

the regiment. He took a quick calculation bearing on the spot—276.55—and 'phoned down to battery.

It was three minutes to ten.

VI

The Pocket, Left Wing
(Morning—About 9:30)

Cullen was a trifle stricken at having so summarily dismissed the prisoner who was human after all, though a German and a solemncholy duck. He crawled along behind the man for a little distance, with some confused idea of seeing both that the man got through all right and that he did not try to escape. The prisoner seemed both safe and docile enough, dodged around a tree out of sight. As he did so the Lieutenant turned back, noticing to his surprise that his hand and one knee were covered with something white and chalky.

He looked up; just above him was the post where one of his corporals, assigned there on the first night, had been burrowing like a badger at every interval. The pit he had digged must be all of seven feet deep by this time, its entrance crowned with a couple of huge logs the man had dragged from God knew where. Evidently he had run into a stratum of soft white clay as he penetrated the hillside, for that material was flung out in a long apron across the crest of the pile at the doorway of his cave.

As Cullen gazed at this exhibit, there was the shriek of a sniper's bullet. He flattened against the hillside, rolled over, then wiggled back to his own post, filled with interior chucklings, in spite of the situation. Across the valley within the German lines that white apron at the entrance of a deep hole must have been as visible as a bar of soap in a coal scuttle, and the logical Germans, working on the old military maxim that the deeper the hole, the higher the officer, had evidently assumed it to be the battalion post of command. So that was why his flank had been honored with all the attention from the trench mortar and the machine guns.

VII

Headquarters, 254 Reserve-Infantry-Regiment
(German), Near the Pocket
(Dawn to 10:00 A. M.)

The German military machine was an exact but rather ponderous instrument which displayed a tendency to get tangled in its own efficiency. The French movements in the sector facing Wellmann's corps during the two previous days had been repulsed with ease and with much loss to the Gauls. According to the *Schemas* prepared at headquarters it was known that the French system did not provide for renewed attacks by beaten troops. Therefore unless the arrival of a fresh French division at the right or westward section of the corps line were noted, it was reasonable to suppose that no fighting would take place there. Both the General and his new Chief of Staff, Major von Ditfurth, felt that this portion of the line no longer needed so much attention. The latter worked out a program for a further slide eastward along the corps front, the troops to the west taking over more ground, and Quadt-Wykradt-Hüchtenbruck's 76th Reserve Division becoming more concentrated by narrowing its front to the section from La Palette to the junction with von Kleist's Army Group. This would enable the 76th Reserve to put considerably more men into line around that *Amerikanernest*, possibly wipe them out with brief delay, and certainly to turn back all efforts at relief.

The movement had started on the afternoon of the 4th, after a few weak and local French attacks had been beaten off. It came to an end during the night, with the German 252nd now established in La Palette, the 253rd mainly in reserve and the 254th devoting its whole attention to the surrounded Americans with the help of the pioneer companies that had been brought into the battle at the beginning and what aid the 122nd Landwehr of von Kleist's group could give.

In the meanwhile Lieutenant Leak had told his mendacious but highly credible tale of at least twelve hundred Americans full of fight and with plenty of food in the pocket, and von Sybel had warned Major Hünicken to proceed with caution against this nest of Americans. Hünicken does not appear to have been very willing to hold his hand. He had lost a good many men and had gained no ground against Whittlesey, and this hurt. His orders were permissive enough to give him a little latitude; and he apparently determined to construe them as forbidding heavy and continuous attack against the knot of Americans, but not forbidding occasional movements as long as they were well organized and carefully planned.

Their position, he decided on examining his map, was most easily approachable from the side of the hill at its center, where his own men could come down with a rush, the slope aiding the preliminary barrage of potato-masher bombs. In the morning mist nothing was to be done. It was too risky in those woods, one might hit friends; but as soon as it cleared he opened up on the Americans with the *Minenwerfer,* and just before ten he began forming his men for the attack, using a clearing near the crest of the hill for formation.

An Allied airplane flew over and fired a rocket while the concentration was in progress.

VIII

The Pocket
(10:00 to 10:45 A. M.*)*

At ten the men of the surrounded battalion heard the shock of guns southward, the same sound they had heard the day before, when the disastrous American barrage fell on them. Every head turned and every heart stood still; there was a crash, and the shells, all in beautiful line, landed along the edge of the stream. Once more the thud of artillery, once more the line of shells—nearer. In spite of the morning chill men began to break into perspiration and to swear under their breath.

—Oh, my God, again?

Then, as they waited in heart-breaking suspense for the lightning to come down on their heads, the dancing line of explosions came one step nearer, skipped a beat, and then all the bursts together sounded gladly from the hill above and to their front. Again! The slope up there vomited branches, torn leaves and singing fragments of steel, this time in the lines where they knew Germans were. Again! Someone was hit up there, two or three unearthly howls rose and fell with the accent of fire-sirens.

"Jeez, Jim, listen to those bastards yell!"

The men of the command, who had hugged themselves to the ground when the firing started, sat up, half-rose. The kraut trench mortar had gone silent, the machine guns coughed a half burst more and stopped, all up the slope in the intervals of the shell-bursts you could hear commands and shouts in German and the hurry of forms crashing through the bushes. The auto-rifle teams let off a few bursts in the direction of each rush. In spite of its cold, hunger, wounds and weakness the battalion, for the first time since it entered the pocket, began to enjoy itself. Nothing is so pleasant as seeing the man who bullied you take the same treatment from a bigger bully.

October 5

IX

Between Lançon and Briquenay
(About 9 A. M.)

The orders came down during the night. In the morning the captured Americans were taken off for further questioning by Lieutenant Prinz, the divisional American expert. During the trip Leak and Harrington were with the privates for a few minutes under guard of ordinary German privates, not very bright. Leak seized the occasion.

—Listen, you fellows (he said rapidly) we may be prisoners, but you want to remember that we are still American soldiers. Don't give them anything you don't have to and when you do give them anything let it be bull.

Half an hour later he was being ushered into a big room where a fire burned cheerfully, and a tall, blond man who announced himself as Lieutenant Prinz, was asking in excellent English whether he knew anyone in Seattle and how many Americans were in the pocket.

X

Headquarters, 77th Division, U. S. A.
(12:00 to 1:30 P. M.)

It would be just before noon that Johnson of Brigade got through on a 'phone to Alexander and informed him that the morning attack had not been delivered, what with Stacey's request for relief and the time he him-

171

self had spent getting to the front and working out the minor tactical situation. The General was furious, especially since Klotz and de Coppet, who had remained in close touch with the French division on the left, reported that they had really made an attack that morning, a supreme effort. For five minutes they had held La Palette; but there had been no American support on their right, the Germans gathered strength, counterattacked fiercely from the direction of Charlevaux Mill and drove them back to Binarville. If messieurs the Americans had made good their part of the contract, the position had been won.

To add to his pleasure there was a message passed through by Corps from Army, that is, from John J. Pershing himself; an order that it would be extremely dangerous to dodge or flout:

Bonehead 3 to Dreadnaught 7:

> Direct that a vigorous effort be made this afternoon to relieve the companies on the left of the 77th Div. that are cut off. Suggest that they be notified by airplane of the attack so that the action of the people cut off will be co-ordinated.

Brigadier Johnson, as a result, got one of the prize wiggings of his career; he was to drive through that line in spite of losses. The 153rd Brigade was stirred to new effort; if the 305th had suffered badly, put in the 306th with the other regiment in support. Another message asked Corps for all available airplanes, one of which was to deliver a message to Whittlesey immediately.

172

The Brigade Commander is now attacking the German trenches in the ravine southeast of the Moulin de Charlevaux.

The Division Commander directs that you retire and fight your way through, attacking the Germans from the rear while our troops engage them in front.

HANNAY, CHIEF OF STAFF

The aviator who carried this important missive had trouble with archies and low clouds—the sun had hidden its red face again, shortly after noon—and through the intervals of trailing mist below could only make out the undulating green waves of the Argonne, without landmarks, only here and there the flicker of a stream slicing across the featureless forest. Taking his bearing from one such silver line he swooped and circled. That headland westward must be La Palette, (he decided) the brook that of Charlevaux. He tripped the bomb-release and down floated the weighted message on its little parachute.

Three days later it came back to divisional headquarters with this endorsement:

5 Oct 1:25 PM dropped after aeroplane had circled for 25 minutes. Also six pigeons all ok. This in box with pigeons.

PRIVATE E. B. AHRENS,
53rd Coast Artillery, Battery F.

The 53rd Coast Artillery was an outfit of heavy guns, firing high-angle, interdiction shoots on the German railroads, off the map. Their position was three or four miles behind the hill where Whittlesey was holding out.

XI

Headquarters I Reserve-Korps (German), Briquenay (About 2:00 P. M.)

After lunch Graf Schulenberg, the Chief of Staff for the Army Group of the Deutscher Kronprinz, dropped in at Wellmann's headquarters. He did not attempt to conceal that the situation, taking the front as a whole, was serious. Another retreat in the Rheims sector had become necessary; and von Kleist was having an extremely difficult time in the Aire Valley, where the Americans had put in what appeared to be a whole division of *Stosstruppen* against him, supported by one of the most powerful artillery condensations yet seen on the front. Von Kleist had used Prinz Eitel Friedrich's First Prussian Guard against them, but the Prince was complaining bitterly that his men were showing the effects of war-weariness and needed a spell in a quiet sector to bring them up to storm-troop quality again. There were many replacements of low grade and the good men who remained were becoming bored with the endless repetition of the same series of movements. The Herr Graf quoted Nietzsche to the effect that against boredom even the gods struggle in vain.

Wellmann had begun to grow suspicious that this elaborate introduction would be followed by more demands on him, and sure enough, they came in the next sentences. They were taking away from him the 45th Reserve Division, one of the best units he had, and giving him in its place the battered First Prussian Guard. His protest was stifled:

—Consider the front as a whole (the Graf said); surely it is obvious that if the Americans continue to hold Fléville and Exermont they are in a position to take Apremont and the Chêne Tondu by an attack from flank and rear. The retreat of the whole of the 2nd Bavarian Landwehr Division would then be cut off.

—I have only one division in the Argonne myself, the 76th Reserve, and its line of retreat is through Lançon (urged Wellmann).

—But its left flank will be entirely open if the 2nd Landwehr Division is forced to leave the line (von Schulenberg retorted irresistibly).

There was nothing to do but consent, though Wellmann was moved to inner sneers at the idea that his own could be considered a quiet sector. His disposition was somewhat improved by the discovery that the French had made a surprise attack on La Palette, which had been repulsed with the capture of sixteen prisoners and no less than twelve machine guns.

XII

The Pocket
(*2:00* P. M.)

The morning sun, which had helped the shivering and weary men on the hillside, ducked under shortly after noon, when the men caught fleeting glimpses of airplanes among the clouds, but so far away they were unable to spot them as either Allied or German. The Boches were very quiet today; apparently the shelling they got this morning did them a lot of good. Most of the men crawled out of the funk holes and sat on the edges, happy to breathe. Up toward the firing-line floated a disembodied voice:

—By God, I wish I had some chow.

Sergeant Tuite murmured something about the first hundred years being the hardest, then noticed that Lieutenant Schenck was reading from a little leather-bound book, about four inches by three. The Lieutenant closed it when he saw he was noticed and held the volume so the Sergeant could see the gold stamping on its back—*Science and Health,* by Mary Baker Eddy.

"This is food and drink to me," he remarked, "a wonderful comfort."

"This is my comfort," replied the Sergeant, unbuttoning his tunic and pulling out a rosary.

XIII

The Ravine Near La Palette Hill
(*1:30 to 3:00* P. M.)

A few Mississippi and Alabama replacements had come up and been ployed into the 308th when the fighting started on the last of September. Like the Westerners who joined the division a day or two before, they were a mixed lot as to military experience. One or two had fired rifles around the farm in civilian life, some had had a certain amount of training with the issue Springfield. But none had so much as seen the French Chauchats they were to use in this drive. Instruction in the use of the strange weapon had to be given hastily, at night when the men would rather be getting their shut-eye, or by day in the heat of battle.

Did it matter?—for the *sho-sho* is practically fool-proof. It did not matter in the earlier attack when the East Side city rats, veterans of the Vesle, did the auto-rifle work. But that afternoon of the 5th it suddenly began to matter very much, as Johnson's attack went corkscrewing forward. Better than the New Yorkers the men from the West understood how to care for themselves in the open, how to lie comfortably at night, take cover, protect themselves against illness. The losses of those first October days in the wild woods fell heavier on New York, not because the city men were more courageous, but more ignorant. And when Johnson's move got under way the new men who did not know auto-rifles were perforce handling these weapons because there was no one else to handle them.

Result:—"We were subjected to terrific machine-gun fire. The fire of our own artillery did not seem to damage the wire much. They could not find it among the trees. The green men fought remarkably well; you never saw such bravery. But unfortunately, their lack of knowledge of automatic rifles soon exhausted our supply of ammunition, as they fired whole clips at a burst and we were soon within ten feet of the German's strongly entrenched position with our ammunition gone. We took what we could from our fallen comrades and looked in vain for supporting platoons. Instead of supporting platoons Germans came around behind us as well as in front. My knowledge of the Argonne drive from here on is hearsay, for I was captured and sent to a German hospital."

By three o'clock it was all over and Johnson's attack broken down like those that preceded it.

"I am being held on general line 73.5," he reported by runner from the front. "Heavy artillery, machine-gun and rifle fire. French upon our immediate left or slightly to our rear. Two of their liaison groups are with me. I am attempting to advance and pass company through interval in wire which exists at bottom of ravine. I am myself with this company which is attempting to pass through and who in the last few minutes have lost over 20 killed and wounded out of 85."

Things had come out no better rightward, where Houghton had his 307th Regiment in action after a hot meal, the first the men had enjoyed for days. They were just digging in, imagining their mission to be support, when the orders came for the advance, and out of the fox holes, up through a narrow and winding trail they made their way, toward a hill, with Captain Blagden at their head and Captain Eddie Grant, who played third base for the Giants, somewhere along the line.

At the foot of the hill a barrage of potato mashers came down; Blagden was hit and went back wounded, with several of his men. Half the company took cover and fired over the heads of the other half, but even that was no good. They had only made a hundred yards, losing a man for every yard, when word came through from the Colonel to break off, the losses were too heavy.

XIV

The Pocket
(*3:00 to 4:00* P. M.)

The afternoon attack was announced, about three o'clock, by a few ranging bursts from the German machine guns.

"Duck, everybody," said the noncoms, and the men flattened into their funk holes like frogs diving into a swamp. Over on the right young Hennessey was just finishing the butt of a cigarette, the only one of the day, and he had only a couple of pulls at it, hated to lose it by burying his face in the dirt.

"Down, you fool!" called someone below him.

"I'm sitting low."

The machine guns ground out again, a regular concentration, with grazing fire. There was a clank; young Hennessey gave a leap and came rolling down on the men below him, his limbs flopping like those of a decapitated chicken, the cigarette crushed beneath him without his getting that last puff. "I'm hit," he managed to articulate. His face was a funny greenish color and there was blood at the belt of his tunic.

—Got it through the guts.

Tiedeman picked up Hennessey's canteen (which the owner would not be needing) to see whether there was any water left in it, but it held only the bullet that had spent itself penetrating one side after passing through the Irishman's body.

Whittlesey and McMurtry were lying side by side, their heads not a foot apart, where they had pancaked out when Peabody yelled "Down!" A storm of bullets rushed just over their heads. "*Most* unpleasant," remarked the Major as easily as though he were criticizing the flavor of a cup of tea.

For twenty minutes to the tick it went on; with a crash and a fountain of earth it closed as the first bomb of another potato-masher barrage announced a German rush.

—Everybody up!

Excitement is a wonderful restorative. The weary, starving men, worn with sleeplessness and hopelessness, double-timed up to the line of the road where the bombs were falling. Revnes was with them, dragging his wounded ankle; McMurtry was in the van in spite of his wounded leg. The latter was out on that right wing where the cliff gave the enemy so good a bombing-point, with a sort of glacis rolling round its foot in the protect-tion of the trees, which would bring the charge right down into the lines on a run before defense could get set. The Captain planted the auto-rifle teams to cover the point, warning them to fire hip-high up the slope. Out beyond, the few American snipers were letting go, single shot; along the center the new men were firing faster—"just to have something coming out of the end of that gun."

The Germans must have had a new supply of potato mashers. They were using them faster than ever, and in bunches now, five or six of them bound together with wire, so that the bunch made a hole as big as a trench-mortar shell. One blew the legs clean off a man in one of the fox holes at the center. "Mama—mama—mama," they heard him cry frightfully before pain brought its own anesthesia, then in a faint ghost of a voice that trailed to a whisper on the last word, "Good-bye, everybody. I forgive all."

Not ten feet from where he stood McMurtry saw Lieutenant Pool go down with a bullet in his back from a sniper who had somehow worked around that flank. The Captain shouted first aid; one of the medical men came running through the fire in a manner that won him the D.S.C. and lugged the officer off to the dressing station, where his wound had to be covered with a bandage taken from a dead man and so folded that the blood clot did not come in contact with the new wound.

The main German effort fell near the center. Sadler was up there, one of the two artillerymen who had accompanied Lieutenant Teichmoeller on his liaison mission. He fired; then leaped suddenly to his feet, yelling, "I got him! I got him! I tell you I got one!"

"Get down, you damn fool. Do you want to get your head blown off?"

A surprised grin spread across the artilleryman's face. He subsided into his funk hole and began to work the action of the rifle that he had taken from one of the wounded, and was firing for the first time.

Evening report from Reserve-Infantry-Regiment 254 (Hesse) to 76th Reserve Division. Noted; passed to headquarters, I Reserve Corps, General Wellmann:

A hand-grenade attack was undertaken this afternoon against the *Amerikanernest*. It was repulsed by extremely heavy machine-gun fire.

XV

NEWS FLASH

AMERICANS GAIN AS ENEMY'S FRONT WEAKENS

Germans Give Every Sign of Preparing Withdrawal in Argonne

UPTON MEN IN HARD TEST

since the offensive started.

A battalion of American soldiers were surrounded by the Germans and cut their way out. These troops held out against the Germans attempting to corral them and were protected by our artillery.

Officers at General Pershing's headquarters were inclined

German machine-guns camouflaged in the forest, fired into the Americans from all sides.

XVI

The Pocket; Funk Hole for Wounded
(*About 4:00 P. M.*)

Lionel Bendheim was feeling pretty sick, what with his smashed leg, all bloody and gangrened, and a wound in the other gam, too, so that even the company of his friend the enemy prisoner was not much use any more. He felt a touch on his shoulder and looked up into the Major's eyes. Whittlesey was extending a small piece of chocolate.

"Just imagine," said the officer, and with every appearance of meaning it, "you'll be down on the Riviera while we're still soaking through these woods."

Well now, that was an idea.

XVII

Headquarters, I Reserve-Korps (German) Briquenay
(*6:30 P. M.*)

A telephone message for General Wellmann came through just before the dinner hour from the Army Oberkommando. The situation in the Aire Valley and along the eastern edge of the Argonne had become serious. If any further retreat became necessary there, the whole line was to withdraw to the position known as the Kriemhilde Stellung, at the north edge of the Grand Pré gap. The Kriemhilde Stellung was not as well organized as that now occupied by his corps, nor was it so rich in the vital lateral communications, and the General saw fit to voice an objection.

This was not, he was informed, an order to retreat. It was merely a warning order. Have your Chief of Staff prepare directives for such a move; if it becomes actually necessary to carry out the retreat, further orders will be sent to you.

Wellmann seized the occasion to complain of the little knot of Americans behind his lines, who were giving him so much trouble; already they had caused the dislocation of his whole corps sector. The troops engaged in surrounding this *Amerikanernest* were in a most difficult position and outnumbered by the Americans around them. The 254th Reserve Regiment was not equal to the task of both beating off the constant efforts to relieve and attacking the Americans in a manner to wipe them out. The good Major Hünicken had been forced to resort to all kinds of shifts; his pioneers were useless except for bombing attacks to which the Americans always replied by intense machine-gun fire, and the small detachment of the 122nd Landwehr present were useless for any kind of attack work.

His divisional intelligence officer had, besides, obtained information from prisoners that made it appear the Americans were even stronger in numbers than appeared in the beginning and that they were well supplied with food and ammunition. He was inclined to credit this information; the conduct of the *Amerikanernest* had been such as to support it. Therefore, he had ordered that the attacks against them be not pressed closely. He begged the loan of a battalion of first-class storm specialists with full equipment. It would be a reproach to the German Army if these Americans were allowed to survive.

The 'phone emitted sounds expressive of the grinding of a mill of thought, and then promised the arrival of a battalion of *Stosstruppen*. Equipment, including especially flame-throwers, would be sent in the morning.

XVIII

The Pocket
(*Twilight*)

As McMurtry came down the hill in the falling twilight to the battalion P.C. in its hole in the dirt, Whittlesey noticed that there was something sticking straight out of his back at right angles.

"What have you got there?" he said, and gave it a yank. It came loose—the stick of a potato-masher grenade. "Murder!" yelled the Captain. "If you do that again, I'll wring your neck."

Whittlesey grinned. "Go get it dressed," he said. "I won't do it again. There's only one. Didn't you know you were wounded?"

When he came back the two officers conversed for a few moments. It was, both of them felt, becoming more than ever important to get exact information of their plight through to regimental and brigade headquarters; not only because they were in urgent need of many things, but also because a messenger going through would serve as guide along whatever path he had taken, and could thus bring relief through whatever gaps existed in the German defense system.

—Will any of you runners try to get through? (asked Whittlesey, raising his voice).

—I will (said Joe Friel, and swallowed) if someone will go with me.

—How about you, Botelle?

The Major turned to the battalion messenger who had crawled across that fire-swept hillside half a dozen times already on errands from company to company. Already he was marked down in Whittlesey's mind for a citation.

—Well, you see, sir—do I have to go?

—I can't order you to go, if that's what you mean. But a man's duty as a soldier sometimes goes beyond the performance of orders.

—It's ... (His voice was not as decisive as it might be.)

—It may be suicide for all of us if headquarters doesn't learn the situation here. Now look, Botelle; you have been one of the best men in the unit. It's more or less up to you to keep up that standard and set an example for the rest. As I say, I can't order you.

—I'll go.

—Good for you. Ask to be taken to brigade headquarters when you get through. Tell them ...

Out on the flanks the night outposts were being set

once more, watching for the snipers and machine-gun nests of the Germans, who occasionally fired a few shots, especially around the water hole. Newcom was loading for Indian Martinez; he spotted a trace of movement behind a bush.

—There's one (he whispered).

He passed the gun up to the Indian, who lifted his head over the edge of the log and drew a cautious bead on the spot. At the same moment there was a flash and a report; Newcom saw Martinez' whole frame shiver convulsively, and his hands cramp once round the rifle, then let it drop. When he turned the Indian over he found a hole square in his forehead and the eyes popped right from their sockets with the impact.

—Never knew what hit him.

All quiet now along the front, save that faint and far, the men in the pocket could hear across the night the chug-chug of Chauchats from the direction of the American lines, the direction whence they had come, a thousand years ago.

—Listen (said the Major) it's like the pipes at Lucknow. (Then, he paused a moment, and added:) If we can hear them they can probably hear us. Wouldn't it be a good idea to let off a few bursts to let them know we're still alive and kicking?

McMurtry nodded and crawled away toward one of the auto-rifle teams. With gun pointed up the slope, they fired several bursts. Ten shots—a pause—ten shots—a pause—ten shots, spaced at regular intervals to make sure the hearers understood it for a signal. The Germans understood it so whether the Americans back there did or not; the third or fourth time the signal-bursts were fired, they tried to cover the intervals with the clatter of their own mechanical weapons and night and rain closed round the command with an occasional Very light flickering weirdly among the falling drops and the wounded moaning.

"I'm going, boys, I'm going. Write to my mother—please—please!"

I

Headquarters, 77th Division, U. S. A.
(Early Morning)

DURING the night Corps and Army had been in touch with Alexander and had again impressed upon him the importance, in their eyes, of getting Whittlesey relieved. The conversation, which was telephonic, apparently convinced men at both ends of the wire that on that day, the 6th, more attacks against the German positions at La Palette and Hill 198 would be futile. Our hope lay in the east, where the 1st had driven its thrust home to the German nerve-centers. Now there was a gap along the Aire; the general commanding, who was Mr. Pershing, was going to use the fresh 82nd Division there, driving westward into the Argonne; would flank the whole German line in the forest and roll it up, if all went well.

Meanwhile the whole of the 50th Aero Squadron was placed at Alexander's disposal, for communicating with Whittlesey and carrying him the needed provisions. Their orders were simple—make repeated flights over Charlevaux Valley, check the co-ordinates of Whittlesey's position, and carry him the necessaries. All these matters being settled Alexander trotted off to find out what he could by personal first-line observation.

II

The Pocket
(*Dawn to* 8:00 A. M.)

Human routine establishes itself under the most extraordinary exterior circumstances and regardless of them. Men falling through space into the sun would do it by timetable; bank robbers work according to a predetermined schedule—and in the heart of the Argonne Major Charles W. Whittlesey crawled about his posts in the morning, inspecting them in a sequence familiar and therefore comforting by repetition. Nothing new, nothing new; there was never anything new. The same soldiers who lifted heads and said, "Do you think we'll get out of this, Major?" The same wounded; little Griffin, surprised and bewildered, his face expressing "This can't happen to me"—but plenty brave about it; Peabody, the worst wounded of any of the officers, wry lips cheerful when any of the men looked his way or spoke, but moaning softly to himself for pain when he was for the moment alone. "Can I have some water, sir?"

—We'll try to get it to you.

Pass on: to the next post, an auto-rifle post where the same soldiers end a conversation half heard with a faltering dropped sentence—subject, probably, how the hell can we get out of here—which it would not do for officers to overhear.

Yet, curiously, there was less of this than there had been three days previous. Commanders and commanded were discovering the secret of siege, the thing that had been learned in all the great beleaguerments of history—Tyre and Rhodes, Leyden, Humaytà and Paris—that the human capacity for endurance, for mere passive defense, exceeds all belief and possibility as long as there be a leader to say, Don't give up, we're not licked yet.

Galloping Charlie was such a leader; yet even he, who had thought the situation desperate two days before, when he sent the morning pigeon with the message ending "Cannot support be sent at once?"—even he must have been surprised to find his men still much alive, still uncaptured and still unbroken in spirit after forty-eight more hours foodless and after that misfortunate barrage.

—Where did you get that? (A soldier munching away on a fragment of black bread, the size of a tiny biscuit.)

—Off one of the dead Boches, sir. Will you have some?

—No, you deserve it. Eat it up.

Carry on; the danger was not now that the battalion would crack. City rats and Westerners, with a few from the south, they had been welded into one by the external pressure. The danger was failing physical strength. A man's dragging feet would trip over a pebble no bigger than a baby's thumb and he would go sprawling, fail for a long minute even the effort to rise. Close action of any kind was no longer possible to men so enfeebled; if the Heinies came strong enough to break into the position they could mop up with the bayonet and not find much resistance. To win, even to hold out, the guns must be kept working; and there were not many cartridges left and not too many guns. Three of the machine guns were definitely disabled and would never shoot again; and the auto-rifles had suffered a proportionate diminution.

Even the effort to bury the dead was altogether too heavy. Not only would it further exhaust men's slender reserves of strength, but it was dangerous for them to stand up, even in a crouching position. The German snipers had all the open places marked; the cover was being stripped by the constant rain of bullets. Men whose reflexes had been slowed by fatigue and hunger were less adept at dodging, would suffer heavier casualties.

Yet,

—It won't do them any good to see their buddies lying there dead (mused McMurtry).

—Cover them with branches and leaves, then (replied the Major).

He told off burial parties as usual. The men were warned to continue using the official latrines.

III

Headquarters, 307th Infantry, U. S. A.
(6:30 to 7:00 A. M.)

On the extreme right flank of the division the 306th was now in the front line and in fairly good shape for an attack, but a movement there offered little prospect of success. The General inspected briefly; he passed on to the other brigade and Colonel Houghton of the 307th, a remarkable man, who had led a banana revolution in Honduras, organized his own machine-gun battalion and took it to France with the Canadians at the outbreak of war (he was in business in Winnipeg at the time), fought through first Ypres when the chlorine gas came rolling down, won decorations and a repute for reckless daring, was transferred to the Americans when we came in, and by high officers consulted as an expert on trench war.

They offered him a cushy staff job; he refused it with revulsion—What! Him a brass-hat?—and went to live in fox holes, commanding a regiment, with his Chinese striker, Lee, who fed him rum when the weather made the Colonel's old wounds hurt. Houghton and Alexander were ducks from opposite sides of the pond; had already been in a row down on the Aisne, when the General ordered him to carry through some attack or else. Houghton 'phoned back that he needed no threats to make him do his duty and would be glad to turn over the regiment to someone else if high command thought the duty could be better done so. A fighting man, whose nerves jangled with the impact of many battles, but who responded to the sound of machine guns like an old fire-horse to the gong.

The General found him in his fox hole, dug under the roots of a big tree. The hole was wet and Houghton was yellow with jaundice—"I can't tell myself from Lee sometimes," he used to joke grimly—the interview between the two was clear, frosty and precise as autumn. Houghton remarked that the Germans facing him did not seem particularly stern stuff, but that their position had been chosen with great care and developed by good engineers. They had excellent trenches, camouflaged both by art and time; everything was heavily protected by wire.

That wire was the difficulty. He had asked for an artillery concentration to cut it on the afternoon of the 4th, and again on the previous day; he had heard the guns banging away and had seen explosions, somewhere on the slope of Hill 198, tripping along the valley and on the opposite crest. This had not done the business. He did not blame the artillerymen, who had fired a good shoot, well timed and well aimed, but of course they had to do it off the map, had no observation on the fall of their shells, and could not be accurate enough to deal with the irregularly running belts of wire. That was what had brought the failure of the relieving attacks on the last two days.

(The two men had been walking cautiously forward as the Colonel spoke and Alexander could see for himself what kind of country it was; mentally agreed that everything Houghton said was true as the Gospel of Mark. They were at a junction where two ridges ran together and could see a little way down the tangled valley. An occasional bullet went past—zip—zip—zipee.)

—If we had some Bangalore torpedoes (continued the

Colonel) we might do something with that wire.

The General's adjutant coughed for attention and remarked that the Colonel had mentioned the idea over the 'phone on the previous evening and that the Bangalores had been ordered—but you know what transportation is at this time.

The Colonel nodded understanding and swept on with his exposition. The German wire was not absolutely continuous. His Lieutenant Tillman, a good officer, had found the end of a switch of wire and had a few men up front; had been ordered to work along inside the wire and cut more gaps, noting those already existing. Small parties of men would be filtered forward to these gaps in ones and twos. They would take cover near the gaps; and by night filter through the wire. When a sufficient concentration of men had been worked up, forward there, an attack could be delivered, laterally along the German line and behind it, with some prospect of achievement. The operation, however, was an extremely tricky one, depending upon catching old Fritz by surprise, a thing that did not often happen. To hurry it would be absolutely fatal; the men must be worked forward by such gentle stages that the Germans had no hint of their presence there. It would probably be forty-eight hours before the assault could be delivered.

—Approved (said the General).

He went off to see Breckinridge and Johnson on the extreme left flank, whom he found in the dumps with a ruined regiment around them, truly in no shape for attack. If anything more were done to relieve Whittlesey soon, Houghton or the 153rd Brigade would have to do it.

IV

The Pocket
(6:00 A. M.)

Botelle came back just about dawn, while Whittlesey was making the rounds and before the German trench mortar started its daily concert. The Major found him at the dressing station, where Bragg of the medical detachment was engaged in adjusting to his head a bandage raped from a dead man and binding it into position with a spiral puttee. Half his scalp had been laid open by a slashing bullet, there was blood in his eyes, and it was more or less a mystery how he managed to get back.

—Where's Friel?

—Dead (croaked the messenger). We got into a machine-gun burst. They was all around us. I must of laid there half the night. He done his best, Major.

A little later potato mashers began to drop from the cliff above Holderman's position.

V

Valley of the Aire
(*Dawn to Noon*)

In the morning the engineers began to sift up toward the front at Montrefagne and Hill 272, where they were to build the division in for a strong defense. General

Summerall had no illusions about the German counter-stroke he had smashed the day before; that is, no illusions about its marking a last desperate effort. The position the 1st had won was altogether too important for the Germans to give up without having expended the last ounce of effort and the last drop of blood to recover it.

He was right; just after daybreak, a hurricane of a barrage fell on Hill 272 and the Montrefagne, and behind it the waves of a German assault division, a new and fresh unit, brought into that part of the line for the first time. The 1st's own artillery was well to the front now. They treated the German assembling points beyond Ariétal Farm to a lovely concentration, and when the infantry got through that, the machine gunners of the 1st put on a fine imitation of hell for them. The division had a lot of casualties, mostly from the German barrage, but the Germans themselves had more. About noon they were licked and going back, leaving a star-spangled colonel in the 1st's hands. The gas started coming over immediately.

VI

In the Air, Above the Pocket
(Morning)

Thirteen planes took off from the 50th Aero Squadron field, with objective point still the bottom of the Charlevaux Valley. Among them they carried about a thousand pounds of food, ammunition, medical supplies and pigeons. Fortunately, the Allies had air superiority over that part of the front; there was no German interference to worry about except that from archies and ground machine guns, but these were plenty bad, what with the low ceiling under clouds that had been spitting rain all night, and the necessity of low flying if the place were to be seen at all.

The machines were all two-seater DH's. Brown and Phillips, swinging in near Binarville toward a ravine that looked as though it might be the one they were after, got peppered by a ground machine gun and their engine conked out. They put her into a glide and managed to get down near Binarville before she cracked up, but the wings went all to pieces against some trees and the two lieutenants were lucky to get out with their lives. Bird and Bolt never got over the objective at all; a badly glued prop flew apart, they crashed near Vienne le Château, and both men were injured.

The others made it all right and sowed their bags of joy all along the ravine in the hope that they were hitting the right spot at least part of the time. Not a sign of our men or of any disturbance they might be causing was visible from the air, but this surprised nobody, given the fact that the trees were so thick.

VII

*Headquarters, I Reserve-Korps (German) Briquenay
(Morning to Noon)*

General Wellmann and his Chief of Staff, Major von

Ditfurth, had an uncomfortable and not a very fruitful Sunday morning. At breakfast a report from the latter was laid on the General's table. It spoke feelingly about the preparation-for-retirement order received the day before, the weakness and battle exhaustion of the front-line elements, the difficulty of conducting a retiring operation with them and the fact that the pioneers, who were needed to prepare for retirement, were being used as combat troops against the *Amerikanernest.* The General postponed his meal while he telephoned to Army headquarters and succeeded in wringing from them the promise that two machine-gun battalions which had been serving with the Guard should be sent to him; also an additional pioneer battalion placed at von Ditfurth's disposal to mine the Aisne-Aire bridges.

Toward noon another Job's messenger came from Army. The drive against the American position on von Kleist's Aire Valley front was going badly. The Americans had brought up artillery in overpowering quantities. General Wellmann would withdraw his left wing to the neighborhood of the Grand Pré gap, Kriemhilde Stellung, beginning the movement within thirty-six hours. Confirmation coming by messenger.

The General launched into a protest in the most vigorous terms he could find. It would have the worst possible effect on the morale of the troops, his preparations were not made, he . . . no use.

—At least give me two days more to eliminate the Americans behind my lines. They are practically pris-

199

oners now. We must really wipe out that detachment or the investment in time and lives already expended there becomes a loss. The *Stosstruppen* battalion promised to me should be at hand at any moment; with their help I will guarantee the crushing of this group.

The instrument was silent for a few moments.

—You are granted thirty-six hours to eliminate the *Amerikanernest*. At the end of that time the retreat order will be carried out.

As Wellmann hung up the receiver a front-line report arrived that the French were shelling the whole district around Autry with extreme intensity and had shot down fixed balloon No. 19. The 9th Landwehr Division, which held this part of the line, did not believe this bombardment to be the preliminary of a new attack. Most of the guns engaged were heavy calibers, and the effort appeared to be in the nature of a destruction fire, but it was extremely galling and the 9th wanted counterbattery work by the heavies.

VIII

Charlevaux Valley, the German Lines ### *(10:00 A. M. to Noon)*

When the American planes started coming on the day before, the men of Reserve Infantry Regiment 254 cursed, flattened themselves to the earth and let the machine guns take care of it, having long ago learned that it was no good making a stir or firing rifles. The fliers only got a better target on you for their bombs and machine guns. In the morning there were more airplanes and still more—a perfect pest of insects. The anti-aircraft batteries, which were pretty well back at this point because of the trees up forward, did not seem to be able to do much with them.

"*Kein Zweck.*"

"*Man soll Erharrung haben. Grüss Gott, auch keine Tank.*"

In the early morning one of the daring flyers swept too near the lines on the La Palette headland and a machine gun got a hit, so you could see the splinters fly. The plane wobbled perilously, spiralled and then tilted in among the trees with a rending crash, but the artillery observation post reported that both men escaped from it.

The discovery that these machines were not dropping bombs or propaganda but packages of delicious food, such as no man in the German Army had seen for two years and a half, did not date from any precise moment. It seemed spontaneous; before noon of this day every one of the airplanes was being greeted as an old friend, and there was something like a disorderly rush to spots where the packages landed. Butter! Conserves! Chocolate! Cigarettes!—and a lively system of barter growing up along the line, with five cigarettes worth half a bar of chocolate. Another plane wheeled across the valley, and as a machine gunner drew a bead on its turning point, a veteran shoved him roughly to the ground.

"Don't shoot the delicatessen-flyers!" he cried. "They are doing us more good than the enemy."

The Oberhauptmann, who had kept night watch, was dead beat, so tired that he slept all through the artillery firing that morning. He didn't stick his head out till afternoon, by which time most of the chocolate was gone, and when he found out about it he grumbled a good deal.

"Little things like that," remarked an old *Gefreiter* named Dünne, "the company-troop can handle for itself without orders."

The Oberhauptmann said nothing, and half an hour later orders came down the line for the afternoon attack, in which a couple of flame-throwers which had just come in, were to be used.

Battalion Klemm of the 252nd had been sent over to join in the operation; and the Herr Major had just encouraged the soldiers with a personal message from S. Kgl. Hoheit the Grand Duke of Hesse, expressing the thanks of the people for the good bearing and true fulfillment of duty of the division.

IX

Front Line, 77th Division, U. S. A.
(*12:30* P. M.)

A little after noon a message came down to the front line from the general commanding, to let all the troops know that the Germans had wirelessed Paris asking for a peace on the basis of the fourteen points.

—Oh, yeah?

—How does that help us get seconds on chow?

—What are the fourteen points?

—No, listen you guys, don't you see? The Boche knows he's licked, and . . .

X

The Pocket
(*3:00* P. M. *to Twilight*)

Not a man of all those in the pocket but felt his heart-strings tighten a little when the clock touched three, with the hour's presage of a German attack. The murmur of conversation anxious or interested during the first three days of the siege, had died away to grunts and growls. All tempers were short, every question brought a snarl for an answer; the men seemed to be growing to dislike each other as much as the Germans. During the first day everyone had been horribly, frighteningly hungry; it seemed as though one could not go another ten minutes without eating. But that was at first; now all other sensations had sunk into a vast morass of weakness and bad temper, out of which sympathy lifted its head only when the wounded cried for water.

Worst of all were the airplanes that wheeled overhead without cease—Allied airplanes, American airplanes, with the cockade under their wings showing as the sunlight caught them in a bank. The panels had lain out constantly, but the machines never seemed to pay any attention to these signals, not even when during the artillery shelling McMurtry had Schanz lying on his back in a funk hole, waving a towel toward the skies.

Down from the wings of those friendly, unseeing planes, dripped a rain of packages that glimmered in the light across the hills, slowly settling to rest, always just too far down the hill, too far to one side, where one could see them among the trees, and hear the glad, guttural German shouts as the Boche plundered the packages for which they were starving.

Every time one hit hunger seemed a thousand-fold increased. The men swore under their breaths or, like Private Hollingshead, dozed off and dreamed of a gigantic steak with a mountain of mashed potatoes beside it, looking down on a gravy lake. The dream shifted; the company cook was shaking him;—"Why the hell are you lying there?" he said. "Come over to my kitchen and I'll fill you up till you bust your web-belt." Hollingshead, still in his dream, started to his feet and followed the cook toward a camp kitchen, not one of your little rolling affairs that followed them on the drive, but a real camp kitchen such as he had seen in training, from which an aroma of steak—always steak—floated deliciously. He began to run; there was the crash of a German shell, Hollingshead threw himself to the ground, noting as he did so that the kitchen had been knocked into singing fragments of metal and all that steak—

. . . And woke to find a piece of hot aluminum lying on his shoulder, the chip of a mess kit from the man next to him, just hit by a shell from the trench mortar. The afternoon attack was on.

Trench mortars and then machine guns—zip-zipping through the underbrush, the usual concentration. On the hill, slightly above the headquarters group was the funk hole where young Peabody, the machine-gun lieutenant, sat, twisting his lips to a smile when anyone was looking at him, giving quiet intelligent answers to questions. The pain of his shattered leg was fierce; when no one looked he moaned. They had given him the one overcoat in the outfit for his gallantry, but as he sat draped in it that afternoon under the machine-gun barrage, his tired reflexes did not respond quick enough to the danger signal.

Without a sound he came flopping down the hill right on top of signal-man Larney, through the hole and out again into another depression, his limbs flung grotesquely wide.

Larney looked at Richards and Cepeglia, who were in the hole with him, then edged down on his belly like a crawling lizard, and with the remark that the Lieutenant must have been alive when he fell and dead when he stopped, began to pull off the overcoat.

—Don't do that! It's bad luck to take a dead man's coat.

—I couldn't have any worse luck than I got right now.

—Butts on the coat then.

They wore it in turn.

Up hill on the right, by Holderman's company, Mc-Murtry had wriggled to the front as soon as the machine guns stopped their chatter. Berroum!—Bang! Here come the bombs.

—Take your time (said Captain McMurtry); they don't know where they're throwing those things. They can't hit anybody.

There were sudden shouts and a man came charging down the hill to Whittlesey. "Liquid fire!" he shouted.

"Liquid hell!" retorted the Major. "Get back there where you belong." Everybody could hear him.

A long pennon of sissing, smoky black slashed through the leaves and among the brown trunks, a hundred feet or more, its drops shedding into little fiery pools whenever they touched anything—liquid fire sure enough, the most dreaded, though actually one of the least dangerous German methods of attack. All around on the flank where it had come men were swearing and sobbing, letting off their guns blindly in a kind of wild fury over this final barbarity. Another slash of it and another, half a dozen of them, and arching above it the potato mashers with their violent shock.

McMurtry was there. Sergeant Jim Carroll was there—"Cream Puff" Carroll, they used to call him before they found that beneath the pale exterior he was hard as yesterday's toast—and he aimed straight and true at the big German sergeant who was plowing along behind the flame-throwers, and brought him down without even a cry, shot between the eyes. ("How do you know you hit him?" twenty years after. "By God, I ought to. I found him that night dead; went out to see if there was any bread on his body.")

A bomb got Noon, the other machine-gun officer, and his gun with him, blew them to pieces. In the center a wave of the attack washed right into the outpost line. Whittlesey himself was on the spot, gathering up men from C to plug the gap. Al Summer was getting himself a D.S.C., the little Englishman with the Cockney accent. It happened when Strickland was hit and went down with a yell just as one of the German waves came welling down. Summers slid through the bullet-hail to drag him in, tie up his wound and then through it again in the other direction to get water. It was the wildest, most incidented conflict of the siege. Lower on the hill looking out across the brook Stan Kozikowski was squatted on the ground behind one of the Chauchats with Corporal Hinchman beside him. Suddenly a trickle of blood burst from the latter's lips, his legs flexed and he pitched forward as though in the final movement of a swan dive. Koz caught the flicker of movement in a bush and saw above it the smooth contour of what could only be a coal-scuttle helmet. Brrrt! went the Chauchat; the helmet dropped and the bush was still.

Out on the left a bomb splinter killed Armstrong of C, and a voice shouted, "Come on, they got him. Let's go up there and kill some of those bastards."

Almost simultaneously on the right the grinding Chauchats caught the men with the flame-throwers.

Noise, flames, bombs and attack all stopped together and there was no sound but the moans of the badly wounded.

Report to 76 Reserve Division Headquarters from Reserve Infantry Regiment 254; transmitted to I Reserve Corps headquarters; approved, von Sybel:

In a long attack with the support of hand-grenades and *Flammenwerfer,* we succeeded in winning some ground from the *Amerikanernest.* Two light machine-guns captured and one heavy; nine prisoners taken, all badly wounded. Not expected to survive.

XI

NEWS FLASH

FOE SLOWLY YIELDS TO YANKEES

Pershing's Men Continue
Desperate Advance in Argonne

---

on the Rheims front.

In the forest of Argonne the Germans managed by sneaking through the underbrush in small parties to encircle one American battalion, which found itself attacked front and rear at the same time, but it made a courageous fight and when last heard from had got help and was making a strong bid for freedom.

East of the forest the veteran troops

XII

Headquarters, 50th Aero Squadron, U. S. A.
(5:30 P. M.)

Late in the afternoon Lieutenants Graham and Mc-

Curdy brought their airplane back from one more trip over the pocket. When they had swooped in to drop a basket of pigeons, they had been fired at from the ground. McCurdy had a wound in the neck, and it was God's grace that the plane had come through.

"Several Huns came out of a dugout exactly where our men are supposed to be," they said.

Telephone message from Birdie 7 to Dreadnaught 7:

Lieutenant McCurdy returned shot in the neck and was unable to drop his pigeons at five o'clock. He reports the Germans were mopping up the ravine. One machine is now missing.

Dreadnaught 7 to Birdie 7:

What time did that man go up who is still missing?

Birdie 7 to Dreadnaught 7:

About four. Have not heard anything from him at all.

At division H.Q. it was agreed that this looked as though the battalion had been wiped out and the Germans were mopping up.

XIII

The Pocket—Conference
(Twilight)

Dark was shutting in early on another evening that promised rain. In the silence that followed the attack a man crawled over from the dressing station to Whittlesey and handed him a note. It was from the one machine-gun officer left alive, Revnes, the dark, handsome actor who, though crippled by his wound, had slung his pistol and gone hobbling up the hill to be in on the repulse of every German attack.

He was suffering much pain; listening to groans all about him. Surrender was not to be thought of, but the enemy might be persuaded to permit evacuation of the wounded.

Whittlesey went over to the wounded man, squatted down, and spoke with him at some length. When he left Revnes was more cheerful, but the Major who walked back to the headquarters funk seemed to have taken upon himself something of the Lieutenant's depression. There followed a long conversation with McMurtry, conducted in low tones and out of earshot of the men in the key of—What to do next?

The thing that bothered both officers was the weakness that seemed to be sucking the command in like a quagmire. Weakness in numbers, first; it was doubtful whether there were as many as two hundred effective fighters left. After the loss of the machine gun and the death of Noon, it had been necessary to contract the position. Further losses and further contractions would have the special objection that they would lay the position open to being attacked in every part at once.

Weakness in the physical efficiency of the men, second; how many more afternoon attacks could they beat off?—

for the one today had been the most difficult to beat back thus far. At a given, unpredictable point, if the force of these German thrusts kept mounting, they could cross the curve of the unit's resistance power. The command would then simply be crushed.

Worst of all was the mounting spiritual weakness engendered by the combination of the others. Another mark was the temporary break when the flame-throwers came. It was not a bad break and it had been quickly repaired, but the flame-throwers themselves had hurt nobody. (Late that night Corporal Altiera was to find two burned bodies, far out, but they did not know this then.) The really dangerous thing was the whispering going on on the heels of that flame-thrower attack. If the mounting feebleness these whispers represented had reached up into the officer ranks the mental state of the command was bad.

Nor was this all; for at this moment, when officers of ability were more than ever necessary, the battalion was losing officers faster than either Whittlesey or McMurtry cared to think about. Both felt as though they lacked an arm since the passing of Peabody. Even wounded, he had still been one of the most useful men in the pocket. Holderman was standing up nobly, but with his gangrening wounds, could not stand up much longer; now Noon was gone, and Rogers, who took the German prisoners coming over the hill, had also been killed.

On the other hand the persistent effort of the airplanes during the day showed that the division . . .

—Aeroplanes are under Corps (interrupted McMurtry).

Well, Corps then, is perfectly aware of our plight and probably of our exact position, since our panels have been out continually.

—Let us reason this out. If our friends have located us and we have not been relieved, it must then be because they are having trouble getting through. But the experience we had coming in shows that the German lines across Hill 198 and through these ragged valleys are not absolutely continuous. Indeed, they cannot be. If a chink can be found, if a messanger can get through going out, elements can also filter in.

McMurtry thought he could arrange for some more men to try that desperate adventure and slipped away to do so.

XIV

First Army Headquarters, U. S. A.

The situation is now that the 77th Division has been unable to effect any substantial alteration in its position or to make any progress in the effort to relieve the mixed battalion behind the German lines under command of Major Whittlesey. Nor, after four days of fruitless effort to this end, is it likely that General Alexander will accomplish this task unaided.

On the right the 1st Division has broken through, dug

in, resisted all counterattacks and played hob with at least two of the five German Guards divisions. They hold and will. Between them and the 77th is the 28th, now facing almost due west; its left held up before the steep fortified butte of the Chêne Tondu, the pollard oak, its right reaching up to join the 1st in the outskirts of Fléville. It lies squarely astride the Haupt-Widerstands-Linie, the main German defense line. Its right is definitely in the rear of that line. But the 28th is badly used up by having been in heavy continuous attacks, and the division needs rest before attempting so strong an enterprise as storming the fortified woods and summits of the Argonne.

On the roads, now marching up, is the 82nd, a stout, battle-worthy division, with some experience. It will be used to relieve Whittlesey's command; but there are two possibilities as to the manner of its use. One is to put it in on the extreme left, at La Palette and up to the Charlevaux Valley in direct relief. The other is to put it in right-center at Fléville, at the joint of 28th and 1st, a right-hook, cutting across the German communications all through the Argonne, prying their line westward and relieving Whittlesey by indirect action.

Decision—for the second plan. 'Twill serve Whittlesey as well and the general battle better, for we may throw the Germans into some disorder and round up a lot of prisoners, besides some artillery; perhaps clear the whole Argonne. Attack at dawn; let the artillery of the 28th support the thrust, with some of the 1st's guns and such of the 82nd's as arrive in time to reach position.

Whose decision? General Pershing's, unquestionably. Whose plan? There are various claims, but the best evidence is that it leaped from the brain of Colonel Malin Craig, Chief of Staff of the 1st Corps.

XV

The Pocket, Right Wing
(Night)

Captain George G. McMurtry possessed the rare characteristic of looking for the best in any character or incident that fell under his notice. Informed that one of his men had (let us say) stolen a thousand dollars, his reaction would infallibly be, "Oh, I don't believe that! He's quite incapable of such a thing." If irrefragable proof were furnished he would hesitate a moment—then, "Well, if you're sure, he probably did. But there must have been some strong reason for it that we don't know anything about. You notice that he didn't steal two thousand, which he might easily have done."

It was not so much the existence of mistakes or evil that he denied as the existence of evil impulse. His attitude was that men are fundamentally honest, generous and brave. He was charitable to every error of conduct because in no action could he perceive anything more than an incorrect application of genuine and highly creditable principles.

The Lost Battalion's second-in-command; Major George G. McMurtry.

Not that he excused divergence where the line of duty was clearly and precisely delineated, or that he failed to point out with energy that only muddy thinking could keep this line from being obvious, but rather that he had not a trace of that assumption of moral superiority which so often accompanies physical authority.

Such an attitude is, in the long run, impossible to conceal, particularly in the army, where the question of how a man conducts the details of his daily life comes under the review of his officers. McMurtry's non-punitory but unsentimental approach to the problems of social contact had long ago made him a kind of lay confessor to the men in his company—"Captain, I'm having a little trouble with my wife. You see—" or "Captain, thees letter, I can't read him so good."

In return for these services and this appreciation the enlisted men accorded McMurtry a degree of confidence not usually given to officers in the draft army, where the relations between commander and commanded were always new and were often felt as temporary. If the Captain said something to you it was okay; he knew his stuff and he wouldn't have you go breakin' your back for no gold bricks.

Therefore, when the Captain crawled out to the right of the position in the darkness which was already becoming intense to see whether he could get a messenger to try the lines, both his approach and the response it evoked were predictable.

—Come here, you men.

215

Pause, punctuated by rustlings in the dark.

—Somebody has got to get out of here, back to the division. I think the best way is along that creek and out there to the right. It's a dangerous job. Will anybody volunteer for it?

There was a momentary hesitation and a cough. "I'll go," said Jeremiah Healey, the New York perfumer. Bob Yoder nudged his buddy, Newcom, who answered for both. "So will we." "Me too," said Bill Begley. "I go,"—that was Lipasti the wop, "And me," which was Johnson. Eight all together. They got their instructions in a low tone and started away into the night in a crouching walk. It was raining.

For the first few steps the way was clear enough and they had to keep pretty much together, though the word was to spread as much as possible. Suddenly a flare soared through the falling drops. All eight dropped, but the two New York boys, Begley and Lipasti, not quick enough, for right in the glare of the Very came a burst of machine-gun fire and they pitched down, dead before they hit the ground.

Now the rest spread indeed, working along close to the ground, no use taking chances like that again. Newcom, sliding rightward and down, felt his hand touch something wet.

—The creek (he whispered, with his lips close to his comrade's ear).

In return he received a smack in the stomach from Yoder's elbow, with such force as almost to knock him out. His mouth was all opened for a snarl of protest when, right beside his ear, he heard the unmistakable click, the action of a machine-gun before it starts firing. In a split second he was grovelling; in another the frightful thing was hurling a torrent of steel-jacketed bullets into the brush right over his head, so close that one of the sparks from the discharge burned the back of his neck. Newcom never knew how the Boches missed seeing him and depressing the weapon, but miss they did. After about fifty shots it cut off, and by reaching out his hand, he could feel that Bob was still alive.

For a long while they lay motionless as ice; then, with one muscle stirring at a time, gradually transferred themselves an inch, another inch, a foot, a yard, to the right till they hit a fresh shell hole with mud in the bottom and crawled in, peering through the dark to discover the whereabouts of the machine guns and get between them.

Futile effort; not an object, not even the outline of the hill visible in that wet dark. The bushes crackled with movement near them, then someone stumbled, it seemed right over their heads, a voice said, "*Achtung! Granatenloch!*" in a stage whisper, and the sounds of movement went past them, down the bank of the stream, away from the two shivering.

Yoder nudged Newcom again; the same thought had flashed wordless through the minds of both. If they followed that German patrol, they would be led somewhere. They did not dare follow close; and after a moment both voices and path were lost ahead. Newcom, going first, tripped suddenly and pitched into another shell hole—squarely onto Johnson and Healey, who were already in possession.

—Where are we?

—The position is right behind us (said Healey). Johnson found it.

—Did anybody get through?

—I don't think so.

OCTOBER 7

I

The Pocket
(*About* 8:00 A. M.)

WITH the day the buzz of airplanes overhead began
again; not so many as on the day before, but still per-
sistently dropping food, which always fell just beyond
reach. In the pocket men raised haggard faces and looked
hungrily at each other, or exchanged scraps of dirty
paper with a few words written on them—the literary
activity of the siege.

—Listen, Jack, this is a letter to my mother. Here's
her address, see? 26 West 38th Street. If you get outa
this and I don't, see that she gets it from me, will you?

There was a shortage of writing materials, particularly
of paper. A few men wrote these final messages on
scraps of bandage or pieces of shirttail rudely whacked
off with pocket knives, with blood for ink, not in a gesture of melodrama, but out of necessity.

Whittlesey found them at it everywhere as he made
his morning inspection trip. It disturbed him, one more
sign of crumbling morale, which breaks long before
bodies in such a situation. Bodies were weak enough,

too—almost impossible to find anyone to bury the fresh dead this morning. One could only cover them with leaves and hope that the siege would not go on to the point where the last of efforts, that of pulling a trigger, became also too much labor.

Captain Cullen on the left was uneasy.

—Nine of my men went over the hill (he stage-whispered to the Major as the latter slithered along through the position). This morning at daybreak. They were looking for some of that food the airplanes dropped. I just found out about it. One of them was that New York Chinaman. Chinn was his name.

The command was beginning to break up.

II

Headquarters, 77th Division, U. S. A.
(7:00 to 10:00 A. M.)

The night arrangement had been for an artillery concentration along Hill 198 to cut the German wire and make a gap through which Johnson could try one more relieving attack by filtration in the morning, with those two flank battalions reorganized and put in with care. The French had promised ample help. Their means were no better than before, troops none too plentiful and weary with four years of war, country without cover between them and the German lines, which ran through strong positions—the French means were weak, but the French spirit had been stirred by the tale of the six hundred against an army; Gallic emotion was up to a point that transcended means, and they would attack. At a quarter to eight this message from the front:

Delaware to Dreadnaught (*runner*):

At this hour French have not moved forward but my troops have reached position from which assault on the trenches could be made. I cannot see or locate the French. At this hour I have therefore ordered my troops to assault without them. We are meeting machine-gun and rifle fire. I shall be beyond communication for a while but will return later.

JOHNSON

At eight another:

Delaware to Dreadnaught (*runner*):

I have just received this message from the French: *Laissez-moi savoir où est votre gauche, parce que je veux faire feu de l'artillerie de 75 et de 37. Le gros de l'aile gauche s'arrête sous la mitraille, et il nous faut faire feu à la tranchée par la droite. A cause de ceci il me faut savoir votre position exacte.*
I have told the French they must not fire until we hear from you.

JOHNSON

What did the French mean? Some error due to haste, surely, in saying their left was held up; the left of that French Army was way over beyond Autry, and one could find out about it in the communiqué next morning. "He surely means his right," Alexander wrote across the message by way of annotation, the thought flitting through his head that perhaps it had been French artillery fire that Whittlesey had complained about by that last pigeon message, the "For heaven's sake stop it!" one. Still it would be a poor idea to have the Gauls shooting off their guns down the Charlevaux Valley even now. Almost certain they would manage to pink some of poor Whittlesey's men. The General sent for Captain Klotz and dispatched him to the French with an urgent message not to do any artillery shooting in the direction of the valley.

A moment or two later Johnson was reporting again:

Delaware to Dreadnaught:

Am attacking. Arty fire apparently has had no effect. Wire not cut. Machineguns and high explosive shells being used against command. French on our left not attacking.

JOHNSON

III

The Pocket
(*8:00* A. M.)

Whittlesey found Holderman slouched down in the funk, smoking an amateur cigarette made of yellow issue-message paper and dried leaves, which had been given him by one of the privates.

—Are there any men in your company who would

volunteer to take a message through by daylight? George and I think it will offer a better chance than in the dark, when they can't see where they're going.

The Captain considered, puff—puff.

—If anybody can do it Krotoshinsky can. Abe!

A little, stoop-shouldered Polish Jew slithered over to them, his uniform more than usually untidy. Pale, a long, hooked nose, not very erect posture. The Major glanced at Holderman, who nodded encouragingly, and then began to give the man the usual instructions. As he was speaking two more men came up and joined Krotoshinsky, evidently additional runners somebody had picked up.

It was full daylight by this time, but pretty quiet. The three men slipped away among the bushes downhill toward the water hole, taking that direction as the best route. The machine gun bracketed on the hole began to chatter and the Major saw the bushes near it stir in different directions as the three spread.

—I hope they make it (Holderman said without conviction).

IV

Valley of the Aire
(*Night to Noon*)

The town of Cornay lies in a fold of hills across the Aire from Fléville, which had by this time been tagged Fleaville in the A.E.F. South of Cornay another fold holds Châtel Chéhéry, while between the two, Hill 180 throws out a projecting buttress to turn the stream aside for a brief space. Around Châtel Chéhéry the fold splits into two peaks, each taller and each sharper in outline than Hill 180—Hills 223 and 244. South of them again are Apremont and the Chêne Tondu.

Here was the spot of the 82nd's attack, which many officers in the 82nd itself thought mad; which had been protested by a French officer who arrived at I Corps headquarters at midnight to deliver the official remonstrance of his country's military men. There were the hills, fortified; the stream, unfordable; the German artillery—

While they were listening Colonel Malin Craig was at the front with Stonewall Jackson's march at Chancellorsville floating through his head—was this not such another occasion? He thought likely, but as the key of Jackson's move was knowledge of the country so was this, and he was making personal reconnaissance. The main question was the river and its western bank; he waded the stream himself in the night, to and fro; marked that the west side was higher than its mate, but not impracticable and the stream not too deep.

There had been trouble about getting the 82nd's artillery up the jammed roads and by no means all of it was in position in time for the morning attack, but Summerall swung the 1st's splendidly-served guns through ninety degrees and in the morning that cannon-fire fell like an avalanche on the Germans.

They were men of good heart and their position was strong because essential—the high-ground heavy artillery emplacement for a long stretch of front—and their machine guns cost the American division a good deal. But by noon they lost Hill 180; the 28th joined the attack and early in the afternoon the two divisions were working up the slopes of 223 and 244 in a double salient to pinch out Châtel Chéhéry. The communications of all the German forces in Chêne Tondu and farther south and west were in deadly danger.

V

German Dugout Near the Pocket
(10:00 A. M.)

"Noch einander," said the voice. One of the men beside Private Lowell R. Hollingshead dropped his gun and putting one arm around the American's shoulders, helped propel him toward the cavernous mouth of the dugout, with a gentleness that surprised the prisoner as much as that of the bearded doctor who had dressed his wounded knee.

The steps were hard to negotiate even with help and the leg hurt like billy-hell. The passage turned sharply at the bottom and ended in a vast dugout, the largest Hollingshead had ever seen, with bunk space for as much as a company. A primus stove at one end under a ventilating duct made the place comfortably warm. Beside it and behind a table littered with papers sat a blond young man of about thirty-five with his cap off and decorations on his collar which Hollingshead took to indicate he was an officer, especially as when he snapped something out one of the other Germans saluted.

The officer fixed him with a friendly gaze. "Well, how do you do?" he said, in perfect American English. "Did they give you something to eat? Did they fix you up? Sit down."

He indicated a box on which Hollingshead seated himself, stretching out his leg to ease the pain from the knee. "They gave me a bowl of cabbage soup," he answered, "and the doctor dressed my leg."

"Too bad you got hurt. Too bad we have to fight this war, anyway. Have a cigarette. I was in Seattle. Are you a Westerner, too? Some of your men are, aren't they?"

The prisoner accepted the cigarette and the light that accompanied it. A feeling of comfort began to invade his members in spite of the wounded knee. Information of this kind surely could not be dangerous.

—No, it's mostly (he began and then stopped). I cannot answer any questions.

The man behind the table laughed.

—Oh, never mind that stuff (he said gaily). We know all about you already. We have captured several of you chaps before. You are the second battalion, 308th Infantry, with an attached company from the 307th. No secrets. We know everything; we know even that a

French airplane has carried the Honor-Legion cross to your commander. I'm Lieutenant Fritz Prinz. What's your name?

—Hollingshead, sir. Lowell R. Hollingshead.

—Good. We admire you people very much. You are brave soldiers, you know. How did you happen to get there? We have not taken any of you fellows except those that were wounded.

Hollingshead swallowed.

—It was the sergeant, sir. He told us we had to get through and bring up the relief. There were eight of us.

—Yes. We captured four of you. Your friends are back there, wounded. One of them was an Oriental, no? Now look here; we have treated you well, haven't we? I want you to do something for me. I want you to take a message back to your major.

Hollingshead gaped and then looked puzzled.

—I don't see how I could do that, sir.

—Well, look at it this way. You people have done well. I give you credit for being good soldiers. But now you've made your showing there and there isn't any use of the rest of them holding out in that place until they're all dead. They have their reputations. All I want you to do is take them a message stating the case and giving them a chance to surrender in time to save their lives. As a matter of fact we have another battalion of *Stosstruppen* coming this afternoon and we are going to make a flame-thrower attack, with enough flame-throwers to burn the whole side of the hill off. You'll just be saving the lives of your comrades if you take this message in, and they give people medals for saving lives. What do you say?

Hollingshead fished vainly into the pool of his small experience of life and war (he was eighteen and a replacement from an ammunition train) for something that would help him steer his way through the turbulent ocean of thoughts the German had set in motion. It was a proposal from the enemy; therefore there should be something wrong about it. But he was unable to detect the flaw. He fully realized that as a prisoner of war his rights included those of safe transport to an internment camp, with food and medical care for the balance of the conflict. Surely it would be taking the braver part to carry in the message and then take his chances with the rest of the battalion. As for the battalion surrendering, that was a matter not for his decision, but that of the Major. On the other hand—

—I'd like to think it over a little, sir.

—Rest up a bit? I don't blame you with a wound like that. Take your time. I'll ask you about it again after you have a chance to lie down. Adolf! *Zum Bett mit dem Gefangener!*

VI

Headquarters, 77th Division, U. S. A.
(About Noon)

Toward noon, the 305th, on the extreme right flank

of the 77th Division, found the German resistance weakening at the point where it was in liaison with the troops of the 28th Division. It began to gain, though its left was still held so that the gain was the motion of a swinging door of which the regiment's left wing was the hinge. The news was passed along; an excited officer of the 306th also reported that that regiment also had pushed ahead a quarter to half a mile, which would take it through most of the defense system opposite.

In view of the general situation and of the army conferences where they had been talking about prying the Germans out of the Argonne from that direction, General Alexander found both reports sufficiently easy to credit. He had them 'phoned up to Colonel Houghton with an interrogatory note as to why he was not advancing in conformity with the regiments on his right.

Houghton's move to infiltrate up to and through the German wire, concentrating for attack close in, was going forward smoothly, but it was still far from complete. An assault now, with his formations so spread, would sacrifice surprise and ruin everything. On the other hand he was convinced that if he could deliver the attack the way he had planned it, toward evening, it would break through. He could then go rushing down the Roman road behind the German lines, reach La Palette from the rear, break off a long section of the German lines and make a heavy bag of prisoners.

—Give me back my 3rd Battalion (he asked) and I will ruin this whole German line.

Nothing doing, was the reply. That battalion was needed leftward with General Johnson.

—Well, then let the 306th slide three or four hundred yards leftward (he pleaded) to take over my front. I with what I have will work farther left and bottle those Germans on Hill 198 and in La Palette just as they have bottled Whittlesey.

"Your job is to get Whittlesey out," replied Alexander. "We simply can't spare the men for any other operation—" and went on to repeat his indignant question as to why Houghton had not advanced in tune with the 306th.

—The 306th isn't up that far. They can't be (protested Houghton).

—The brigadier of the 153rd brigade has confirmed their location (retorted the General).

"Then for Christ's sake tell them to stop machine gunning and bombing my men. All the fire we're getting is coming from that direction."

VII

The Pocket
(*10:30 A. M.*)

The two who had started with Krotoshinsky were back, one with a smashed shoulder and face white with pain. A C Company man offered him a bit of candle as refreshment.

—Good for the Eskimos, why not us?

—Couldn't get through. Too many machine guns.

—Where's the other fellow?

—You mean Abe? We lost track of him. Killed, I guess.

Whittlesey turned to young Schenck.

—Can you get a couple of men from your company to take a message through?

—I'll try, sir.

He passed along the line, asking for volunteers. A short, snub-nosed man raised a hand—Stanislaw Kozikowski, the Polish immigrant, and one of the best autorifle men in the company.

"Well, I'll take a chance," said he. "I'll go."

"Good for you. Get another man."

Koz slipped along the line as Schenck had done, asking. Most of the men met him with averted faces and half-excuses, except two of the wounded, but this was no job for a man with a hurt. He was beginning to get discouraged when Cliff Brown called him back, a light-haired man, very religious. He did not admit it in open words, but had been arguing the matter out in the light of his spiritual experience—yes, God would guide him through in safety, the inner voice said, if his trust in his Maker were only complete.

Koz shook hands with him; Schenck took the two aside and told them how serious a matter getting through would be and how many precautions necessary, but they knew that already.

—Drop every kind of equipment (the Lieutenant told them) except your pistols. Even those tin hats you'll have to leave behind. If they hit a stone or a bush they'll make a noise and you'll get it. The idea is to sneak through; don't shoot unless it's a matter of life or death.

He gave them his pocket compass and indicated a route—up the stream; across it higher up, and then following the south side of the valley to 307's lines. Whittlesey wanted to see them before they left.

"Boys," said the Major, "you know our condition as well as I do. Tell them we have not surrendered and they are to reach us as soon as possible."

"Yes," said another officer, "and tell them not to stop dropping us food from airplanes if you get back."

Brown: "We expect to get back. We are trusting the Lord to show us the way."

"You'll make it all right."

VIII

Headquarters, I Reserve-Korps (German) Briquenay
(Noon to 3:00 P. M.)

The noon front-line reports from the 76th Reserve Division had been decidedly encouraging both to Wellmann and von Ditfurth. The French had begun the day by launching an attack between Autry and Binarville, a move of stormy valor, but not very intelligently arranged, the type of whirlwind rush not seen since 1915.

For this the Germans were well prepared. The 76th's artillery had bracketed on the French at the first fire, the attack broke up in bloody loss, and there were twenty-seven prisoners, including an officer who said that the 4th, 9th and 11th Cuirassiers had taken part and that all three regiments were badly broken. The 76th Reserve begged to report that Unteroffizier Jahn and Musketier Kronig of the 252nd Reserve Regiment had especially distinguished themselves in the counterattack which had been carried out along the line of the Binarville-Autry road.

This attack had gained some ground; if there were any troops to back it up a hole might be developed into the French defense system. Wellmann ordered the advance to pull its horns in again. He could not risk salients with the weakness developing farther east.

The battalion of *Stosstruppen* ordered for the assault on the *Amerikanernest* had also reported at 76th Reserve Division headquarters—and satisfied that all was well, Wellmann went off on an inspection trip.

It was after lunch before he returned to Briquenay. The first thing he found was an urgent message from the 76th Reserve and his caller proved to be von Sybel, practically in tears. The storm troops had reported, but instead of a battalion there were only sixteen men. Did the Herr General-Major really expect him to wipe out the Americans with this squad? Or what was he to do? —Anything you can! (shouted Wellmann angrily).

Still boiling with fury over what he felt as a scurvy trick of the higher command, he called Army headquarters for a slanging match.

He did not get much satisfaction. In fact there was another disappointment waiting for him. The Americans had taken the heights east of the Aire; the Army Group Argonnen's whole wing was broken and being held under overwhelming artillery fire. Von Kleist would have to retreat immediately or lose his heavy guns and his line of communication. The Giselher Stellung was lost; and Wellmann's own corps must conform to the withdrawal or be prepared to care for its own left wing.

Angry but impotent Wellmann told von Ditfurth to send out the withdrawal orders, movement to begin by the left. The withdrawal should not start till after dark, in view of the pressure against that portion of the line. If the *Amerikanernest* had not by that time been wiped out, they would have to let the matter drop.

IX

In the Air, Above the Pocket (*Noon*)

The morning had been thick; not quite so thick as the

day before, but bad enough. The 50th Aero Squadron did not feel any too cheerful about going out again looking for Whittlesey after losing two machines the day before, but what the hell, this is war. Therefore Lieutenant Anderson took off, with Rogers, the Texas law school student, as observer.

La Palette was easy to locate; they spiralled down and raced along the valley, lower even than the tops of the surrounding hills, while a storm of red-hot lead from the machine guns blazed at them. The DH took it well, though the bullets tore new holes through her already patched wings and tail and her wireless generator was knocked out. Rogers spied like Tiphys from the side and saw a panel, two black squares in the side of a white triangle, an American battalion signal, sure enough. They flew back over it higher up, to check, Rogers using his glasses. Yes, there was no mistake about it; American battalion panel, and it was not hard either to make out the co-ordinates from the air—294.9-276.3. Found at last!

The plane climbed, Anderson holding her on a level while Rogers scribbled out a hurried message to be dropped at division headquarters, telling of the find and its place.

It was really too bad that this should have been one of the fake panels put out by the Germans at Lieutenant Prinz' suggestion, in order that they might take up collections of good American food, with the possibility that they might reap a harvest of interesting orders as well.

X

The Pocket
(*11:00* A. M.)

It was just about the time when one of the wounded men was begging Baldwin to shoot him and end it all that Lieutenant Schenck started back to his position after having gotten the runners away. There was a big rock in the path he chose, and as he moved around it a trench-mortar shell dropped. The splinter took him right in the face and he never wiggled again.

After the war his father, who lived in Brooklyn, was much interested in talking to any of the boys who had known or served under his son. Most of them went around to see him at one time or another, but none could do anything toward bringing young Gordon back to life.

XI

Hill Beyond the Pocket
(*Afternoon—Time Uncertain*)

When the two were not so close together as to be side by side Brown took the lead, as he had the compass. Minor obstacles tended to separate the pair, and there was always a wait when they came to one, for each feared the separation would become permanent. Brown, for example, would get a pace or two ahead; Koz would hear some small noise inaudible to his companion, and flatten out, wondering whether Cliff had gone on without him. They slanted up the valley to keep away from the water hole, which the Germans seemed to be watching with such care, and it was while they were on this circuit that they heard a crashing from the direction of the pocket.

They happened to be together at the moment. Both whipped out their gats and ducked behind a bush, but they put the weapons away when they saw it was only a couple of boys from C Company, eyes hysterically bright and voices tense as violin strings with emotion. They said they had heard Brown and Koz were going back and they had decided to go with them. Koz glanced at Brown, who gave an imperceptible nod of comprehension.

—Four men will make too big a target (said he). The Boches will spot us. Why don't you two go on ahead?

"No, we'd rather follow."

The Pole's forehead wrinkled, but Brown spoke with juridical calm.

—Have either of you got a watch?

—Best goddam watch in the outfit (said one) and I keep it wound, too. Here.

—All right, I'll tell you. You lay over here and give us half an hour's start. You can follow us easy. Then if we get hit or anything you can branch off another way.

The runaways evidently did not like this but were too

much nerve-racked to find a counter proposal, so they had to squat while Brown and Koz slipped away from them. The messengers had hardly gotten a hundred yards farther, however, before their pursuers came tearing through the brush after them like a herd of elephants. How the Germans missed them is the world's wonder.

—Jesus! (said Koz with feeling).

Brown found himself both shocked and upset. When the pair caught up he bawled them out hard, warning that their ridiculous insistence on company might mean death for all four. They wagged their heads in agreement, but failed to meet the messengers' eyes. It was obvious that a panic beyond rational argument had them in its grip, and when, after another start, Koz and Brown heard them thundering through the brush again, they snapped down behind some bushes. The two runaways went ploughing right past down the path like madmen. Neither of the messengers ever saw them again or ever learned who they were.

It was farther on and Brown had half-risen to spy the way when Koz said, "Look," and handed him something from the ground. It was a pigeon, limp, with glazed eyes and body badly crushed by the heavy service rifle bullet that had killed it. The same idea went through both men's minds, but Koz sniffed, then pinched his nostrils in an expressive gesture. When they turned the bird over, they noticed that the message was attached to its neck instead of to the leg, as with American pigeons. Sure enough, the writing was in German.

Brown stuck it in his pocket with the remark that somebody might like to have it, and they set out again.

XII

German Dugout, Near the Pocket
(2:30 to 3:00 P. M.)

Hollingshead stuck his head out of the bunk and then swung a leg over. The other leg, in which he had not noticed the wound till the big Boche with the Lüger had pointed it out, hurt like hell now, and he staggered when he came down on the floor. He felt sick, but managed a salute.

—Well, my friend (Lieutenant Prinz greeted him) have you decided to carry the message for your companions?

—Yes, sir. (It was the braver thing to do; there was no fun in being a prisoner of war. He had seen them working on the roads and would take his chances with the gang.)

—That's famous! Now you just sit down here, and I'll typewrite a message for you to carry.

He wrote it on a rickety machine, looking up when he had finished to ask Hollingshead his name again, which was inserted somewhere in the letter with a pen; cocked his head on one side, and seeming satisfied with the artistic effect of the production, handed it to the American.

He gave Hollingshead a stick to which was attached

a square of cloth bearing a stenciled design in the German poster style of a doctor applying a tourniquet to the leg of a wounded man "just like me" (thought Hollingshead).

—Here is a white flag that will get you through the lines.

Prinz stood up and looked around the room.

—You'll need a cane, with that leg of yours. How would you like some cigarettes?

The Lieutenant pulled a package from his pocket, shelled out half a dozen onto the table, then reached over and stuffed them into the American's breast pocket.

—There you are. All fixed up. So long and good luck. Adolf!

It was tough work getting up the stairs, but the soldier Adolf helped him. At the top, like the man who had captured him, Adolf made motions indicating that he wished to buy Hollingshead's safety razor, enforcing the idea of the barter by producing a handful of paper marks, but the American affected not to understand. He was thinking hard about what he was doing and whether the sentry would try to shoot at him.

Nothing of the kind happened. Adolf dropped away behind, Hollingshead struggled a hundred yards farther on and heard a voice from nowhere telling him to halt. He held out the white flag. "Message for the Major."

A head emerged. "Let's see it."

—It's for the Major.

—Wait here (said the sentry).

He slithered away through the trees to return with a lieutenant, who also wanted the message. Hollingshead refused to give it up, so the officer took him off to the headquarters funk hole where Whittlesey and McMurtry were sitting together, apparently not doing anything in particular.

The ex-prisoner shifted the cane to his other hand and saluted.

"Sir, I am Private Hollingshead of H Company. I have been captured and I was sent in by the Germans with this letter for the commanding officer."

XIII

Hill Slope 198, South of the Pocket
(Afternoon—Time Uncertain)

Both men were soaking wet by the time they had crossed the stream and were working up the opposite hill, but they had been wet so many times since it started that it didn't much matter now. There were Germans all around; Koz pulled Brown flat behind a brush pile just as a heavy voice spoke up within six feet of them, followed by the clank of a canteen and the gurgling of water. There were five Boches in the party, each carrying a string of the canteens, which they presently took back uphill while the Americans dodged across their track to the protection of another brush heap.

They held a whispered conference there and agreed

that it would be better to work along the slope for some distance away from the pocket before attempting to cross the brow of the hill. When they attempted to put the project into execution, however, they unexpectedly came on a rude artillery road hewn through the wilderness.

That was cause for another conference, resulting in an arrangement to split and attempt the crossing some distance apart. Then, if one didn't make it, the other could try a different place or turn back. Koz said he'd make a lead, but just as he was about to duck across the road two Germans came down it. At the second try he got across; Brown followed, they turned right and went up the slope, working along slowly about ten yards apart, one moving while the other kept watch.

Brown was on one of his turns of moving; had taken a couple of steps and come to a stand behind a tall bush with many brown leaves when he found himself staring almost into the eyes of a well-built German soldier, who had apparently materialized out of the ground. The man had a rifle in his hand, held at the ready. His face looked attentive and suspicious; evidently he had heard some movement, but not yet seen them, since his eyes were not focussed but searching. Brown held his breath and wondered about Koz, but there was neither sound nor motion behind him, and after a moment or two of attention the Heinie turned round and disappeared into the earth with the jerky movement that indicated a flight of steps. Brown lowered himself to the ground and lay almost without breathing. Behind another bush Koz was doing the same, not having seen the German, but copying his comrade's action.

As both men waited, gathering nerve for another step there came the heavy crash of a considerable group through the underbrush, then German words of command. The messengers made out a whole file of men going past, at least half a company, with machine-gun parts on their shoulders. Brown swiveled on his chest to follow their progress; there were more commands and the half-company spread out along the slope just below, and between the two messengers and the artillery road, forming in little knots left and right, each knot around a machine gun which was being assembled for action while some of the others dug.

It was a good two hours before either Brown or Koz dared crawl on. Meanwhile it grew dark, then began to rain. A machine gun, American to judge from its sound, started up somewhere, firing a long-range barrage that cut through leaf and branch just above the level of the prone figures of the messengers. If they had been any fatter the bullets would have cut their butts off.

XIV

The Pocket
(*3:45* P. M.)

As a matter of fact Whittlesey was becoming dubious about the ability of the battalion to hold out and had sat down with McMurtry to discuss the question, not of what to do, but of how to do the obvious thing, which was to beat off the afternoon attack that would surely come within a short time. The loss of young Schenck cut both men deep. He had been a tower of strength; and his fall underlined the growing deficiency of the command in officers with the capacity to lead and to hold the rest up to the mark, just as the mounting weakness made such personalities more than ever important.

It was therefore necessary to rearrange the commands to some extent. Several of the noncoms and a few privates had (fortunately) revealed some ability in leadership—particularly Corporal Klein of A Company, Private Pollinger of G, Sergeants Roesch, Johnson and Mynard of the machine guns, Carroll of Holderman's command, the first two carrying on in spite of wounds.

The question was how to distribute these better spirits so they could fill the gap left by vanished officers. The discussion had just chimed with agreement that Mynard was the man to take charge of the machine guns on the left when Hollingshead appeared with his cane and his letter.

He offered the missive to McMurtry, who turned it over and over in his fingers as he asked sharply;

"Why did you leave H Company?"

"I crawled out with some other men of the company this morning to get a basket dropped by an aeroplane yesterday and we were captured by the Germans."

McMurtry's mild face flushed quick and hot; he opened his mouth, but before the hurricane burst round the private's head Whittlesey remarked, "George, let's look at the letter," accepted it and tore it open. He read:

Sir:
    The Bearer of the present, Lowell R. Hollingshead, has been taken prisoner on October — . He refused to the German Intelligence Officer every answer to his questiones and is quite an honourable fellow, doing honour to his fatherland in the strictest sense of the word.

He has been charged against his will, believing in doing wrong to his country, in carrying forward this present letter to the Officer in charge of the 2nd Batl. J. R. 308 of the 77th Div. with the purpose to recommend this Commander to surrender with his forces as it would be quite useless to resist any more in wiew of the present conditions.

The suffering of your wounded man can be heared over here in the German lines and we are appealing to your human sentiments.

A withe Flag shown by one of your man will tell us that you agree with these conditions.

Please treat the Lowell R. Hollingshead as an honourable man. He is quite a soldier we envy you.

THE GERMAN COMMANDING OFFICER

The Major glanced from letter to messenger. Then passed the note back to McMurtry, who read it through, then handed it to Holderman, who had just joined them. The three officers looked at each other, and as though by a common impulse all grinned—that appeal to "human sentiments" from the man who had been directing flame-thrower attacks against them.

McMurtry pulled himself upright. "We've got 'em licked!" he cried, "Or they wouldn't have sent this!"

Whittlesey was on his feet now, too. "You," he said to Hollingshead, "had no business to leave your position under any circumstances without orders from your officer. Go back where you belong."

The boy turned away—"None of my business," he commented later, "to talk back and tell him that the sergeant called for volunteers," but that was after the war, and for now he went back to the funk hole he had occupied the day before and began to tell another private about his capture, how the Germans had fed him and not taken anything that belonged to him.

Cullen overheard the end of the story.

—If you don't shut up about that (he gritted) I'll bump you off myself right now.

Hollingshead did shut up and drifted off into an uneasy doze with his leg hurting, while back at the headquarters funk the Major was summoning Baldwin. "Get out there and take in those airplane panels. We don't want those people thinking they are a sign of surrender."

"Major, is it true that they asked us to give up?"

"Yes."

October 7

The word went through the command by grapevine in fifteen minutes. Everywhere heads popped out of funk holes.

—What's that?

—The Major told them to go to hell.

—They want us to quit.

—We'll—

And by a perfectly comprehensible reaction in mental chemistry, every other emotion of the dead-weary, starving, wounded, hysterical men was transformed into a wild rage, a furious desire for vengeance.

"Why, the dirty sons of bitches! Just let me get near one of those Dutch bastards!"

Tired men, sick men, sat up and began to sharpen bayonets on pieces of limestone, grinding their teeth. Wounded, who had not fired a gun for two days, pulled themselves out of their holes and began to hunt for cartridges. Sergeant Deahan in Company K, who had been trying to signal an airplane with a towel, hid it under a bush, the whole battalion recovered the tone it had lost and made new gains.

Doubtless this was a temporary effect and would have worn off in time. But the Germans are mechanists, not psychologists; they delivered their afternoon attack strictly on schedule, with the storm troops in the lead. Major Hünicken knew by this time that he would not have above twenty-four hours more to wipe out the command. His kindly offer to receive the men in it as prisoners had been refused, and so the assault was the heaviest and most determined the battalion had yet met, with the whole bag of tricks brought into play—*Minenwerfer,* grenades, machine guns, snipers and even a couple of flame-throwers.

It met the fiercest and bloodiest repulse of any attack yet delivered. Men were snarling with anger all along the line; too weak to walk, the wounded crawled to the front and pulled triggers, those too weak to crawl loaded guns as they were passed back. Holderman, out on the right flank was the hero of the occasion; right in the thick of it as the double attack came down front and flank, shooting with his pistol and whooping with delight every time he hit a man. He was wounded again; stayed on his feet, and with the aid of a sergeant broke up the whole wave on this front in a manner that later brought him the Congressional Medal. On the left there was even something like a counterattack that drove a German platoon back beyond the road, their officer dead and the men in disorder.

Hollingshead woke in the midst of the racket, to see the glare of the flame-thrower far to the right through the dusk. The gold-tipped cigarettes Lieutenant Prinz had stuffed in his pocket were gone, and he was sick.

"Oh, my God!" he said softly.

"Aw, shut up!" came a voice from the next funk. "Here you are, kicking because you're puking. Hell, I ain't got nothing in me to puke!"

The boy did not begin to feel good about his adventure till years later when, somewhat to his own surprise, he found himself becoming popular as a lecturer on the battalion and the war.

XV

Southeast of the Pocket
(*About 5:30 P. M.*)

Major McKinney of 307's first battalion moved his command post through the German wire about dusk. All day the steady seepage through the gaps spotted by Houghton and cut by Tillman had gone on. With dark McKinney had the strength of a full battalion forward, since a good many men of other companies than his own had worked in. To left and right they were spreading out by companies, along and behind the German trench system, and the occasional dull beat of their Chauchats showed they were meeting and beating down resistance. Northwest there was a burst of rifle fire. The officers stood trying to peer through the murk in that direction when their ears caught the crackle of a man forcing his way through underbrush at a shambling trot.

He burst suddenly on them, a horrible scarecrow figure, leaning forward like a skier about to jump, beard on his cheeks.

"For God's sake, stop our artillery! Bring food and doctors—but stop that artillery!"

249

They sent him back with a runner; never found out his name or whether he was an official messenger or not.

XVI

Hill Slope East of the Pocket
(*Noon to 6:30* P. M.)

Abe Krotoshinsky had not been killed. When the machine gun let go at them as they were passing the water hole, he had been lucky enough to take cover behind a protecting stump and after the gun quit held internal debate with himself, made up his mind that he was bound to come on something if he went forward, and crawled on, an inch at a time. A few hundred yards were covered in this fashion with the expenditure of many precious minutes. Then, feeling he was off the sights of the machine gun, he ventured a crouched dash to a spot of cover.

Nothing happened. He tried it again and then a third time, each dash being followed by a momentary pause in which he examined the landscape with care and selected the next available bush. Naturally, these successive leaps did not carry him in a straight line. He had to guide by stream and slope and was by no means sure of his location, only that his direction was generally correct.

It must have been well into the afternoon when he came on the machine-gun post. It was a hole four or five feet deep, its forward lip camouflaged with cut branches, but so heavily that the Boches had not seen him either, and went on comfortably chatting in their dugout while he wiggled past, an inch at a time, as he had left the water hole.

Beyond the machine-gun post, which he left as it began to grow dark, with a drizzle coming down, his right hand abruptly went over the edge of something. He had been looking back; the experience made his heart turn flip-flops till he perceived that the long and deep trench into which he had reached was empty.

Abe, still on his belly, wriggled backward till he had put a screen of trees between himself and the trench, then, it being dark enough now to give cover, began his little rushes once more. Just as he flopped behind a tree after one of these jumps he heard voices again, to his left; strained ears, and to his delight made out the words were English.

"Hello!" shouted the messenger, careless of the consequences now; in an instant men were all around him, half a dozen of them, nervous and businesslike. Krotoshinsky began to gabble, words he himself could hardly understand.

—Do you know this man? (asked somebody).

—Yes sir, I recognize him. This is Abe Krotoshinsky from K Company.

—Hello, Abe, want some coffee?

Through half a daze the messenger recognized Bill Bergen's voice, from Brooklyn.

He drank the coffee in enormous sucking gulps, saying something through it about being hungry, at which someone passed him a can of corned willy with the top cut off. An officer was standing over him as he ate.

—This is the lieutenant of our company, D (said Bergen).

Krotoshinsky told the officer about the battalion and where it was and what condition it was in and the Germans around it—"You should come right away."

"Can you lead us back?" asked the lieutenant.

"Sure. I feel good now."

He stood up with the can of beef, half-consumed, still in his hand.

XVII

East of the Pocket, Location Uncertain *(6:30 to 7:30 P. M.)*

"They're slowing up," said Lieutenant Hamblin of B Company, 307.

"Put the whip on them," replied Lieutenant Tillman. "What's that fire?"

—Boche machine guns but it's high. We don't have to worry about it.

"You bear to the right up that hill, and you'll take whoever's doing that shooting in flank."

Tillman himself took the leftward slant and the men began to scramble through dark and underbrush.

—You lousy bastards go on there, he could hear a sergeant grit, and then a cry of "Boche here."

"Commence firing," ordered Tillman. There was a rattle of rifle-explosions followed by the typical German scream of agony, then the crash of heavy bodies toward the road. Tillman lifted his nose to the breeze. It stank like a glue-factory, and the next minute he was stumbling into a shellhole in the dark, right onto a man who cried at him like a puppy. He just managed to throw himself sidewise from the silvery flash of a bayonet and could make out that the helmet and the arm that held the weapon were American.

"What's the matter with you?" snapped Tillman. "I'm looking for Major Whittlesey."

"I don't give a damn who you are and what you want," said the man with the bayonet. "You just step on my buddy again and I'll kill you."

"I didn't mean to step on your friend," replied the Lieutenant. "I just fell into this hole in the dark. Where's the Major? I'm Lieutenant Tillman of the 307th. You're relieved, and we'll have food up for you right away."

"I'm sorry, sir. I didn't see." He bent, and with his arms around the wounded man who had cried out, lifted him so that the well-built form of the Lieutenant was visible against the night sky.

"See? We're relieved. You're going to be all right."

"Yaaay!" said the wounded man, feebly.

XVIII

The Pocket
(*7:00* P. M.)

McMurtry sat on the edge of the funk in dark and rain, nursing his wounded knee and talking in a low tone to Whittlesey. It was seven in the evening, and Teichmoeller, the artillery lieutenant, was stretched out on his back near by, hardly listening to the conversation. Something had gone wrong with his ears since the friendly artillery fire of the 4th and his head ached. A soldier appeared before them, gave a sloppy salute, and said:

"Captain Mumbleblum (the name was indistinguishable) is up on the road with a patrol and wants to see you, sir."

Whittlesey: "All right. George, you stay here and I'll see what this is about. Come on, Cepeglia."

Cepeglia: "Is it safe now on the road?"

Whittlesey: "I guess so."

His motion, as he climbed to his feet, bespoke the weariness of the siege. The little runner bounced up like a terrier beside him, and they pushed off into the dark. McMurtry, still massaging his knee, let his thoughts run idly till they stopped on the announcement of that saluting soldier with a click.

—*Captain* something-or-other (he had said) and *on the road.*

The road was under German fire, machine guns and

snipers; the only captains were Holderman, who sat half a dozen yards away, and Stromee, who was down among the seriously wounded. McMurtry, invaded by a sense of excitement, suddenly leaped to his feet, and at a half run, took the same direction the Major had.

There was a little group of men on the road, including a lieutenant in a new uniform, beside whom stood Whittlesey, eating a sandwich. "For God's sake," cried McMurtry, "Give me a bite of that!"

The Lost Battalion was relieved; and a few moments later Krotoshinsky was down with the wounded, giving some of his corned willy to Fein who, with tears in his eyes, was saying, "Gee, I never thought I'd see you again."

XIX

Charlevaux Valley
(7:15 to 8:30 P. M.)

The runner came to Major McKinney from Company B at about a quarter past seven. Tillman had reached Whittlesey and had outposted the position to protect it from attack. He had also distributed all the rations his men carried and wanted doctors and medical supplies sent into the pocket at once. It was raining and very dark; McKinney asked Captain Stone, the Intelligence man, to go back with the runner and enough men to establish a line of posts.

They had to feel their way through the woods, but

Tillman's runner was a lumberman from somewhere in the West, who knew his stuff when it came to woods at night. There was no conversation; German parties were moving cloudily all about and the party did not wish to risk anything that would hinder its mission, therefore made no effort to hunt up such parties and fight them. Charlevaux Valley when they reached it, they found beaten into a perfect lumberyard, with trees hewn down and shivered to splinters by artillery fire. The party was a considerable one in view of the double-strength runner-posts that had to be left to bring in rations, and they used low whistle-signals to guide. At the point where the path turned up the slope there was a pile of sticks the lumberman had left as a marker. It was here they first began to smell the battalion, a frightful odor of corruption, wounds and death, long before they could see them. Now they were into the pocket, where men were groaning, muttering and stirring in the fox holes all around. The sound of a bayonet jabbed into a corned willy tin was audible, a voice rose over the murmur, "Lieutenant Pool, Lieutenant Pool, *for God's sake* bring me a drink," and then repeated it over and over, always the same sentence.

Yet every man they met was grinning, an almost foolishly happy smile. Stone had some chocolate and a couple of steak sandwiches in his musette, pushed in there when he started in the morning by Chinese Lee, the Colonel's cook. Whittlesey and McMurtry accepted both greedily. A Stokes mortar somewhere began to toss its ash cans around in the dark, the sound quite different and distinguishable from the explosions of the German *Minenwerfer*. In the morning the advance toward Grand Pré gap would start.

NEWS FLASHES

N. Y. Evening Post

AMERICAN BATTALION SAVED

Rescue of Troops Surrounded by Enemy in Argonne Region

With the American Forces Northwest of Verdun.—Word was received late last night of the rescue of an American battalion which had been surrounded by Germans in the Argonne forest region.

Several efforts were made yesterday to obtain reports from the lost battalion by messenger and homing pigeon. A basket containing a number of pigeons was lowered by a parachute in the vicinity of where the Americans were thought to be. The aviator entrusted with this task declared that the basket seemed to fall exactly where he intended it should, but no word had returned up to a late hour yesterday.

N. Y. Sun

SEVEN U. S. COMPANIES SURROUNDED THREE DAYS

With the American First Army.—Seven companies of Americans surrounded in the Argonne forest for more than three days were rescued yesterday after daring and continuous attacks by their comrades.

The Americans were cut off while pushing through dense timber in single file. Airplanes had supplied them with food, munitions, medical supplies and orders. The full story of their resistance and rescue probably will furnish one of the most dramatic episodes of the war.

News Flashes

N. Y. Times

AMERICANS RESCUED FROM ENEMY TRAP

Surrounded Three Days in Argonne Forest, 463 Men Held Out Bravely

Without Food 36 Hours

Airplanes Helped Them While They Were in Their Plight— French Also Aided

With the American Army.—Surrounded in a fastness of the Argonne Forest three days, target all the while for German artillery and machine guns, without food for the last 36 hours, a battalion of American soldiers has been rescued in an attack by Lt. Col. Gene Houghton of Racine.

The story of these men is one of the classics of the war. On Friday night, participating in an attack on the Germans deep in the forest, they had to advance in single file. Pushing on against opposition, they gained their objective to find at dawn Saturday that the Germans were not only in front of them but behind and on both sides.

Their position was three kilometers northeast of Binarville on the western edge of the Argonne Forest. The Germans had found an opening on the left and using a trench filtered in fully 1,000 men behind our battalion out there. In trenches on the hillside the enemy installed many machine guns, and went about coralling what they regarded as their sure prey.

Saturday morning other Americans discovered the plight of their comrades who were men from seven companies and numbered 463. The French on the left attacked at the same time in an effort to release the Americans. The attack failed but as it developed it probably saved the Americans because it diverted a German attack on them from the south.

Sunday three more attempts were made to reach them and all failed. That day 14 airplane missions were undertaken in their behalf, dropping two tons of food and considerable ammunition for the sequestrated men. Pigeons were also dropped by parachute so that messages could be sent back. Our aviation could not see anything of the missing men.

The Lost Battalion

N. Y. Times

BATTALION SPURNED OFFER OF SAFETY

"Go to Hell!" Shouted Whittlesey When Germans Sent Note Pleading for Surrender

Cheers Heard by Enemy

Beleaguered Force Fell Into Trap Through Eagerness, and Were Ready to Fight to the Last

With the American Forces Northwest of Verdun (Associated Press).—The brightest spot in the heroic and amazing story of how the famous "lost Battalion" which belonged to the 77th Division, as yet untold, was the climax to the fourth day of siege of the troops in the Argonne Forest.

When the men had been for a long time without food and almost wholly without ammunition, and, when many were weak from exhaustion, but not one despairing, an American who had been taken prisoner by the Germans suddenly appeared at the little camp surrounded in the valley.

The man had been sent blindfolded from the German headquarters with a typewritten note reading:

Americans, you are surrounded on all sides. Surrender in the name of humanity. You will be well treated.

Major Whittlesey did not hesitate a fraction of a second.

"Go to Hell!" he shouted. Then he read the note to those around him and his men, despite their weariness and hunger and the fact that they were in imminent danger every moment, cheered so loudly that the Germans heard them from their observation posts.

The enemy had planned to catch the Americans in a hollow surrounded on all four sides by heights, the greatest of which was a steep hill directly ahead. The Americans who were not accustomed to forest fighting and were filled with eagerness, dashed into this hollow without stopping to think that the enemy might be awaiting them. The battalion was at first checked by the American artillery barrage which had worked steadily forward. Nevertheless it had not worked as fast as the troops themselves and the battalion proceeded halfway up the hill and there waited for the barrage to pass in front. Then they discovered that the Germans on both sides had jointly flanked them and had closed in on their rear.

260

News Flashes

Sheltered only by shallow and hastily constructed trenches the men were subjected to sniping machine-gun fire as well as trench-mortar bombardment every time they showed themselves. Only with the greatest difficulty and extreme caution could they move from place to place and keep guard against surprise attacks. The battalion had started with meager rations expecting more to reach them later. These of course, could no longer be transported to them. It was the greatest good fortune that they were fairly well supplied with water.

Nightly and daily too they sent back volunteer scouting parties but, whether these reached the positions in the rear without being captured or killed, the beleaguered force could not tell for none ever returned.

Daily American aviators searching vainly for the battalion flew overhead but no outcry the men could'make brought anything but a volley of shouts and laughter from the Germans in the forest behind and to right and'left.

As the days passed the Americans grew more and more emaciated but they never gave up hope. There was nothing but grim determination to hold out till the last man was finished. Ammunition was depleted to the point where the few machine guns had only one belt left and rifle ammunition was so short that they had received orders not to fire at anyone attacking until within such short range that his death or serious injury was almost inevitable.

Major Whittlesey, who is a well-known New York lawyer, had his entire force behind him to a man. Captain Leo Stromee of San Bernardino, Cal., told the A. P. correspondent that his men jeered at the idea of surrender and men who came out of the four days' siege are united in declaring they never would have given up.

October 8—and Forever

I

KOZIKOWSKI and Brown got through all right, too, but it was later in the night, after the rain had stopped. They worked across the German trenches due south by compass and Brown discovered they were going to be all right when he fell into a hole and incredibly recognized it as one he himself had dug during the advance up to the pocket. He stood up straight then and began to talk aloud to Koz "in the American language." One of Breckinridge's patrols gathered them in after a minute or two and took them to that officer, who gave them a can of beans and telephoned the brigade. Koz and Brown got the D. S. C. with the same citation Krotoshinsky received, the higher command deciding their deed had been as gallant as his.

General Alexander was one of the first men into the pocket the next morning, coming down the road with a cigarette in his hand as though he were strolling along Fifth Avenue, although there was a German machine gun over on La Palette which still fired intermittently. Ambulances were bumping along the road by that time and a long line of ration bearers coming up with sacks of canned meat, molasses, bread, tomatoes and prunes.

Just after the relief. An exhausted Lost Battalion survivor gets a drink of hot chocolate.

They dumped the food in big heaps near the road, while the eyes of the hungry men in the pocket bugged out like the eyes of lobsters and the doctors tried to get them not to eat too much in their first enthusiasm.

"Where's Whittlesey?" asked the General.

"Down at the foot of the hill, sir," said Baldwin, to whom the question was addressed, indicating the direction where the Major was personally handing out food to his men. "Shall I get him for you?"

"By no means. I'll go to him."

The Major looked worn and dilapidated, no press in his torn clothes, overseas cap collapsed and the captain's bars which were the only badge of rank he had taken into the pocket tucked away. He was feeling rather low because one of the relievers had offered him a flask of fine whiskey first thing in the morning and it slipped between their fingers to crash on a rock. Alexander greeted him warmly. "How do you do? From now on you're Lieutenant-Colonel Whittlesey."

The Major, or rather, the Lieutenant-Colonel, murmured something appropriate and indistinct. There was a moment of obscure emotional tensions which the General sought to relieve by glancing at the leafy curtain overhead. "Well, I can see why the airplanes couldn't find this place."

Irrepressible little Cepeglia, from his position on the ground piped up, "General, the artillery certainly found it."

"Oh, no, that was French artillery," said Alexander

263

without batting an eyelash, and flicked the ash from his cigarette.

II

That last remark held the enzyme that set an acid ferment working. The achievement, the collective courage and endurance of the command during its siege, under fire friendly and hostile, beating off daily attacks, had been one of the finest in American history. It was capped on that morning of October 8 when many of the one hundred and ninety-four men who had gone through it without becoming hospital cases, with incredible nerve, volunteered to go up in the line again immediately they had eaten; did go up in the line again while the division harried Wellmann's retreating corps to the rocks of Grand Pré.

Yet at the time and since there was observable at corps and division headquarters, that is, in the professional ranks of the army, a disposition to regard the siege as an unpleasant matter, to hush it up, gloss it over. As matters stood this would have amounted to a tacit admission that so much courage and devotion had been unnecessary, and it would have been the first step in some kind of official process fastening the blame for the cutoff onto Whittlesey.

Such an intent was not specifically announced by any person and would probably be vigorously denied today by everyone concerned. It was merely in the air, existing as impalpably as an odor whose source cannot be traced. Yet by the time the command was relieved it had already become impossible to translate such an intent (if it existed as more than a dinner-table conversation) into action.

This impossibility was fundamentally due to the war correspondents. On the first or second day of the cutoff the UP man, Fred S. Ferguson cabled a dispatch about the position of the battalion. His cable editor wired back, "Send more on Lost Battalion" (which seems to have been the first use of the name), and then all the other papers took it up. By the morning of October 8 Whittlesey was one of the best-known men in the war and the papers back home were printing columns on his stand.

Paris papers with copies of those dispatches were already in Alexander's hands by time the relief took place, and it was perfectly evident that Whittlesey was going to be a "human interest" hero. The process of lionization was also sensibly aided by Arthur McKeogh, who had been Whittlesey's adjutant during the first, September, cutoff, and had bravely broken through with the message for help. McKeogh was a writer; he had just been drafted home, stepping off the boat about the time Whittlesey was relieved. Here was news from the fountainhead. The papers went after him for interviews, and *Collier's* published an article he wrote, describing the first cutoff. But this was a side issue. The main fact was that by the time of his relief Whittlesey was established as a hero.

Both he and McMurtry were voted Congressional Medals of Honor, an action which rendered any further criticism futile.

III

Yet criticism of actions in a war is always gratuitous. There is evidence of the persistence in army circles of the opinion that Whittlesey was somehow to blame for being caught in the trap, and that he should and could have gotten out of it after he got in. Also, not unnaturally or unforgivably, there was a faint undertow of jealousy at seeing an emergency officer receive America's highest award for gallantry in action, an honor most West Pointers go through a lifetime without ever having a chance to win. The fact that the battalion was relieved, in the passive voice, the very name attached to it, "the Lost Battalion" played a rôle in spreading this feeling. There was a joke by a pair of comedians at one of the army shows following the Armistice which expresses the matter nicely:

A: "Gosh, I just lost my wrist watch."

B: "That's nothing; a major over in the 77th Division just lost a whole battalion."

The matter might have passed over into nothing more serious than remarks at reunion dinners but for two factors—the question of that artillery fire on October 4 and Whittlesey's own character. He was a lawyer of the most ethical type and an unreconstructed New

Englander, a combination that caused him to think (as we have remarked) in terms of a duty so strict as to be beyond the comprehension of the average individual. This exquisite sense of duty led Whittlesey, when he got out of the pocket, to recommend an unusual number of his men for decorations. It also led him to make a report on the note sent to him by Revnes, the machine-gun lieutenant.

Such a report can be treated in one way only—by a court-martial to try the soldier affected. There was a considerable arrear of courts-martial in the A.E.F., and it was 1919 before the matter came to trial. The court was a very mysterious business, and it was held in the peculiar post-war, 1919, atmosphere.

The war was over. Everybody wanted to get back home, and nearly everybody had been seized by the first wave of violent revulsion to the whole bloody business, the revulsion that brought *Three Soldiers* as its most characteristic product. Whittlesey had already gone back to the states with his lieutenant-colonelcy, and the newspapers from back there were still ringing with the Rover-boy type of story about the battalion's exploit, in the key set by the first flush of enthusiasm among the correspondents when they heard of it. To a good many people in the A.E.F. it might well have seemed that Whittlesey had received Homeric honors for a grade of heroism not uncommon in the army.

The undercurrent of feeling was still further accentuated when the court in the Revnes case requested GHQ to bring Whittlesey back to France to give evidence at the trial and GHQ refused. The trial thus practically turned into an inquiry on Whittlesey's conduct, and it was a big affair, lasting three days, with McMurtry, Holderman, all the available sergeants and many of the privates, forty men all told, being called as witnesses. Acquittal was a relatively simple matter; whatever Revnes had said, he had behaved very bravely, crawling to the front with his pistol and his wounded ankle to aid in the repulse of every German threat. The more prominent impression left by the trial was that Whittlesey's excessive zeal had led him into a trap from which he later had to be rescued when he might easily have escaped.

That impression has been persistent. Nine persons out of ten believe it today; and it is impossible that Whittlesey himself could not have been aware of its existence.

IV

Consideration of this question not only reveals the fatal weakness of conducting an inquiry into one subject under color of investigating another but also throws open the whole question of responsibility. When one of the members of the court was informed, nineteen years after, of Alexander's general order that any officer giving orders to retreat was a traitor and should be shot on the spot, he cried, "What! Why that was never brought before the court!" Then, more pensively, "If it had been it would have changed our point of view."

Yet had the order been offered in evidence it is difficult to see what the court could have done but throw it out again. The Congressional Medal of Honor was an act of approval and oblivion which prevented the trial of Whittlesey in any jurisdictions but those of public opinion and his own mind. Nor would any court, particularly either of the latter pair, have been likely to give weight to the truly essential feature in the question of responsibility—the operations of the enemy.

For people, and even soldiers who should know better, insist upon regarding war as a matter capable of mathematical analysis, a kind of destructive engineering, a struggle against inanimate, passively resistant forces which must give way if calculable quanta of energy are applied at the correct spot. They fail utterly in grasping the fact that the final fascination about this most dangerous game is its imponderables; the fact that the enemy also is striving to conceal his intentions and to impose his will; and the fact that the ultimate result is a compromise brought about by this clash of wills. Or not so much a compromise as the result of the intention supported by the greater force, moral or material, being modified by the intention of the weaker.

In the case of the Lost Battalion, the dominating intent was indubitably that of the Allied high command; the intent of breaking through the German line. Yet the execution of this intent was subject to numerous limitations, of which the most severe were imposed by the type of mass war in which the parties were engaged.

In this type of war it had long ago become clear that although in general the advantage is with the defense, an attacker once halted loses morale and the rhythm of his movement, and can again go forward only at great cost and after careful preparation. The Germans had lost morale and rhythm at Soissons in the early summer, but they might recover both if allowed a winter in which to rest.

This, then, was the simple and controlling compromise of forces which dictated the orders Whittlesey had received to rush on without regard to his flanks, the repeated attack orders given to Johnson and Stacey by Alexander, and behind them, Pershing's urgency with Alexander and Foch's with Pershing.

But the necessity of keeping the offensive was not the only factor, or Whittlesey would never have been ordered on "without regard to flanks or losses." The Germans imposed the second of these addenda upon a simple attack order; the Germans and geography imposed the first. And this matter of German action is so important to the whole question of responsibility that it is worth remarking that the favorite German method of stopping an attack was to allow it to proceed on a limited front and exhaust itself in extension behind their lines; that is, forcing it into the shape of a mushroom, and then cutting the stalk. Alexander felt on October 1 that he could force enough of these mushrooms into the German front to give them indigestion; therefore he ordered forward his regiments "without regard, etc."

A review of events shows this confidence to have been

far from unjustifiable, for it was only a most extraordinary chapter of accidents that caused the Lost Battalion to become lost. Had Rainsford and Blagden of the 307th not returned L Company to their jumping-off line, there would have been two of these fungoids in that section of the German front, probably a mass beyond the Teutonic digestive powers. But they retreated on the afternoon of October 2 and so there was only one—Whittlesey's. Had Shelata and more than three of the four companies sent up that night not fallen back out of the movement they would have been in the Haupt-Widerstands-Linie in the morning, forming a thick and heavy stem to the mushroom, so that the effort to cut might well have failed. Indeed, on the night of October 2 the German divisional command seems to have been worried chiefly about the fate of its bakery, over the hill, north of Whittlesey. Again, had Johnson vigorously pushed forward his reserve battalion on the night of October 2 as Alexander intended he should, the stalk of the mushroom would have been too thick to cut. Nor does it appear that the morning of October 3 was marked by any attack on the part of the 308th to reach Whittlesey but the foredoomed one of Paul Knight's little body of one hundred men. That these two last "accidents" took place was, however, a condition more than a little imposed by the Germans. Johnson may quite reasonably have felt the danger of transforming his whole wing into an oversize kind of mushroom, subject to being cut off by a strong advance from La Palette on the part of the Germans.

There is still another modifying factor present at this point, which becomes evident when one considers that the 1st Division over on the Aire fought its way forward against opposition, if anything, sterner through country nearly as difficult, and without having any lost battalions, companies or platoons. No colonel in the 1st Division had to kneel in the mud under German fire, as Colonel Stacey did on October 3, and show a recruit how to load his rifle. They understood the importance of liaison, and what was more vital still, knew how to accomplish it. They had men who knew all about scouting, whereas in the whole of the Lost Battalion episode only one man, Captain Holderman, really showed himself able to conduct a scout.

The situation was similar with regard to all the other details of service in the field; which is to say that the men of the 77th Division lacked not for courage, intelligence, patriotism or any other fundamental quality, but simply that they were poorly trained and insufficiently experienced. Seen from this angle the ultimate responsibility rests on the Washington authorities who sent such soldiers to a major war, and the lesson is that democracies should not engage in mass wars, for when they seek a universal military competence they tend to lose democracy.

V

Yet this is not the only angle from which one can

examine the question of responsibility, for the criticisms of Whittlesey are detailed as well as general. He should, say some, have left Holderman's company back in the German trench line on the morning of October 3 instead of rallying it on himself. This criticism overlooks the fact that the seventy-nine men Holderman brought would have formed an excessively long and excessively thin stem to the mushroom—hardly more than a strong line of runner-posts.

There is abundant evidence from the German side to show that the soldiers who filtered into the empty trenches behind Holderman were at least six or seven hundred in number. How Holderman's single company could have stood them off does not appear. Moreover Holderman had crossed the trench line during the night; even before he came over the brook to join Whittlesey the filtering process may have begun without anyone being aware of it.

There is also the criticism that Whittlesey did not establish liaison to left and right. This is the voice of ignorance; for enough has been said above to show that he made efforts in both directions, and that both efforts ran into Germans. Liaison to the rear he had kept by means of a double-strength chain of runner-posts; when that broke, through no fault of his own, he had used pigeons, the correct procedure.

Securing his rear against the encirclement that actually took place was not his business for Alexander's general order, the same one that directed no ground be given up, says plainly and specifically, "Troops occupy-ing ground must be supported against counterattack." That is, it was the function of Regiment, Brigade and Division to furnish supports for Whittlesey once he reached his objective, a function which they conspicu-ously failed to perform.

There remains the question of why Whittlesey did not break out of the pocket rearward, as many thought he should and as Wellmann thought he could. (It must be remembered, however, that von Sybel and Wellmann, deceived by Leak, Harrington or their own estimates, thought Whittlesey had twelve hundred men.) The answer is the positiveness of Alexander's attack orders— "halt at the objective and await orders for a further advance"—reinforced by the last message from Stacey again telling him to get ready for a further advance; and above all that general order, so freshly issued as to be uppermost in the Major's mind, that any officer ordering a retreat was a traitor.

And that general order was itself a case of the modi-fication of the American intent to make a sensible, not-rash advance, by German intent. It was a direct product of the incident on the 28th Division's front when the men who gave retreat orders turned out not to be American at all. Whittlesey thus was, in a sense, obeying German orders transmitted to him through American mouths, and it is not surprising that he got into trouble. The responsibility for what happened did not rest with him because responsibility had been taken out of his hands by higher authority; authority higher than Alexander, higher than Pershing or Foch—ultimately the responsibility rested with the war itself. It was what courts rather incongruously call "an act of God." General Alexander was later to accept fully whatever of human responsibility there was behind the episode. Said he: "Whittlesey's command did what it was told."

That it did this to the satisfaction of the highest authority in the army there is one incident to show. Immediately after the relief Colonel Gordon Johnston came down to take command of the 308th regiment. He was one of the most brilliant officers and keenest analytical brains in the army, a man high in the confidence of GHQ; and he held a long series of conferences with Whittlesey, McMurtry and other officers of the regiment. At the close of these conferences he was transferred to another division; but just before leaving for the new post he publicly transmitted to Whittlesey "the thanks of General Pershing in the name of the American people" for his courageous and intelligent conduct.

From that judgment no reasonable person can dissent.

VI

But Whittlesey lacked the perspective to make Johnston's analysis and still more the perspective to make that given here, both because his almost atrophied religious sense had been compensated by an overdeveloped sense of social duty and because the question of the friendly barrage intruded an issue of responsibility entirely extraneous to the main issue. On the general question he could not—at least many officers who knew him more or less intimately say he could not—ever entirely forget lying at night in the pocket and seeing men dying around him. Of the six hundred-odd men there he presented the most perfect union of courage and brains during every waking hour, but it had been noted of him that he sometimes cried in his sleep.

And there is no question but that the matter of the barrage weighed heavily upon him. Alexander had heard of it the day it occurred—via the "For heaven's sake" message. After the relief he ordered an inquiry, but some of the inquirers understood that it would be desirable (for purposes of army morale) that they give the business a dose of whitewash. They accordingly reached the official decision that the artillery which fired into the battalion was German.

Now it was patently impossible that it could have been German artillery. The slope was out of range of any German guns on the front. The Germans had nothing that would fire so high a trajectory as to land artillery shells in the pocket. Moreover the men there present had heard the warning explosion of guns before the shells fell among them, and those explosions were 75's, the Franco-American gun which makes quite a different sound from the German 77. Nor had all the shells exploded; and the duds were 75 duds.

When it was announced, therefore, that the artillery fire had been German, considerable indignation was expressed by the survivors. One at least (there may have been more) went to Whittlesey and offered to swear an affidavit that the command had been shelled by American artillery. By this time the Armistice had come. "Forget it; the war's over," said Whittlesey.

He, unfortunately, was not permitted to forget it. Mingled with the other criticisms of his conduct was one of which he could not but have been aware—that he had sent the wrong co-ordinates to his position. The artillery (says this version) had fired by those wrong co-ordinates and hence had pounded his men instead of protecting them. The evidence on this point is not altogether complete, since some of the messages he sent back are missing from the records. (It would be interesting to know who got them.) But on the evidence of those messages we have, and which have been quoted *in extenso* above, the co-ordinates Whittlesey sent back were very accurate indeed. Such errors as they contain are not material and are of a character to keep the shells from falling on him rather than to bring them down.

The evidence, admittedly incomplete, always obscure and sometimes obscured, seems to show that the co-ordinates used for that fatal artillery shoot were either those supplied in the message from Lieutenant Teichmoeller or those Lieutenant Putnam brought back from his observation mission with the 308th.

Both those sets of co-ordinates were incorrect. Both

placed Whittlesey's command in such a position that fully to protect him the artillery would have to fire on exactly the spot it did fire—that is, right into the true position of the battalion. And we do not know what infantry officer marked Putnam's map for him.

VII

But this is the result of careful investigation nearly two decades after the event; much too late to do Whittlesey any good. At the time he could only know that the artillery business was leaving a painful impression on his mind.

For that matter, his whole position, on being demobilized, was a painful one. He was naturally a rather modest and retiring individual; naturally, he had always been acutely uncomfortable in the presence of anything that savored of personal publicity or personal display. He had an acute sympathy with the forgotten man and wanted to be one himself. Before America's entry into the war he had accepted the doctrine of the intellectual liberals, voted the Socialist ticket and talked a type of pacifism not unlike Wilson's "Too proud to fight." Not adventure, ambition or patriotism (as with so many ROTC officers) but an enlarged sense of social duty led him to be one of the first to volunteer. Now that the fighting was over he wanted nothing so much as to revert to his previous status, to sink into the crowd and bury himself in his legal work.

But he was not permitted to revert. He had been

named by Pershing himself as one of the "three outstanding heroes of the A.E.F.," and he was the only one resident in New York and instantly available for all kinds of speeches and ceremonies. His office became a rendezvous for job-hunting ex-soldiers—"Not a day but I hear from some of them," he said once. He was not a private citizen, but an exhibition piece, a plush horse.

A plush horse constantly on exhibition in circles where a word about his real convictions on war as a bloody and unnecessary business (which do not appear to have changed) would have caused a violent scandal and made people think him insane. Still more would a word of his real convictions as to the episode for which he was being honored; he thought it fortuitous and futile. Not merely the desire to avoid the publicity such a word would entail, but also his sense of social duty—in this case, duty to his old comrades of the A.E.F. many of whom had given lives to an ideal he regarded with suspicion—forbade him to speak; forbade him publicly to question any detail of the official version. It never occurred to him that the official version might be fundamentally correct; that General Pershing's thanks in the name of the American people might have been not for his courage alone but also because the advance and the siege of the command, with all the events it dragged in its train, had materially aided the victory in the Meuse-Argonne. In a sense, he lacked the long view; saw the deaths without seeing the triumph they bought. We have the word of one of these old comrades that half a dozen times on lecture platforms he seemed on the edge of speaking of that deadly barrage of October 4, but always bit his lip, gulped back the words and turned to some other topic.

Yet every day saw him forced deeper into his false position, every event forced upon him more undesired honors, more elements of a career not of his own choosing. The Organized Reserve was formed; in August, 1921, Whittlesey was offered and did not feel he could decently refuse the colonelcy of the 308th Infantry of that Reserve. "They're always after me about the war," he said, about this time. "I've got to help some soldier or make some speech or something. I used to think I was a lawyer; now I don't know what I am."

But he was a lawyer, and he had a peculiarly difficult case to handle at about the time he was made chairman of the Red Cross Roll Call, and invited to Washington for the dedication of the tomb of the Unknown Soldier, along with some thirty others who had received the Congressional Medal. He sat beside McMurtry, had little to say, listened to the ceremonies with barely the quiver of a muscle. Two weeks later he took a girl to a show and next morning boarded the steamer *Toloa* for a vacation in Cuba. That evening he sat late in the saloon with a man named Maloret, discussed the war for a while, and then with the remark that he would retire, went out and jumped over the rail.

VIII

Nobody saw him go, but when the news came to New York his legal associates found in his desk painstaking notes for the conduct of the difficult case, with the remark that he would not be back. There were also letters for his closest friends; they consulted and issued a brief statement closing with the words "His was a war casualty," but never told what was in the letters.

His brother, Melzar Whittlesey, also received one of those letters, but was not among the consultees who issued the statement.

"What was in it?" he was asked recently.

"I don't know. I never opened it. It's still home in my safe."

"Why don't you read it? It might clear up the mystery of his death."

"If my brother couldn't tell me himself why he did it, I don't want to know. No, now that you have reminded me of it, I think I'll destroy it tonight."

IX

Teichmoeller did not come off much better. His hearing steadily worsened and finally, about the time Whittlesey stepped over the side of the *Toloa,* he had an operation from which he failed to rally. A few of the other wounded died in hospitals just after the war. Most of the rest recovered, even including the man who had begged a comrade to shoot him, and whose name is omitted here for the obvious reason that he made a snappy recovery, got a job and a wife and has been living happily ever since.

Indeed, the most striking general physical character-

281

istic of the survivors seems to be their excellent health and the fact that they have outworn similar bodies of men of the same age.

As for other matters, the New Yorkers in the outfit kept pretty much together after the war, most of them joining veterans' organizations and meeting to keep alive memories of the days in the pocket. The effect of the experience on them has been largely social, providing them with contacts and common interests in life; though as the years since the war have rolled by, they have grown less and less inclined to talk about the experience or to revive its memories, especially among strangers.

Partly this is due to the fact that they have already become figures in a legend. Every time one of them accomplishes anything—birth, marriage, death, new job or political appointment—he gets his picture in the papers, with two or three columns, usually inaccurate, about the Lost Battalion. One can only compare it with the immense hullabaloo made in England over the survivors of the Light Brigade, which also went into action with six hundred men.

A pamphlet came out in the early '20s about them and enjoyed quite a sale; and there was a movie of the Lost Battalion produced about the same time. Both, like most of the newspaper accounts, left the veterans pretty well dissatisfied, complaining of major and minor inaccuracies, and even of the name "Lost Battalion."

—We were never lost (they say with energy). We knew right where we were and so did the general.

Of the specific New Yorkers, Krotoshinsky got into the newspapers most prominently. He was interested in the Zionist movement. After the war Nathan Straus paid his passage to Palestine, where he set up as a farmer, but couldn't make a go of it, what with the natural difficulties and the fact that a dose of gas had left him weakened in health. He came back to New York, and knocked around for a while, drifting from job to job and not very lucky with anything. In 1927 a reporter from the *World* got hold of him and printed his story, with some unkind remarks about the Postal Service, for which Krotoshinsky had taken an examination a year or more before without hearing anything further about it. The story was carried to President Coolidge. He investigated, found Krot had passed the examination in a manner to place him high on the list of eligibles and instantly gave him a job by presidential order.

He is one of the several Lost Battalion survivors who have talked publicly about their experiences. Hollingshead more frequently than anyone else perhaps, but also Brown, Cullen, both Corporal Baldwin who handled Whittlesey's messengers and Sergeant Baldwin who took over E Company after it lost its officers. Pollinger died recently in a Veterans' Hospital; he used to talk about the Battalion from the lecture platform at infrequent intervals and get a hundred dollars for it.

The upstate New Yorkers keep in fairly close touch with the Legion post, especially Larney, the signal-panel man who kept the diary. He went into politics and became a big shot in St. Lawrence County; used to get together with Baldwin, Cepeglia, Cahill and some of the others, and read over what he had written beside Charlevaux Brook. A few years later he took a trip on the same steamer and run Whittlesey took in 1921 and stood by the rail all night, looking down into the black water, trying to imagine himself into the Major's mind and so to find out why he did it.

Holderman was the most interested of all; he stayed in the army, got a Medal of Honor for his part in the exploit, and wrote a monograph on the battalion for the Infantry School, but never quite recovered from his wounds, and is now a colonel in charge of a Veterans' Hospital in California. Stromee, who was more seriously wounded than Holderman oddly enough recovered quicker and more completely than Holderman, though his wounds left marks on him all right. He is now in the reserve.

Most of the Westerners in the ranks were more inclined than the New Yorkers to drop touch with the war after they were mustered out. Except for those in hospitals they have had fewer contacts with the war and no such focal point as the New Yorkers. A good many of them are now in Minnesota, but scattered, and they have tended to form new contacts, or else to take up those dropped with the war, like the three miners from Butte, who went right back to their holes in the ground and are still there, except Indian Rainwater, who died recently.

Hollingshead, of course, presents a special case, but even he has been heard to remark that people often say they'd give a million dollars for such an experience, but as for himself, "Hell, I'll take the million." Another special case was a Minnesota private named Krogh, who wrote a remarkable letter to the 77th Division club house in New York after the war, inclosing a sketch-map of the pocket which he had drawn. He had left a watch and several other articles at a spot marked X on the map when he was carried out wounded, and he wanted to know if these things could be found for him.

X

They never were. Only the dead were found, including the dead runners, the bodies of the latter piled in threes, one across the other, with their shoes removed and their broken rifles beside them. All of them were buried in Charlevaux Valley in a single wide and deep trench under a wooden cross. The valley is now partly drowned by some damming operation farther downstream, but the water has not covered the fox holes, and the curious can still find there bits of equipment marked U. S.

The End

NOTES

NOTES

P. 19, l. 23: Lieutenant Arthur McKeogh died recently in New York, where he was managing editor of *Good Housekeeping* magazine. He was an authority on the Lost Battalion and, before his death, manifested a warm interest in the preparation of this volume.

P. 20, l. 2: Joseph Monson is also dead; Jack Herschkowitz survives, in robust health, in New York.

P. 21, l. 16: Colonel Cromwell Stacey, now retired and living in Port Angeles, Wash. He had begun soldiering twenty-four years earlier as a marine drummer-boy. Some of his officers recommended him for a Distinguished Service Cross for gallantry under fire in attempting to bring relief to the Lost Battalion, but he did not receive it.

P. 22, l. 6: This is the first publication of the important fact that Major Whittlesey himself advised against the attack that transformed his command into the "Lost Battalion." He advised against it not once but twice; not only on the morning of October 2 but on the night previous. Both times Colonel Stacey made the same reply, that he agreed with Major Whittlesey but that he had his orders to attack from higher authority.

The first time, the night of October 1, Colonel Stacey also sent his adjutant, Captain Francis M. Weld, to explain details to Major Whittlesey. Captain Weld found Major Whittlesey, Captain McMurtry, Lieutenant Cullen and several others in a captured German dugout. To his explanation someone retorted: "Then we'll be cut off again." Captain Weld said: "That possibility has been considered, but the attack has been ordered nevertheless."

P. 22, l. 10: Brigadier General Evan M. Johnson, a regular army officer, underwent an operation shortly after the war for an ailment that had troubled him throughout the Argonne fighting and, not long afterward, died.

P. 22, l. 22: Major General Robert Alexander, now retired and living in La Jolla, Calif. Last September at the American Legion Convention in New York he was the guest of honor of the 77th Division veterans.

P. 26, l. 25: Charles Cahill, now living in New York.

P. 30, l. 18: General Johnson so testified in General Alexander's presence at an inquiry into the causes of the cutting off of the Lost Battalion held October 6 by Captain Albert T. Rich, Assistant Inspector General of the First Army which then was commanded by General Pershing. The stenographic record of this inquiry shows that at the same time General Alexander testified that he ordered the attack because it "coincided with the belief expressed by the Army and Corps headquarters, that the Boche was in retreat and my flanks would be sufficiently taken care of by my own people." He added that when he told General Johnson the French were ahead of Johnson's left flank and so in position to protect it, he knew this was not true.

He might have explained that he was not the first officer in the A. E. F. to employ that *ruse de guerre* to spur on a subordinate.

Such were the circumstances under which the Lost Battalion attacked.

Major General Alexander had been an honor student at the regular army's postgraduate schools at Fort Leavenworth, Kansas. He fully realized that the whole battle of the Meuse-Argonne was being fought in a desperate effort to crush the German Army before winter. To do that required a combination of audacity and dogged perseverance, as the orders and exhortations he was continually receiving from his superiors eloquently testified. General Pershing in turn was receiving from Marshal Foch urgent directives, of which one said:

"Troops thrown into an attack have only to know their direction of attack. In this direction they go as far as they can, without any thought of alignment. . . ."

P. 31, l. 20: This conversation was pieced together from the accounts of three men who heard it: Major McMurtry, Colonel Stacey and the Reverend Father Halligan, the regimental chaplain.

The full text of the order Major Whittlesey received follows:

"The advance of the infantry will commence at 12:50. The infantry action will be pushed forward until it reaches the line of the road and the railroad generally along 276.5 where the command will halt, reorganize and establish liaison to left and right and be ready for orders for a further advance. This does not change the plan as given you by Detroit 1 (Colonel Stacey). You still leave two companies on your left as a containing force, that is, the remainder of the first and second battalions. The General says you are to advance behind the barrage regardless of losses. He says that there will be a general advance all along the line."

P. 36, l. 6: Kerr Rainsford, now an architect in New York.

P. 36, l. 13: Crawford Blagden, New Yorker and Harvard graduate, died several years ago.

P. 37, l. 14: Omer Richards, now in Ogdensburg, N. Y.

P. 38, l. 17: Leo A. Stromee, now a city employee in Los Angeles, Calif., and director of the Veterans' Home at Napa, Calif., of which Colonel Holderman is superintendent. The two men had been members of the National Guard together before the war.

The Lost Battalion

P. 38, l. 15: Henry J. Williamson when last heard from was in Opelika, Ala.; Karl Wilhelm, now in Buffalo, N. Y.; J. V. Leak, now a lawyer in Longview, Texas; Victor A. Harrington, now in Detroit, Mich.; Wm. J. Cullen, now an attorney in New York, and a major in the 308th Infantry, Organized Reserves, whose emblem bears a mill-wheel, for Charlevaux Mill and the Lost Battalion; Maurice V. Griffin, now in Denver, Colo.

P. 39, l. 7: George Newcom, now running a "dust-farm" in Oakley, Kansas.

P. 40, l. 3: Walter J. Baldwin, later sergeant major, now in New York.

P. 45, l. 3: Hans William Christensen, now in Denver, Colo.

P. 47, l. 12: Colonel Eugene H. Houghton, now a grain broker in Winnipeg, Canada, where, soon after the war, as an impromptu chief of police, he broke up a general strike and an embryo Soviet, using extremely direct action.

P. 49, l. 8: For what he did, General Johnson had military precedent; indeed, he was preparing, if the Germans struck Whittlesey's left flank, to execute in turn the classic maneuver of striking their right with his brigade reserve . . . always assuming, of course, that in the forest the handicaps to quick observation and movement would not prove too severe, and his counterstroke fall too late.

P. 50, l. 15: Thomas G. Pool, now a deputy sheriff in Beaumont, Texas.

P. 51, l. 10: The authorities here are Colonel Houghton and others.

P. 62, l. 9: Robert Manson, recently in Brooklyn, N. Y.

P. 64, l. 1: Lieutenant Paul R. Knight was one of the more experienced of the 77th's company commanders, having served with the 102nd Engineers, New York State National Guard. He is now a major in the regular army, stationed at La Salle Military Academy, Oakdale, L. I., N. Y.

P. 70, l. 19: To avoid, if possible, interception and translation by the Germans, a code was used that gave designations for all major units, staff and commanding officers in the 77th Division, which was called "Dreadnaught," and General Alexander was "Dreadnaught 1." Code names for all units in the division commenced with "D." The 154th Infantry Brigade was "Delaware" and General Johnson, "Delaware 1"; the 307th Infantry Regiment was "Denver" and Colonel Houghton, "Denver 1." The 308th Infantry Regiment was "Detroit" and Colonel Stacey, "Detroit 1." The Regiment's three battalions were "Detroit Red," "Detroit White" and "Detroit Blue"; so that Major Whittlesey was "Detroit Red," Captain McMurtry, "Detroit White," and Captain Scott's brigade reserve was "Detroit Blue." Companies were numbered 31 to 50 inclusive so Company A, 308th Infantry, was "Detroit 31."

This message has never before been published. It was found in War Department file number 277.37.16; the 77th Division message-center where it was first received; it was not found in the files of the 305th Field Artillery, but neither were some other things that might reasonably have been expected to be there. (The files of all A.E.F. units are, for one reason or another, incomplete.)

Previous published accounts of the Lost Battalion episode have given the full text of six messages Major Whittlesey sent back by pigeon. But, of two crates of pigeons the command started with, one crate was smashed and all the pigeons escaped; and so (*vide* text) did one pigeon in the other crate which had contained eight.

The Lost Battalion

P. 76, l. 8: The orders spoke of a narrow-gauge railroad running alongside and parallel to the Apremont-Binarville road; the maps showed such a road; but neither the Lost Battalion nor anyone else could find it. The map-makers must have mis-read an airplane photograph.

P. 76, l .15: After the Lost Battalion was relieved, this message was given to Major Henry H. Curran, then commanding the 302nd Ammunition Train, now deputy mayor of New York City, by one of his men who had found it on the body of an American soldier lying dead amid the thickets covering the route the Lost Battalion had followed. Doubtless he was one of Whittlesey's runners, and his important message never reached Colonel Stacey. The previous message had reached the Colonel, however, as the records of the 308th Infantry show, and the files of the division message-center show that at 4 P.M. the afternoon of October 2 division headquarters had been notified that "308th Infantry is nearly at its objective." The record disproves the statement sometimes made that Major Whittlesey was so slow and inaccurate in reporting his position that no one knew where he was until the first pigeon message of October 3.

P. 79, l. 30: Harvey M. Farncomb, now in Sacramento, Calif., lost touch with Otto Volz, the man who helped him. "He should," says Farncomb, "have a scar on his face, running from one corner of his mouth almost back to the lobe of the ear." Perhaps Otto Volz, or someone who knows him, will see this.

P. 81, l. 7: Farland F. Wade, Prospect, Pa.

P. 87, l. 25: Arthur Fein still lives in New York, and at a recent reunion greeted Carroll as "the man who saved my life." There also was ruddy, blond Sergeant Joseph P. Heuer who in that same fight commanded a platoon of K, 307th, and shot the only German he knows he killed in the whole war: "a big fellow,

294

with a machine gun." Heuer is now a vestryman of the Episcopal Church in Cranford, N. J.

P. 93, l. 14: The impelling motive behind General Alexander's order received endorsement a short time later from General Pershing, who visited commanders of several divisions and impressed upon them that "ground once taken should be quickly organized for defense and then held at all hazards." (*My Experiences in the World War*, John J. Pershing; Frederick A. Stokes Company.) But neither General Pershing nor any other historian records that he said anything about shooting anyone on the spot; or that in the 77th Division anyone said anything to anyone about the ignoring of this order by Major Blagden and Captain Rainsford of the 307th on October 2, which was partly responsible for the cutting off of the Lost Battalion. Perhaps this was because no one knew about it; the first Colonel Houghton heard of it was ten years later.

P. 97, l. 14: William J. Leonard, now a machine-operator in Little Falls, living in St. Johnsville, N. Y.; father of five children.

P. 106, l. 2: Major General Hunter Liggett, later a lieutenant general who succeeded General Pershing in command of the First Army, was then commanding the I Corps of which the 77th Division was a part. He and General Alexander were on the best of terms. General Liggett died some years ago.

P. 113, l. 23: Captain Lewis M. Scott, later a major, now an engineer in New York.

P. 119, l. 3: G. Endicott Putnam, now in business in New York.

P. 119, l. 23: Harry F. Wanvig, now in the insurance business in New York and a colonel of Field Artillery, Organized Reserves.

The Lost Battalion

Lieutenant Putnam still has his own map, marked in accordance with the unknown captain's directions, showing the Lost Battalion half a mile north of west of where it actually was.

P. 121, l. 7: Lieutenant Putnam believes these six shells were ranging shots from his own guns, that he had called for by telephone. But he could not know that they had struck among the very troops he thought he was helping his guns to protect; even from his treetop, he could never actually see the Lost Battalion—only distant smoke.

P. 124, l. 4: A. H. Shepard, now with the Los Angeles County Sheriff's office. "I have carried a gun all the time," says he, "but I have never shot a man since leaving the Argonne."

P. 127, l. 16: The file number is 277.32.16.

P. 133, l. 5: Colonel Stacey and Captain Delehanty remember this clearly. Lieutenant Hattemer was killed soon afterward. Bradley Delehanty is now an architect in New York City.

P. 141, l. 8: The authority is Corporal George Gault, now in the real-estate business in New York. Major, now Lieutenant Colonel, Charles M. Milliken of the regular army is now at Fort Monmouth, N. J.

P. 144, l. 28: The remnant of E Company finally came out under command of Sergeant Fred W. Baldwin, now a major in the New York National Guard, and living in Brooklyn.

P. 144, l. 29: So Baldwin says today. Other reports say there were "thirty casualties."

P. 146, l. 1:

THE "FRIENDLY BARRAGE"

There is irony in the term so frequently applied to the hurricane of fire that struck the Lost Battalion; there is tragic irony in the circumstances. There was even irony in the investigation at the time, since some of the investigating officers well knew they were not expected to report that the 77th Division's generally efficient artillery had been firing into the backs of its own infantry. They reported it must have been German artillery.

And after the Lost Battalion was relieved, they did find in the Pocket fragments of some German projectiles of some sort. Perhaps they were fired from trench mortars, perhaps from a single front-line fieldpiece, perhaps by more distant enfilading guns. But if the last were possible why did the Germans do it only once? A few more times and they would have wiped out the *Amerikanernest* without an infantry attack. One of their principal worries was that they could not reach it with artillery fire. For this statement there are several authorities including Hauptmann Petri, who during the firing of the barrage commanded the troops of the German 254th Reserve Infantry Regiment that surrounded the Lost Battalion and watched the shells fall in their midst, and Major Bickel of the Division staff, an artillery officer. They were not German shells, they say. Even had we not heard of the discovery there of one Franco-American dud shell, we have heard from any number of Lost Battalion survivors that the shells of the "friendly barrage" came from the south.

To the south were American artillery, and French. The French on the 77th's left sometimes showed a vagueness bordering upon aphasia as to the whereabouts of our front line or their own; but scarcely as to the whereabouts of Charlevaux Valley. It was plainly marked as in the 77th's sector of advance, where French divisional artillery could fire only by the 77th's permission which they did not ask until October 7 and were then refused.

But there was French artillery other than that with the divisions on the 77th's left. It was attached as reinforcement to the I American Corps of which the 77th was a part, and this French Corps artillery was called in to support the Lost Battalion, according to Brigadier General Manus McCloskey of the 152nd Field Artillery Brigade, now at Fort Bragg, N. C. Piecing together his narrative with that of his then operations officer, Major Reginald Field, now a New York lawyer, gives this result:

When Major Whittlesey's pigeon messages of October 4 showed the increasing seriousness of his position General McCloskey determined that the artillery would try to help by surrounding Whittlesey with a ring of exploding shells, through which the Germans could not penetrate and in which they could not live. The forging of this ring was a delicate operation, sight-unseen, without direct observation of the Lost Battalion it was intended to protect, at long-range where accuracy is most difficult to attain. To keep the shells from exploding too close to where they believed the Lost Battalion was, General McCloskey and Major Field tried to make ample allowance for the "probable error" in the fall of the shells.

They figured it out on the large-scale French artillery map. From exactly what information they figured, is not certain. If they used the Teichmoeller message or the Putnam message— and there is no proof that they did—inevitably they were off 500 yards in one direction or 1,000 yards in another. If they figured from Whittlesey's pigeon messages, they were troubled by the fact that his 294.7-276.3 was a single point where, to be sure, Whittlesey was, but which did not delimit the whole extent of the three to four hundred yard front his command held. It has since been rumored that even his 294.7-276.3 was incorrect, that Whittlesey was not where he said he was.

At our request the American Battle Monuments Commission

has furnished an accurate check of the exact location of the fox holes in Charlevaux Valley which to this day mark off the exact limits of the Lost Battalion's position. This check shows that "apparently Whittlesey reported his position quite accurately" and submits data indicating that there is no truth in the gruesome stories that by reporting it inaccurately he brought down the "friendly barrage" upon his own men and kept from them the food American aviators tried to drop.

So, not quite certain, but doing the best they could, the artillerymen planned to forge their ring around the Lost Battalion. On the ridge 500 yards north of him, the French Corps Artillery were to fire; on the ridge south and on either side, the 75's of the American 305th Field Artillery; at remoter points, the 155 Howitzers of the 306th. And so, they fired.

Did they fire into the Lost Battalion, as the Lost Battalion from Whittlesey down said they did?

The official records of the 152nd Field Artillery Brigade and its component regiments are incomplete and inconclusive. The files of the 154th Infantry Brigade do show, however, that when General Johnson received his copy of Whittlesey's last pigeon message written amid bursting shells he endorsed it:

"When this message was received, our artillery preparation had stopped."

"Preparation" was hardly the technically correct word, but the endorsement clearly answers those who say that "our artillery had not been firing." Colonel Fred A. Doyle who commanded the 305th denies that it had been firing "a barrage"—again a matter of terms, but General McCloskey makes the unequivocal statement:

"From checking up firing data after Whittlesey's battalion had been relieved and we knew positively its position, I am absolutely positive that no fire of our divisional artillery (the French Corps artillery habitually fired very accurately and I cannot recall a single instance of any mistake having been discovered) could have fallen on Whittlesey's position. When Whittlesey's battalion was relieved, I had the artillery liaison officer who had been with it all the time brought to my command post and I got first-hand information from him. He was positive that none of the artillery fire on the battalion had come from our guns."

This officer was Lieutenant J. G. Teichmoeller, a conscientious youth who had left Wittenberg College where he was preparing for the ministry to become a field artilleryman. During the five days and nights in the Pocket he wrote in a notebook headed: "Notes—Talking Material," things like this:

"Lad calling for mother first when hit.

"Lad reading prayerbook.

"Lad hit beside me beside tree."

He emerged from the Pocket so exhausted that he could not speak, and General McCloskey put him to bed for twenty-four hours before questioning him. The remembrance of several officers who then talked to him is that he could remember little of what had happened. In a letter to his brother, Leonard Teichmoeller, now an attorney in Newport, Ky., he wrote that on October 4 "the artillery gave us a two-hour reception. The shells burst right in our midst and many were killed and wounded." He never explained whether "the artillery" was friendly or German—his runner, Thomas G. Sadler, Jr., of South Attleboro, Mass., who was with him throughout, says flatly that it was friendly—or why he had sent his message the day before, calling for artillery support from a point 1,000 yards south of the Lost Battalion.

Notes

That misdirection, and perhaps even more likely, the misdirection of the unknown captain through Lieutenant Putnam, may "not incredibly at all" have caused errors in calculating the data for the "friendly barrage," says Major Field. All along the line were chances for miscalculation and, with the French Corps Artillery, of mis-translation. Officers of the American 305th say a checkup makes it appear that of 1500 shells its D Battery fired, some may have struck the Lost Battalion—which D's Captain, H. H. Pike, denies.

Whatever shells fell upon the Lost Battalion were not German, but "friendly," says Major Henry O. Swindler of the American Battle Monuments Commission, Washington, after exhaustive study. The shells came from the southeast, where some of the artillery was French but most was American.

At any rate, there was Whittlesey's message: "Our own artillery is dropping a barrage directly on us. For Heaven's sake stop it!" After that message, all authorities agree that the artillery, American and French, did a thorough checkup. And next day, October 5, when again the Lost Battalion heard gunfire to the south, it surrounded them with a ring of shellbursts well and truly laid.

P. 148, l. 27: A. O. Kaemper, now in the Veterans' Hospital at Fort Harrison, Mont.

P. 156, l. 19: Lucien S. Breckinridge, now employed by New York State in White Plains, N. Y., and commanding the 308th Infantry, Organized Reserves.

P. 156, l. 28: Colonel Douglas Campbell is now dead.

P. 160, l. 2: Philip Cepeglia is living in the Bronx, still agile of mind and body, and proud of his Distinguished Service Cross—the first one awarded to a Lost Battalion man.

"After the first day we were surrounded, I got used to it," he said, at a recent reunion. "Didn't get all worked up—just took things as they came. So did Whittlesey."

Then, his bright eyes dimming at the name and the memory:

"I don't know why he disappeared afterward, but it wasn't because he was afraid of anything. He was the bravest man in the A.E.F."

P. 164, l. 24: Lionel Bendheim is still in New York, father of a family. His stump of a leg troubles him sometimes—nerve pains—and he has to go to bed.

P. 165, l. 1: Daniel P. Morse, Jr., now in Winchester, Mass.

P. 171, l. 3: Fritz Prinz, now in Kassel, Germany, won celebrity, in this country especially, but pretty much all over the world, as author of the "surrender letter." He always protested its complete sincerity in interviews with American newspapermen on the Rhine after the Armistice and when he revisited the United States. On that occasion Hollingshead did not see him but "would have walked all day to do it."

P. 173, l. 1: It was so greatly desired to get this word to Major Whittlesey that General Johnson ordered Lieutenant Paul Knight to send a patrol with a sealed letter on the desperate mission of trying to wriggle through the Germans and into the Pocket.

"Don't go straight down this hell-hole of a ravine," Lieutenant Knight told Sergeant Mike Davis. "Circle around to the left, through the French sector. You just may squeak through."

With ten men, the Sergeant crawled away. Some hours later he returned, with six men left, and handed back the letter.

P. 173, l. 1: The Washington file number is 277.32.16; 592; No. 2.

P. 177, l. 25: A quotation from a letter from Lieutenant Clarence M. Davis, of Hempstead, L. I.

Notes

P. 177, l. 11: A machine-gun bullet passed through General Johnson's puttee and he was recommended for a D.S.C.

P. 177, l. 12: The Washington file number is 277.32.16; 565; No. 16.

P. 181, l. 28: Thomas G. Sadler, Jr., now in the wholesale jewelry business in South Attleboro, Mass.

P. 186, l. 11: George W. Botelle died recently in Oakville, Conn.

P. 189, l. 1: In these attacks the 77th Division's infantry were unaided by tanks, but this was not for lack of asking. Believing tanks might crawl through into Charlevaux Valley by way of a road in the eastern part of the forest, Colonel John R. R. Hannay, the 77th's Chief of Staff, asked the I Corps for tanks. The answer was that there were none to spare.

P. 196, l. 13: Joseph Friel's citation says:

"Toward the end of the period he was reduced almost to exhaustion. He tirelessly and cheerfully ran messages to all parts of the position, showing an utter disregard for his own safety. Sent to carry a message to regimental headquarters through the enemy's lines. Several other attempts had been made, as this soldier well knew, which had resulted in the death or capture of the runners. He willingly and cheerfully made the attempt, but was killed in the performance of his mission."

P. 204, l. 5: J. A. Schanz, now living in St. Paul, Minn.

P. 204, l. 16: Lowell R. Hollingshead is now in Mt. Sterling, O., employed by a gas and oil company.

P. 206, l. 14: The practice of burning the enemy to a crisp with liquid-fire was reintroduced into war by the Germans. The French took it up, but so far as known, no American troops did. The German *Flammenwerfer* threw, not flames, but a liquid that did not wholly flame until it struck the target. This liquid

303

was usually petroleum distillate and coal-tar fraction. It was ig-
nited by electricity or friction at the nozzle of the hose held by
the soldier who operated it, and was pumped from a tank carried
on his or another soldier's back. The liquid could be thrown
about a hundred feet. They say that bigger and better *Flammenwerfer* have been devised for the next war.

P. 206, l. 25: James B. Carroll was acting first sergeant of K
Company, 307th. Before the war he had been a drapery sales-
man in New York. Afterward he went back to the same house,
and is still with them.

P. 209, l. 8: The number of this message in the files is
277.32.16.

P. 211, l. 11: Samuel A. Altiera, now living in Brooklyn,
N. Y., was an auto-rifleman. "Nobody else in my squad knew
how to handle one."

P. 214, l. 4: General Malin Craig is now Chief of Staff of the
United States Army.

P. 216, l. 7: Jeremiah Healy is now with Coty, Inc., in New
York.

P. 221, l. 16: The English translation was:
"Let me know exactly where is your left because I want to
make fire of the 75's and 37 mm. guns. The whole left wing is
stopped by machine-gun fire and the trench must be fired by the
right. On account of this I must know exactly where you are."

P. 224, l. 26: Major General Charles P. Summerall then
commanded the 1st Division. He later became Chief of Staff of
the Army, and is now retired and heads the Citadel Military
College, Charleston, S. C.

P. 226, l. 25: The Germans seem really to have believed this.

P. 231, l. 11: Kozikowski is now employed at the Brooklyn
Navy Yard. He weighs two hundred and twenty-five pounds

and seldom fights the war over. This time, as he talked, he strode the floor, fists clenching and unclenching, eyes flashing. Suddenly he quieted, and sat down, back again in the present. "Well, it's only history now," he said.

P. 231, l. 20: Clifford Brown, now running an electrical equipment service in Jamestown, N. Y.

P. 243, l. 4: These men's citations for decorations especially mention their having shown initiative. Others not mentioned elsewhere who were commended include: Sergeants James J. Murphy; Joseph P. Heuer; Herman G. Anderson who acted in command of the remnant of A, 308th; Joseph Boffa; Walter P. Donogue; Peter Wick; Corporals George P. Sims, Boyd S. Hatch, Arthur Eggler, John Davis, Herman J. Bergasse; Privates William Sipple and Tobias Meyerowitz.

P. 244, l. 19: E. Stanley Mynard is now a farmer near East Homer, N. Y., not far from Clyde, where Patrick D'Amato is still barbering, as he did for C Company, 308th, until he got into the Pocket. There was little shaving done there, and he does not like to remember it now, or any other war experience. He does not even like to see war movies.

P. 244, l. 23: Various descriptions of this episode have been published. This one is based upon the recollections of Captain McMurtry, Captain Holderman, Hollingshead and others.

P. 246, l. 22: Larney was wounded, so his panels were pulled in by Private Irving L. Liner of New York, who received a D.S.C. for his daring as a runner. The 2nd Battalion panels were pulled in by William J. Powers, now a mill foreman in Hoosick Falls, N. Y., and living in Stillwater, N. Y. Lieutenant Cullen received a Distinguished Service Cross which mentioned bringing in panels as part of his generally gallant conduct and stubborn defense of the left flank.

The Lost Battalion

P. 247, l. 4: Major Whittlesey never said, "Go to hell!" if only because there was no German present to whom to say it. But, German and all, the myth has been perpetuated by a colorful artist's painting, and even by a fake photograph allegedly snapped by one of the Lost Battalion. The myth probably originated in headquarters of the 77th Division. Thence someone sent an official report giving the text of Lieutenant Prinz's surrender letter and the concluding line: "The reply to the above was 'go to hell!' " back to Lieutenant E. Kidder Meade, at I Corps headquarters. A former New York *World* reporter, he was press officer with the duty of collecting and relaying news of events on the I Corps front back to Field Press headquarters at Bar-le-Duc whence correspondents cabled it to newspapers at home.

A day or two later, on a visit to the 77th Division headquarters, the co-author of this volume, Thomas M. Johnson, asked General Alexander:

"What did Whittlesey tell 'em?"

"What *would* he tell 'em?" General Alexander retorted. "He told 'em to go to hell."

Shortly afterward, Mr. Johnson asked Major Whittlesey the same question. The Major replied:

"We told them nothing."

He and Captain McMurtry wrote in their official report that: "No reply seemed necessary."

But typewriter, cable and linotype—to say nothing of headline writer—had done their work; millions of Americans were throwing down their newspapers to give three rousing cheers for "Go-to-hell Whittlesey" and the "Lost Battalion" that had not lost its nerve. Whoever invented that story was a genius at wartime propaganda. He could have put into the mouth of the

New England lawyer no words that would more endear him and his men to average Americans—or more inflame their war spirit.

On those rare occasions when he retold the story of the Lost Battalion, Whittlesey would say drily: "The men swore a good deal."

P. 247, l. 14: This was Sergeant James A. Deahan, now proprietor of a tavern in Brooklyn. A recent account of his experiences in a tabloid newspaper "might be good for business," he explained, genially.

P. 247, l. 22: The Lost Battalion's scorn of the German surrender letter, voiced by some of its German-speaking members, moved the 76th Reserve Division's Intelligence Officer, Major Bickel, to write in his diary this intriguing entry:

"So we must shoot down descendants of German peasants! Must such a thing be? But it is the drop of true, Nibelungen-true, German blood in these men that made them answer to our parliamentarian that they must do their duty as soldiers. We will try to starve them out!"

P. 252, l. 16: Lieutenant Richard K. Tillman, who got to be a major, won high commendation from Colonel Houghton for his leadership in bringing succor to the Lost Battalion. He is now in Rochester, N. Y., with the Tillman Oil Co.

P. 254, l. 15: Just before, on the right, Captain Holderman and K, 307th, had heard the Germans leaving the hill crest above—but thought it must be another trick.

P. 255, l. 21: Later Major Thomas E. Stone, now living in New York and still interested in his old regiment; still has its operations reports and detailed battle maps.

P. 264, l. 8: One of those who kept on with the front line was Sergeant Carroll, of K, 307th. He stuck until Grand Pré was reached. "We skinny guys are the tough ones," he laughs.

The Lost Battalion

But most of those who tried had to drop out. The killed numbered 107, seriously wounded and sick, 253.

On the afternoon of October 8, 194 of the 554 who had reached their objective the night of October 2 began their march rearward to brigade reserve and rest. Ragged, haggard, some of them trembling with weakness, but in formation, led by Major Whittlesey and Captain McMurtry, they tramped back across Charlevaux Valley to the mouth of the ravine. From beyond La Palette, the raw wind brought a faint rapping sound, and above their heads came the whipping and snapping of machine-gun bullets, almost spent—the enemy's last groping finger-tips. Those who were left of the Lost Battalion did not even turn their heads; they looked neither to right nor left. One, who saw them pass, remembers today their eyes. "When I looked into those eyes, there was nothing I could say to them."

Back in the Pocket, along the scarred hillside heaped with broken equipment and broken bodies, walked Lieutenant Paul Knight. His tender soldier conscience hurt him, and does today: "We didn't do our job—didn't come up with them." He, with his corporal's guard, had come nearer than anyone else in the 308th. Alone, he started down toward the brook, past many a crumpled form in olive-drab. From one of them, came a sound, almost a whisper:

"Take me. Take me."

It was Lionel Bendheim, with his gangrened crushed leg; very weak, scarce any voice. They had missed him; there was neither stretcher left nor ambulance, until Paul Knight brought one, to take Bendheim away, sure enough, to that warm clime Whittlesey had promised him—the last of the Lost Battalion to be found.

P. 265, l. 8: Probably the first "beat" on the dramatic situa-

308

tion of Whittlesey's surrounded command was in the dispatch
of Fred S. Ferguson, then United Press correspondent with the
A.E.F., now president of the Newspaper Enterprise Association. But he did not call it the "Lost Battalion." That inefface-
able title was added in this country by Harold D. Jacobs, then
cable editor of the United Press, and now editor of the Santa
Barbara, Calif., *Morning Post.* He thinks that "any newspaper-
man, under the same circumstances, would have labeled Whittlesey's outfit the 'Lost Battalion.' (The Associated Press immediately followed suit.) It was purely automatic at the time. The
adjective 'Lost,' of course, was used mostly in the sense of being
done for, of being in a hopeless situation."

But most newspaper readers pictured the battalion as literally
lost in the Argonne Forest, surrounded by Germans, unable to
find its way. An eerie picture, distorting as a Coney Island
mirror, nevertheless, the picture that was held up to the world—
to all, that is, but the Germans, who got it straight: "the Beleaguered Battalion" or "the *Amerikanernest.*"

P. 267, l. 6: It was only on the advice and even insistence of
other officers that Lieutenant Colonel Whittlesey reported this
to higher authority which, in turn, preferred the charges and
ordered the officer in arrest.

P. 275, l. 10: Colonel Gordon Johnston died recently, a brigadier general.

P. 275, l. 22: General Alexander wrote us October 28, 1937:

"Colonel Whittlesey led his command to the place to which
he had been directed, occupied the position as he had been
expected to occupy it and did, in a word, what he had been
expected to do. Had others responsible for the remainder of the
front line of the division at that time done half so well as did
he, there would have been no difficulty about the accomplish-

ment of the mission with which that front line had, by competent authority, been charged—and hence, no 'Lost Battalion,' so called. There was never any reason for adverse criticism by either myself or anyone else of the conduct of their commands by either Colonel Whittlesey or Major McMurtry."

In 1930 General Alexander wrote the American Battle Monuments Commission:

"The rumors which have impliedly criticized Major Whittlesey's command on the apparent ground of unjustifiable action on his part are entirely unfounded. The order for the advance was given by myself on what I believed to be good and sufficient grounds. The responsibility was mine, and was and is, accepted by me. Whittlesey's command did what it was told."

Colonel Stacey writes: "There is not the slightest criticism of Whittlesey's splendid conduct."

There are rumors that General Johnson once thought of court-martialing Colonel Whittlesey on two grounds: that by ordering Captain McMurtry to close up on him, he left his rear unprotected; and that he reported his position incorrectly. After considering the facts set forth in this narrative, the reader will probably conclude that there was not much in either charge; and so, apparently, did General Johnson.

P. 279, l. 22: The fighting in the forest was but a part of the vast battle that played so great a rôle in ending the war—the battle of the Meuse-Argonne. This battle the American First Army waged on the twenty-five-mile front from the Argonne Forest to the Meuse River with the object of advancing forty miles and cutting the main German railroad supply line at Sedan. One of the principal obstacles was the dense, rough and strongly fortified Argonne Forest that the 77th Division had to force by frontal assault.

310

Notes

When the Lost Battalion broke the German main line of resistance, the effect on the Germans was to disarrange their defense of most of the forest front; and on the Americans; to speed up their efforts to rupture that defense completely. The inspiration to these efforts—of the 77th, 1st, 28th and 82nd Divisions—sprang in no small degree from the desire to relieve their surrounded comrades who were holding out so heroically. For this statement there is the authority of Generals Craig and Hugh A. Drum; then Chiefs of Staff, respectively, of the I Corps and I Army, and of General Pershing—*My Experiences in the World War;* "There was another important factor that entered into the decision to force the withdrawal of the enemy from the Argonne at this time. This was the predicament of the 'Lost Battalion.' "

Although the German official records show that they were about to withdraw even before the 82nd Division's attack was launched, they had been brought to that pass by the unceasing attacks of the 77th, 28th and especially of the 1st Division, and all three divisions had been spurred on by urgings to break through and bring relief to their surrounded comrades, so that the Lost Battalion episode demonstrably hastened the ousting of the Germans from one of the strongest positions they held on the most important battlefield on the Western Front, at the climax of the most decisive series of battles there fought.

P. 280, l. 15: Two weeks before Major Whittlesey went to Washington Major Francis M. Weld saw him and was distressed at his worried appearance and manner.

"With all these distractions, how do you get through the day?" asked Whittlesey.

In Washington, at the dedication ceremony, he told Major Scott:

311

The Lost Battalion

"Not a day goes by but I hear from some of my old outfit, usually about some sort of sorrow or misfortune."

Yet George McMurtry, with whom he stopped at Atlantic City en route back from Washington, says he was very cheerful.

Twenty-four hours before the steamship *Toloa* sailed, he lunched with Fitzhugh McGrew then, as now, associated with the law firm of White and Case, and now a trustee of Hobart College. They talked of Egyptian funerals, but the subject was not of Whittlesey's choosing.

P. 281, l. 5: Just before leaving, Colonel Whittlesey gave to the landlady of the bachelors' boardinghouse where he lived, a check for a month's rent in advance.

"You'd better cash this right away," he told her, not explaining that elsewise she would have to await settlement of his estate.

He left less than a thousand dollars in cash. The Medal of Honor he left to his mother; the German surrender letter, to Major McMurtry. The latter gave it to Colonel Whittlesey's father, who in turn presented the letter to Williams College, whence his son had been graduated in 1905. It is now in the college library, with Whittlesey's helmet and other articles.

P. 281, l. 6: For the account of Colonel Whittlesey's disappearance and the analysis of its causes, we are indebted to evidence from numerous sources, of which many have been named already in these notes. We add, however, Melzar Whittlesey and two of his brother's former lieutenants in the Headquarters Company, 308th Infantry; Meredith Wood, and Edward R. Bartlett; also, Colonel Whittlesey's former law partner, John B. Pruyn, and John S. Shedden, his roommate at Williams College, together with Max Eastman from whom Whittlesey absorbed some of the Socialism he discarded later.

P. 283, l. 1: "I don't talk about it much any more," Krotoshinsky said quite lately. "It gets me all excited and doesn't do me any good."

But he is a regular attendant at reunions of K Company, 307th, and in the American Legion parade last fall helped carry a big banner inscribed: "The Lost Battalion."

P. 283, l. 27: Although Colonel Holderman still suffers from the old wounds—his only sickness since the war—he writes, with the optimistic enthusiasm of twenty years ago, that he is proud to have been a member of the Lost Battalion, proud to have known every man in it.

His lieutenant, Tom Pool, although he is a Texan, remembers that the defenders of the Alamo knew that there was no way out; if they fought, the Mexicans would kill them; if they surrendered, the Mexicans would kill them anyway. The Lost Battalion knew, especially after the surrender letter, that there was a way out; if they surrendered, their lives would be spared.

Captain Stromee says: "I think the Lost Battalion episode deserves a place in history with the Alamo, and I'm proud to have been in it. But—never again!"

One side of his face is still partly paralyzed by that trench-mortar bomb.

P. 285, l. 13: By those heaps of Whittlesey's dead runners, on the morning of October 8, Lieutenant John G. Taylor led K Company, 308th, toward the Pocket, across now-deserted Hill 198. There they saw how the Germans had held out so long. The plateau dominated the ravine and surrounding country, and was fortified more strongly than had been supposed. Some of the trenches were of concrete, and along the parapets were heaps of machine-gun cartridges, empty. There was a heap every ten yards . . . a mute answer to those who have said that the Lost Battalion outnumbered the Germans who had cut it off. Even

313

though the Germans had fewer men—and all available German sources indicate they had more—a machine gun every ten yards. . . .

Postscript: For all the shelling American artillery was supposed to have given those German trenches, he saw very few shell holes there.

Lieutenant Taylor found Colonel Whittlesey calm, collected and, he thinks, clean-shaven, asking for food and surgeons. At the double Taylor sent his men back across the valley for rations, but when they came—corned-willy, bread, butter and syrup—many of the famished men gulped down their first food in five days, and vomited it up again. Sick and wounded were taken back by ambulances or by the narrow-gauge railroad the 302nd Engineers under Major Frederick S. Greene had just finished repairing. As they lay on the small flatcars, Knights of Columbus workers fed them chocolate.

The dead were buried by a detachment of the 53rd Pioneer Infantry under Lieutenant Walter B. Herendeen of New York. They removed from each body the two identification discs ("dog-tags"); one, with any identifying personal articles found on the body, they sent to the rear for dispatching home; the other they fastened to a rough-hewn wooden cross, which bore the name of virtually every man buried there. Later the bodies were exhumed, identification completed where possible, and, as the relatives wished, sent to this country or re-interred in the beautiful American cemetery of the Meuse-Argonne at Romagne-sous-Montfaucon, northeast of the Argonne Forest, which was finally dedicated last summer.

There, at the American guest house, or at the French *Hostellerie de l'Argonne* maintained at near-by Vienne le Château by M. L. Piot, visitors may and do stay. If they go into Charlevaux

Valley, and along the road, they will come upon a granite marker erected by the American Battle Monuments Commission. Upon it are chiseled only the words "The Lost Battalion," and an arrow. The arrow points down the slope, to the scars of old fox holes, not yet quite healed.

ACKNOWLEDGMENTS

ACKNOWLEDGMENTS

Many of those mentioned in the Notes have assisted us in our work, and we thank them. For help especially valuable our thanks go to Major McMurtry, Colonel Holderman, James F. Larney, Walter J. Baldwin, Colonel Stacey, General Alexander, Colonel Houghton, George Newcom, and Leon E. Moxley of Gouverneur, N. Y.

We are indebted to many not mentioned in the Notes, of whom the following are now in New York City:

Conrad Schuster, Allen L. Lindley, Arthur L. Robb, Colonel J. R. R. Hannay, Colonel Marion W. Howze, A. S. Griffiths, Russell Golde, William F. Tighe, Charles T. Greenwood, Medley G. B. Whelpley, Arthur A. Gammell, James Madison Blackwell, Alexander L. Barbour, Robert K. Haas, Ward B. Chamberlin, Ercole Sozzi, Frederick R. Rich, Philip Kearns, Thornton C. Thayer, Reginald Field and Colonel Julius O. Adler.

And also to the following:

Evan M. Johnson, IV., Major General Charles P. Summerall, Major General Hugh A. Drum, Brigadier General Manus R. McCloskey, Colonel Fred A. Doyle, Colonel A. P. Watts, Colonel Charles A. Dravo, Reverend J. J. Halligan, Mr. Leonard Teichmoeller, of Newport, Ky.; Maurice E. Johnson, of Scranton, Pa.; Dr. Edgar F. Powell, of Fishkill, N. Y.; Arthur H. Robbins, M. D., of Milwaukee, Wis.; Bernard M. Burns, of Cleveland, O.; John A. Fitzgerald, of Ilion, N. Y.; Stanton K. Nethery, of Baton Rouge, La.; Edwin L. Lewis, of Washington, D. C.; Benjamin H. Doctor, of Scandia, Kansas; Arthur K.

The Lost Battalion

O'Keefe, of Worcester, Mass.; Robert Marchant, of Hartford, Conn.; Arthur Hicks, of Butte, Mont.; Cecil O. Leach, of Moravia, N. Y.; Frank G. S. Erickson, of Bismarck, N. Dak.; Fred Main, of Jacksonville, Ill.; Melvin Tronson, of Medicine Lake, Mont., Sherman W. Eager, of Bloomington, Ind.; Bradley Martin; Charles R. Riley, of Philadelphia, Pa.; Harold B. Wiltze, of Tacoma, Wash.; Clarence M. Davis, of Hempstead, L. I.; L. R. Beeson, of Lima, O.; Otto H. Eifert, of Brooklyn, N. Y.; Charles H. Chavelle, of Stanford, Calif.; Henry P. Flanning, of Glendale, Calif.; Howell Stevens, of Brookline, Mass.; Reuben H. Ahlstedt, of Herington, Kan.; Henry J. Cadieux, of Jewett City, Conn.; William J. McGinley, of the Knights of Columbus; and the following from Minnesota: J. A. Schanz and A. J. Le May from St. Paul; Edward Baker from Minneapolis; Herbert Tiedeman from Elkton; Arnold M. Morem from Harmony; Gust Dahlgren from Crosby; Hans Hansen from Canby; and Clyde Hintz from Hutchinson: Peter De Pasqua and Bernhard Ragner, of Paris, France; Judge Pelham St. George Bissell, of New York; Colonel Thomas J. Johnson, of Washington, D. C.; Edwin L. James, of the New York *Times;* Frederick A. Rupp, president of the 77th Division Association; John T. Winterich, editor of the *American Legion Magazine;* Lieutenant Colonel E. F. Harding, editor of *The Infantry Journal,* Washington, D. C.; Barney Yanofsky, of *Foreign Service;* the Rev. Dr. Murray Bartlett, ex-president of Hobart College; and the national adjutants of the American Legion, Veterans of Foreign Wars and Disabled American Veterans.

Besides these men of the Lost Battalion and their friends, we are indebted to others who have made easy our access to the official records and have otherwise assisted in research. These are Colonel Oliver L. Spaulding and Major S. S. Eberle of the His-

Acknowledgments

torical Section, Army War College, Washington; Colonel X. H. Price and Major Henry O. Swindler of the American Battle Monuments Commission, Washington; Brigadier General Frank C. Burnett and the staff of the Adjutant General's Office, Washington; The Veterans Administration, Washington; and Professor E. Wardlaw Miles, Johns Hopkins University, Baltimore, Md. Thanks are due also to Keats Speed, managing editor of the New York *Sun*, for permission to use material contained in Thomas M. Johnson's dispatches as Accredited Correspondent with the A. E. F., and to the Newspaper Enterprise Association for permission to reprint certain extracts from articles.

The most valuable accounts of the Lost Battalion episode from the American side that have been published hitherto are contained in these three books:

The History of the 308th Infantry, by E. Wardlaw Miles, published by G. P. Putnam's Sons.

The History of the 77th Division, published by the 77th Division Association, 28 East 39th Street, New York City.

Memories of the World War, by Major General Robert Alexander, published by The Macmillan Company.

Valuable sidelights are cast by:

From Upton to the Meuse with the 307th Infantry, by Kerr Rainsford, published by D. Appleton-Century Co.

The History of the First Division, published by the Society of the First Division.

My Experiences in the World War, by John J. Pershing, published by Frederick A. Stokes Company.

From the German side, by all odds the best and virtually the only published account is that of General Wellmann—*Das I Reserve-Korps in der Letzten Schlacht*, published by Edler and Krissche. We are also indebted to accounts written by General

The Lost Battalion

Hansen and Major Hünicken, who commanded the 254th Reserve Infantry Regiment during the fighting against the Lost Battalion, supplied by Hauptmann von Sybel formerly of the staff of the 76th Reserve Division, who has been most helpful in many ways. So also has Rittmeister R. Maempel, formerly Adjutant of the 252nd Reserve Infantry Regiment of that division; Hauptmann Petri who commanded the troops that actually closed the gap and completed the cutting off of the Lost Battalion; and Major Bickel, Intelligence Officer of the 76th Reserve Division. We wish also to thank the editors of the division's *"Nachrichtenblatt"* for appealing to their readers to assist with their reminiscences this American effort to present, for the first time, the German side, and General Wetzell, editor of the *Militaer Wochenblatt.* In this connection we also thank Colonel E. R. W. McCabe and Major J. R. Ratay, U. S. A.

For assistance with illustrations, we are in debt to Captain Richard R. Schlossberg and the Army Photographic Service.

The relief-map was modeled in clay by Fletcher Pratt, from the detailed French contour map that the Lost Battalion used. The model was photographed by Mrs. Pratt.

INDEX

Index

Index

Index

Index